More Doctor Who
and Philosophy

Popular Culture and Philosophy® Series Editor: George A. Reisch

For full details of all Popular Culture and Philosophy® books, visit www.opencourtbooks.com.

Popular Culture and Philosophy®

More Doctor Who and Philosophy

Regeneration Time

Edited by

COURTLAND LEWIS AND PAULA SMITHKA

OPEN COURT
Chicago

Volume 93 in the series, Popular Culture and Philosophy ®, edited by George A. Reisch

To find out more about Open Court books, call toll-free 1-800-815-2280, or visit our website at www.opencourtbooks.com.

Open Court Publishing Company is a division of Carus Publishing Company, dba Cricket Media.

Copyright © 2015 by Carus Publishing Company, dba Cricket Media

First printing 2015

This book is also available as an e-book.

Printed and bound in the United States of America.

ISBN: 978-8126-9900-5

Library of Congress Comtrol Number: 2015947719

Contents

SERIAL 4
Gallifrey Falls No More

Once More into the Time Vortex

COURTLAND LEWIS AND PAULA SMITHKA

Some stories are too big, too complex, and just too brilliant to try and tell them all at once. For fifty years, *Doctor Who* has been telling its story; and, happily, there's no sign this story will end any time soon! So, it should come as no surprise we need another volume to tell *more* of the story of *Doctor Who and Philosophy*.

New Moments in Time

Since *Doctor Who and Philosophy: Bigger on the Inside*, much has changed. We have a new Doctor, a new full-time companion, a few new enemies, and this little thing called the Fiftieth Anniversary Special, which seemed to create a whole new crack in the wall of space and time by completely reframing the New Series.

We've learned a lot of new things about the Doctor. His number one rule is to lie, he's quite a ladies' man (just how many wives does he have now?), and he has some pretty deep-rooted personality issues. To everyone's astonishment, the Doctor (in at least one timeline) died at Trenzalore, and he didn't EX-TER-MIN-ATE the Time Lords, after all (what a revelation!). And now, he's been granted a whole new set of regenerations. We've met a hidden incarnation of the Doctor— the War Doctor, (talk about Transmat shock!); and . . . oh yeah, the Fourth Doctor somehow landed a gig as a museum curator.

Okay, we're still uncertain what to make of the last one, but we sure hope to see more Classic Doctors in the coming years! We've also learned that Clara has saved the Doctor more times than he's reversed the polarity of the neutron flow, that Daleks have a concept of divine beauty, which is, of course, divine hatred, and that there was a whole planet serving as an asylum for insane Daleks. And the big reveal: the Master is now "the Mistress"! All of this is, of course, just the "tip of the console of the TARDIS." There's so much *more* to this story!

New Puzzles in Time and Space

More Doctor Who and Philosophy's team of companions includes many new travelers, but some Classic ones too. We address many of the scientific, moral, epistemological, and metaphysical issues that have made their way into the Whoniverse over the past five years. Grab a jelly baby and reflect on a sample of some of these new puzzles we've included. Is the "impossible girl" really impossible, or is she just a figment of the Doctor's psyche—or maybe both? Is an interspecies lesbian relationship morally wrong? What's the nature of the Doctor's knowledge? Can the Doctor deceive himself? Is it okay for the Doctor to lie, especially to his companions? While we're on the topic of companions, what's so special about them? Are they his friends or his pets, and if one day he feels a little puckish, would it be wrong to eat them? (Mmm . . . Clara fingers and custard.) On a higher dimensional level, we even have two companions who've figured out how to build a TARDIS—instructions included!

But that's not all. In this volume, we ask lots of tough questions that challenge readers' understanding of their favorite Time Lord. Does it make sense to say the Doctor could've avoided Trenzalore? Seriously, how can you die on Trenzalore, yet at the same time survive? Thankfully, we have our own Great Intelligences to help us figure out the answer. We also challenge the new hero-personae of the Doctor. What happened between the Ninth Doctor's mantra "coward, any day" and the Twelfth's "never cowardly?" Has the world changed so much that being clever isn't enough anymore, and instead, a less-pacifistic "cowboy" approach is required? Or does the Doctor, from time to time, simply lose his way, diverting from his "magnetic north"—being a good man? Spoilers . . . ! We're not telling. You have to read the book to find out what sort of answers lie inside.

Jammie Dodgers

As a special treat for the new volume, we've invited some *Doctor Who* fandom insiders to join in our journey. These are companions who run hugely successful conventions, play in *Doctor Who*–inspired Steampunk bands, and run wildly popular podcasts and websites. They'll take turns serving as your "Time Lord Presiding" over each Serial of the book. These Presiding Time Lords share their insights into why *Doctor Who* is so culturally important and transformative, as well as philosophically deep and compelling. Besides, it's the dog's bollocks!

Enter a New Relative Dimension

All in all, *More Doctor Who and Philosophy* promises to engage and excite all readers, cybernetic, human, or otherwise. And, if recent *Doctor Who* storylines are any indication, *More Doctor Who and Philosophy* might just become the new companion of the show. With the series' continued emphasis on personal identity, time paradoxes, and everything in between, showrunner Steven Moffat obviously loves philosophy. (Steven, we're available as consultants!) Luckily, we're here to help you make a little sense of the Whoniverse.

Well, we could jabber on, but like all new companions, you can't wait to board the TARDIS. Hop in, hold on, and let *More Doctor Who and Philosophy* take you on a journey in a new relative dimension in time and space . . . Geronimo!

(Oh, and did you pack the jelly babies, Jammie Dodgers, fish fingers and custard? And don't forget the banana!)

SERIAL 1

The Real
Never-Ending
Story

R. Alan Siler
TIME LORD PRESIDING

Magnetic North

R. ALAN SILER, TIME LORD PRESIDING

TWELFTH DOCTOR: Clara, tell me: Am I a good man?

CLARA: I . . . don't know.

— "Into the Dalek," 2014

In the 2014 season of *Doctor Who*, starring Peter Capaldi, we've seen a somewhat darker Doctor portrayed, evident in the actions he takes and the decisions he makes. We've seen him encounter Robin Hood, re-meet the Clockwork Droids, face his own childhood fears, confront Cybermen, and re-encounter one of his oldest and deadliest enemies. At the beginning of "Into the Dalek," the Doctor asks the above question of his companion, Clara, and she responds with a genuine "I . . . don't know."

Now, if anyone should be able to answer that question definitively, it's Clara. As we saw in the Season Seven finale, "Name of the Doctor" (2013), she's seen every point in the Doctor's timeline, so she should know better than anyone the Doctor's true nature. Though, to be fair, there's some question about how much of that experience the "current model" of Clara is actually aware of or can recall. But why ask the question in the first place? Isn't the answer obvious?

Most of us have asked that question or something similar at some point in our life, privately and internally if not voiced aloud to trusted friends. It's one of the basic questions of human existence, along with the old standards "Who am I?", "Why am I here?", and "What should I have for lunch today?"

(All right, I'll admit that not everyone sees the same level of primal importance in that last one as I do.) The old adage, that if you're asking the question then you probably already know the answer, applies in most cases. But the Doctor isn't an average case.

He's a Time Lord, a being not of our own species. The people of his race have the ability to undergo bodily regeneration when they reach the point of death. Regeneration is a cataclysmic process. Every time the Doctor regenerates, his whole cellular structure undergoes a transformation and consequentially his personality gets a bit of a shake up; so the possibility of the negative sides of his personality being brought more to the fore is a very real one. The Doctor may have been "a good man" in all of his previous lives, but a quirk of regeneration could result in his next life being darker, more dangerous. When "The Twin Dilemma" (1984) first aired, the audience was being led to believe that that's exactly what had happened—that a quirk of regeneration had produced a Doctor who was dangerously unstable.

I would argue that "good" is the Doctor's magnetic north—the pole to which he's intrinsically drawn, the force to which his compass points. It's what drove him to leave Gallifrey in the first place. We know the Doctor's opinions of his fellow Time Lords. While on trial in "The War Games" (1969), the Doctor takes an accusatory stance against the Time Lords: "While you have been content merely to observe the evil in the galaxy, I have been fighting against it. True, I am guilty of interference, just as you are guilty of failing to use your great powers to help those in need!" When on trial a second time in the imaginatively titled "The Trial of a Time Lord" (1986), the Doctor describes Time-Lord society as "decadent, degenerate, and rotten to the core"—"Ten million years of absolute power. That's what it takes to be *really* corrupt!" The Doctor rebelled against his own people and their strict policy of non-interference in the lives of other species, and has lived his life, for the most part, championing the downtrodden, saving planets from invading forces of despots and conquerors, helping colonies ravaged by disease or poverty, risking his own life to help someone else, and saving children from the things that give them nightmares. There are countless examples of the good deeds that the Doctor has done. In fact, in 2013's "The Day of the Doctor," we learn that the Doctor's name represents a promise: "Never cruel or cowardly; never give up, never give in." That's the credo by which the Doctor lives his life.

The Doctor's Darkness

But the Doctor definitely has his dark side. We see examples of this right from the very beginning of the Classic Series. When we meet the Doctor, he's a much different person than the one that we've come to know. In the earliest adventures we see, he's a selfish, irascible, paranoid, and controlling old man. He kidnaps Barbara and Ian to keep them from telling others about Susan and him ("An Unearthly Child," 1963); he clearly has the intention of bashing a caveman's brains in with a rock just so that he and his fellow time travelers can escape their pursuers ("The Tribe of Gum," 1963); he lies about needing a mercury refill for the TARDIS just so he can get his way and explore an alien city, ultimately putting himself and his party in grave danger ("The Mutants," 1963). On the occasions that he gets involved in an adventure, it's because he's forced to do so by circumstances or by outside influences, such as Arbitan coercing the Doctor and crew to serve him by imprisoning the TARDIS and vowing to only release it once his assigned task is complete in "The Keys of Marinus" (1964).

The more he travels and interacts with his companions, the more the Doctor evolves. By the time of "The Sensorites" (1964), the seventh story to be broadcast of the Classic Series, we see the Doctor decide to help the titular beings not because he's coerced or cajoled, but because it's the right thing to do. This represents a major turning point in the Doctor's life.

But it's not all smooth sailing from there on. Like any thinking, complex being, his life is littered with mistakes, misjudgments, and occasionally evil acts. We can't ignore the many examples of cruelty or cowardice we see throughout the Doctor's life. No, we aren't letting him off the hook that easily, and neither do his enemies, who delight in accusing the Doctor of being bathed in blood, of being made of fire and rage, of turning his companions into weapons, and all the rest of it.

And certainly, they have a point. In "Warriors of the Deep" (1984), the Doctor is unable to help either side of a conflict, and with the bodies of humans, Silurians, and Sea Devils alike piled around him, the Doctor admits, heartbreakingly, that "there should have been another way" to find a peaceful solution. In "Attack of the Cybermen" (1985), the Doctor misjudges Lytton so badly that Lytton, in his attempt to help the Cryons without the Doctor's aid, is captured by the Cybermen and converted into one of them, the Doctor unable to save him. At the end of "The Runaway Bride" (2006), the Doctor floods the Racnoss, destroying them, and stands triumphantly over the act. Probably his darkest moment comes at the end of 2009's "The Waters of Mars," where the Doctor proclaims himself to be "The Time Lord Victorious," above the laws of time and above reproach for his actions. It takes the suicide of a horrified and frightened woman to bring him out of his arrogance.

Yes, the Doctor has blood on his hands. Yes, the Doctor makes mistakes and sometimes does reprehensible things. We know in fact that there's enough darkness within the Doctor for a separate being, the Valeyard, to be created from it, which we see in "The Trial of a Time Lord." A similar argument can be made about the Dream Lord, another being that's revealed to be a manifestation of the Doctor's darker side in the Season Five episode "Amy's Choice" (2010).

But at his core, he's good, and will always turn back in that direction. We see it time and again. In the 2013 mini-episode "Night of the Doctor," which takes place during the Time War, we have this exchange between the Doctor and Ohila, high priestess of the Sisterhood of Karn:

> EIGHTH DOCTOR: I help where I can, I will not fight.
>
> OHILA: Because you are the "good man," as you call yourself.
>
> EIGHTH DOCTOR: I call myself the Doctor.
>
> OHILA: It's the same thing in your mind.
>
> EIGHTH DOCTOR: I'd like to think so.

There we have, in a nutshell, the Doctor's assessment of himself, his most basic personal philosophy. The Doctor believes himself to be good, or at least sees the life he's led as a good one, and wants his name to be synonymous with 'good'. Even in the midst of the Great Time War, the Doctor attempts to separate himself from his people, from the fighting, and be a force for good in a dark and violent universe. And when the Doctor finally does take up arms to put an end to the Time War once and for all, an act that results in the destruction of his entire race, it's a decision that he recoils from in guilt and horror, even though it's an action that he deems necessary.

Evidence of the Doctor's True Nature

Yes, the Doctor lives in a violent and dangerous universe, and lives a life that puts him at risk and into conflict with that danger. And yes, he sometimes acts in questionable ways in response to that danger. But before we (or his enemies) judge him too harshly, we must take a look not only at his own actions but also to the actions that he inspires in others. In other words, the clearest reflection of his true nature might be in the effect that he's had on the people around him—his companions and associates.

Barbara and Ian were scared and unsure when they first met the Doctor, overwhelmed by the circumstances that they found themselves in, and wanted nothing more than to return home to Earth and London. But eventually they embraced their strange new life, learned to enjoy their travels and experiences, and cultivated what the Doctor called "a real spirit of adventure." They, in essence, learned to live.

Katarina, a lowly handmaiden from ancient Troy, sacrificed herself in order to help the Doctor escape the planet Desparus ("The Dalek Master Plan," 1965). Held hostage in an airlock on a spaceship by escaped prisoner Kirksen, she opened the hatch, blowing both her and her captor into space. She knew that the Doctor's mission, to warn Earth of the threat of the Daleks and Mavic Chen, was urgent and deeply important—more important, in her eyes, than her own life.

When we first meet Jo Grant (1971–1973) she's an awkward, clumsy and not-terribly-bright (but nonetheless enthusiastic) young woman who botches the Doctor's experiments, runs blindly into trouble, gets captured in an attempt to be helpful, and gets hypnotized by the Master and used as a threat against the Doctor. As she spends more time with the Doctor, she learns from him, slowly adopting some of his mindset and outlook, gradually becoming more confident and competent. She eventually attempts to sacrifice herself to save the Doctor from the demon Azal ("The Dæmons," 1971). By the time she leaves the Doctor's company, she's become a mature, caring, passionate woman, able to take up for herself and even resist the Master's attempts at controlling her; she goes on to explore her own causes and live a life making a difference in our own world.

Leela (1977–1978) is an interesting case, since her journey mirrors that of the Doctor's. Both of them were part of a society that they were critical of, challenging the accepted beliefs of their people. Both of them had the courage to walk away from those societies in order to explore truth. When they meet, Leela is just beginning her journey and she finds an apt teacher in the Doctor. As she travels and learns, she abandons thoughts of magic and superstition and learns to trust experience, reason, and evidence. She even chides Adelaide in "Horror of Fang Rock" (1977) for consulting a spiritualist on a monthly basis. "A waste of time," Leela tells her. "I too used to believe in magic. But the Doctor has taught me about science. It is better to believe in science."

Both Tegan and Donna started out as brash and self-absorbed until their travels opened them up to becoming more caring and selfless. Tegan leaves the Doctor's company in "Resurrection of the Daleks" (1984) out of disgust at the death that seems to follow them; "A lot of good people have died today, Doctor. I don't think I can go on." The Doctor is clearly shaken that his lifestyle has driven away one of his friends. "It's strange," he tells remaining companion Turlough, "I left Gallifrey for similar reasons—I'd grown tired of their lifestyle. It seems I must mend my ways." Donna has her turning point in "The Fires of Pompeii" (2008), in which she's horrified that the Doctor would walk away from the imminent destruction caused by the eruption of Vesuvius without saving anyone; and she rails against him until he gives in. It's her passion and her persistence that sways the Doctor into doing an act of kindness in an otherwise fixed point in history.

Ace (1987–1989) was a rebellious, angry teenager, estranged from her parents and stranded on an alien trading colony before meeting the Doctor. Being taken up in the TARDIS gave her a sense of direction and purpose, a sense of home that she'd not had before. Her travels through time and space matured her, tempered her, without diminishing any of her spirit. It's as if she'd never fit in in any of the settings in which she'd previously lived, but in the TARDIS she found her niche. We eventually learn in the *Sarah Jane Adventures* episode, "Death of the Doctor," (2010) that Ace goes on to found an organization called Charitable Earth (which Sophie Aldred will tell you is just a front for Ace's Dalek hunting operation!).

Possibly the most striking example of the effect the Doctor had on a companion can be seen in Rose Tyler. Rose was an average teenage girl with a boyfriend, working in a shop, living her day-to-day life, until the day that her shop gets blown up by the Doctor. After helping him defeat the Autons, she joins him in his travels, meeting Slitheen, Daleks, Gelth, her father, and Charles Dickens along the way.

In Season One's "Parting of the Ways" (2005), the Doctor, while fighting off a Dalek invasion fleet in Earth's future, sends Rose back to her own time where she'd be safe. We see her sitting with her mother Jackie and her boyfriend Mickey in a café. They're trying to engage her in light conversation, but she's distraught that the Doctor is in danger and she isn't there to help him. They tell her that she has to forget the Doctor and start living her normal life, the kind of life that the Doctor could never have. She asks Jackie, "What do I do every day, Mum? What do I do? Get up, catch the bus, go to work, come back home, eat chips and go to bed . . . is that it?" Mickey accuses her of thinking that she's better than they are, but she corrects him, delivering one of my favorite moments in all of *Doctor Who*:

> No, I didn't mean that! But it was . . . it was a better life. An' I don't mean all the travelin', seein' aliens and spaceships and things, that don't matter. The Doctor showed me a better way of livin' your life! You know, he showed you, too. That you don't just give up. You don't just let things happen. You make a stand! You say "No!" You have the guts to do what's right when everyone else just runs away!

This moment sums up the cumulative effect that life with the Doctor has on his companions. He makes his companions better people for having traveled with him. He shows them a better way of living life. Only a good man could do that.

"Into the Dalek" closes with the Doctor returning Clara to her school, thirty seconds after they left, and as she steps out of the TARDIS, she turns back to address the question that the

Doctor put to her: "You asked me if you're a good man, and the answer is, I don't know. But I think you try to be, and . . . I think that's probably the point." I wholeheartedly agree. We may find, as we learn more about this new Doctor, that something about the circumstances of his most recent regeneration has caused a radical shift in the Doctor's personality, but even if his initial moral stance is questionable, he'll eventually prove to Clara and to the audience, that he's still a good man, because 'good' is his magnetic north, the pole to which he's intrinsically drawn, the force to which his compass points.

Yes, Doctor, you are a good man. Not a perfect man, but a good man nonetheless.

1
A Good Man Goes to War

DEBORAH PLESS

> The real hero is always a hero by mistake; he dreams of being an honest coward like everybody else.
>
> —UMBERTO ECO

When did we become so afraid of being called cowards? Or, more accurately, at what point did the BBC determine that it was unacceptable for the Doctor to be a coward? Over the past nine years, as *Doctor Who* has come roaring back to life, blown expectations away, and become the international phenomenon that was always promised by the premise but only recently realized, one simple thing has changed: the Doctor isn't a coward anymore. Rather, he's an action figure who sometimes uses a gun when his screwdriver would do and possesses the moral high ground in every discussion. Why?

Cowards are, after all, essential to the survival of any species. Our ancestors, for all that we appreciate great stories of heroism, weren't the men and women in the front lines of the battle. We're all descended from the cowards and traitors who ran and hid from the fighting, who got lucky or were knocked unconscious by accident or who just didn't turn up for the battle. The human race depends on cowardice to perpetuate itself. And yet, we consider it one of our lowest traits. Heroes are brave. Heroes are good. Those two words, 'good' and 'brave', are almost synonymous. How can one be good without being brave? How can one be brave without being good? And how could the

Doctor, who represents all of our hopes and dreams for who we could be in an idealized world, be a pacifist?

Yet, at the start of the New Series in 2005, he was. Whether or not he could be categorized as a coward in the classical sense is debatable, but the Doctor himself identified his actions as cowardly in the first season finale, "Journey's End." As the show went on and became more popular overseas, though, he changed. The Doctor went from being a man who embraced his inner coward to a man who happily put on a silly hat and fired a gun to get attention in "A Town Called Mercy" (2012). Part of the reason for this transformation undoubtedly can be put at the feet of the War on Terror and a global landscape where cowardice was no longer an option. But another part, possibly a larger part, might be due to the increasing worldwide popularity of the show. It's all well and good for the Doctor to be a coward when Britain's watching the show, but it's another matter entirely when the world is watching too.

In other words, he changed, markedly and drastically, going from the man who couldn't flip the switch even to save the universe to a man who called himself "The Oncoming Storm"—in "The Lodger" (2010)—and preferred to stand up to his enemies and tell them to run. And as the show became more popular globally, it seems that the Doctor shifted away from representing a British idealized self-perception. By the Eleventh Doctor, the character had become an angry god, self-directed to dispense moral judgment on humanity and its enemies. In a world rocked by terrorism and war, the Doctor's moral ambiguity and preference for non-violent options became less appealing than a strong, decisive Doctor who could stand up to threats and get physical if needed. We didn't want to see ourselves; we wanted to see someone better.

A Coward, Any Day

In the first season of the New Series, starting in 2005 under head writer Russell T Davies, the Ninth Doctor, portrayed by Christopher Eccleston, wasn't just a coward, but a self-admitting one. In his final episode, "The Parting of the Ways," when faced with his greatest enemy, the Doctor was asked what kind of man he is, and his answer was simple. "Coward, any day." The Doctor ran from his problems. He ran and hid, and he wasn't ashamed of it. Given the backstory of that character, the new timeline where the Ninth Doctor had awoken at the end of the great Time War, the last of the Time Lords and the only survivor of his race, it made sense. He'd survived because he was a coward, and he wasn't going to stop now. Cowards live longer.

As the series progressed, however, the story changed a little. First we learned, in "Dalek" (2005), that he'd been a part of the final battle between the Time Lords and the Daleks. Then, we discovered that not only had he been there, he had been the one to pull the trigger, so to speak, to end the war. The Doctor wasn't a coward, but a hero! Still, the Ninth Doctor insisted on viewing himself as a coward. Perhaps this was because he believed that cowardice was a preferable option to his actions in the war. He was ashamed of his courage, the courage that had led him to commit a double xenocide, and would prefer to live without it. Eccleston's Doctor represented a self-perception of the modern British man—not idealized, but scared, and unsure of his place in a shifting universe of potential enemies.

What's interesting isn't so much the Ninth Doctor's insistence on cowardice, but rather the show's later repudiation of that stance. When *Doctor Who* aired in 2005, it came to the screen in the wake of a renewed global understanding of terror and war. Tony Blair, while still Prime Minister and head of the Labour Party, was under attack from his constituents and the media for his role in involving Britain in the war in Iraq. In short, war wasn't popular in 2005, and the Ninth Doctor's philosophy reflected this.

The Oncoming Storm

Just a month after "Journey's End," on July 7th, 2005, London was rocked by a series of co-ordinated terror attacks. Over fifty-two civilians were killed, as well as the bombers themselves, and more than seven hundred civilians were injured. The national mood changed rapidly, as did the desire for a less nuanced, more clearly "heroic" Doctor. Into this milieu came the Tenth Doctor, played by David Tennant, a brave, genial, yet still somehow menacing figure. While the Ninth Doctor called himself a coward, the Tenth Doctor was a man who sometimes needed to be stopped. Rather than running away, this Doctor ran towards the danger, and scorned all those who didn't. In the Christmas Special, "The Runaway Bride" (2006), the Doctor yet again committed xenocide, killing off an admittedly hostile species—the Racnoss—to save Earth, but here he didn't seem conflicted over it. He seemed almost gleeful, a fact that his companion Donna pointed out. "Doctor," she yells, in one of the more famous lines from the episode, "you can stop now!" The point was clear. This Doctor, this new Doctor, wasn't the sort of man who needed to be afraid of anything. Rather, everything else, from Daleks to humans, should be afraid of him. And they were.

What's also interesting in this timeframe is the popularity of the show. While the first season back was a modest success in Britain and barely exported, the later seasons, starting in the Tenth Doctor's run, were increasingly successful abroad. The Doctor went from being a British icon, to being internationally recognized, and particularly popular in America. The show has even gone so far as to acknowledge this, making increasing mention of the United States in its episodes, and even filming some of the sixth season in Utah ("The Impossible Astronaut" and "Day of the Moon," 2011). The Doctor became more than just a representation of British idealized action, he became a stand-in for the rest of the world during a time of crisis. The show no longer had the luxury of letting the Doctor be a coward, not if they wanted to continue exporting the show for a global audience.

The storylines in the Tenth Doctor's run, similar to those of the Ninth's, frequently dealt with issues of "no-win situations" or overwhelming odds or unintended consequences. With this Doctor, however, the stakes were rarely seen as being quite so nuanced. A wide variety of episodes specifically dealt with xenocide, but with less of a regard for the affected species. As we've seen, the Doctor eradicates the Racnoss with a clear conscience in "The Runaway Bride." Shortly after that, in "The Shakespeare Code" (2007), he allows the Carrionites to remain banished to a nether-realm for the rest of eternity, determining that to be the better fate for the world. In "The Family of Blood" (2007), he enacts revenge on the titular Family—a revenge that's merciless and literally eternal. While all of these plots involve the destruction of openly hostile species, it's still worth noting that no episodes during this time featured a peaceful resolution or a compromise with the villains. In the Tenth Doctor's tenure, it was better to kill and possibly regret it than to walk away.

The real stream of violent episodes, or rather episodes in which the Doctor unrepentantly destroyed a species, began in the third season of the New Series. This is perhaps because the second season, which aired in the spring and summer of 2006, was already mostly written and conceptualized before the July 7th bombings in London, as well as before the abrupt departure of Christopher Eccleston, who played the Ninth Doctor. As a result, the episodes of the second season have a different tone than the rest of the Tenth Doctor's run, and featured more lighthearted plots centered on the human relationships of the Doctor's companion, Rose. It's not until the Season Three that a marked philosophical shift appears.

This shift continued throughout the Tenth Doctor's time, changing each season and becoming more pronounced. In the fourth season, the Doctor refused to interfere and save the city during the "The Fires of Pompeii" (2008), but not out of cowardice. Here, he was presented as brave and sacrificing, albeit stern. The city of Pompeii must be destroyed, the Doctor explains patiently, but he does allow his companion, Donna, to save a single family. Later, in "Planet of the Ood" (2008), the Doctor goes so far as to seek out the trouble on a planet and actually help foment a systems-wide slave rebellion. He refuses to sit back and watch idly, and condemns those who do.

Notably, in the Season Four finale, "Stolen Earth" and "Journey's End" (2008), the Doctor is joined by all of his previous companions from the New Series in order to take on the Daleks who, yet again, threaten to destroy the universe. Strangely, it's the Daleks who most recognize the Doctor's changed attitude, and they refer to him as "The Destroyer of Worlds." It's a title that carries with it some level of respect, which is alarming when coming from the Daleks. Furthermore, in that episode the Daleks point out how much the Doctor's influence has changed the humans around him. His companions, all originally peaceful civilians, have become soldiers, each of them willing to sacrifice themselves and possibly the planet in the hopes of stopping the Daleks. The Doctor has become a general, and he's at war.

Good Man Gone to War

Still, in the Tenth Doctor's time, the emphasis was more on the moral strength of the Doctor himself, and less on his physical strength. This changed in 2010 with the regeneration of the Doctor into his eleventh form, played by Matt Smith. Here, the Doctor became almost an action hero, brandishing his sonic screwdriver and the occasional gun with the bravado of a gunslinger in the Old West. Literally, as it turned out, when Season Seven's "A Town Called Mercy" took the Doctor and his two companions, Amy and Rory, to the Old West and the Doctor became temporarily the Sheriff, complete with gun. But this wasn't the first gun the Doctor held in the Matt Smith era.

Starting relatively soon in the Eleventh Doctor's run, we saw a marked increase in violent situations, as well as an increase in the Doctor's emotional detachment from them. The fifth season episode, "The Time of Angels" (2010), featured a dramatic scene where the Doctor fires a gun at the ceiling of a crashed spaceship—admittedly this is so that the gravity will reverse and save their lives, but it still marks an important moment. Up to this point, the Doctor has religiously avoided guns, preferring to carry around a useful but intentionally pacifistic screwdriver as his tool of choice. Here, though, we see that the Doctor is eschewing pacifism for bold action. It's a conscious choice, because he so easily could've made that choice differently. He could have used the sonic screwdriver, having no defined function or limits, to alter the ship's gravity. The Doctor chooses to fire a gun instead. The action is bold and cinematic, but also contrary to the Doctor's previous strong stance in favor of pacifism.

Just after that episode, in "The Vampires of Venice" (2010), the Doctor allows yet another race of aliens to perish in favor of saving the human race. While this is a good moment for humanity, it's notable that the Doctor doesn't seem to feel any regret about his decision here. Rather, he barely even seems emotionally affected by it, preferring to leave immediately afterwards with hardly a backward glance. In the next season's episodes, "The Impossible Astronaut" and "Day of the Moon," the Doctor actually goes so far as to brainwash the entire human race into exterminating a species of aliens on sight. What makes this even more morally suspect is the revelation that said aliens, the Silence, while not particularly friendly to humans, had coexisted with us for thousands of years and seemed to have no immediate nefarious plans. Yet, the Eleventh Doctor has them systematically eradicated with the understanding that his moral judgment in this matter is above humanity's and therefore to be trusted above all else.

Finally, in "A Good Man Goes to War" (2011), the Doctor seemingly completes his emotional journey when he chooses to violently assault a mysterious organization in order to save his companions' newborn child—the rest of the Eleventh Doctor's time on the show is largely a continuation of his character from this episode. Again, the bad guys are clearly bad, and the Doctor's motive seems quite sound. But the tonal shift, from a Doctor who'd rather find a sneaky way to solve the problem, or just talk at everyone until he could do something clever, is gone. This Doctor, the Eleventh Doctor, was more action hero than reluctant tourist and his storylines reflected that.

In a complete reversal from the Season One episode "The Parting of the Ways" (2005), where the Doctor refused to perform an action that would destroy the Daleks but also endanger humanity, the seventh season's episode "Asylum of the Daleks" (2012) featured the Doctor's decision to not only destroy an entire planet filled with Daleks, but to destroy along with it a single sentient human mind. Arguably this mind, Oswin, was the one choosing to destroy the Daleks, but a close look at the episode shows that the Doctor is both aware and supportive of Oswin's decision. There's no more room for moral ambiguity or doubt. The Doctor is right and therefore any action he contemplates, no matter how violent, is considered justified.

But perhaps the most alarming moment in the Eleventh Doctor's run comes in only his second episode: "The Beast Below" (2010). In this episode, the Doctor and his companion, Amy, find themselves aboard *Starship UK*, a ship that can't fly and is being kept aloft by the continual torture of a giant Star Whale—the last of its kind. The Doctor, on discovering this, becomes utterly horrified by humanity. While the Doctor had, in previous episodes, expressed contempt for human actions, it's in this episode that he shows the venom behind his words. "You're only human." He spits them out at his companion, condemning her for a choice—to forget her knowledge of the Star

Whale—that she doesn't recall making, and in these lines, it becomes clear that the Eleventh Doctor doesn't consider himself one with humanity. He's above us. The rest of the Eleventh Doctor's time on the show reflects this belief, as he becomes further and further alienated from the humanity that was once his calling card. As you may remember, in the Classic Series, the Doctor was often chastised by other Time Lords or aliens for being *too* human, too soft and sentimental. Here, he's changed. He isn't a coward, he's the good man gone to war.

Never Cruel or Cowardly

The Fiftieth Anniversary Special, "The Day of the Doctor" (2013), took the Doctor's shift away from nuanced moral responsibility and avowed cowardice into a place where not only was cowardice not an option, it was anathema to the Doctor's entire ethos. The Ninth Doctor was defined by his actions in the Time War. His decision to act as a soldier and destroy both the Time Lords and the Daleks in order to save the universe was the cornerstone of his personality and decisions. He became a pacifist, a coward, because he saw firsthand the devastating effects of violence in the name of courage. The Ninth Doctor's line, "Coward, any day," is a direct result of his actions in the Time War. Fitting, then, that in the episode where we discover what precisely those actions were, the Doctor himself repudiates that identity, choosing to be, "Never cowardly or cruel."

In the special, the Tenth and Eleventh Doctors are transported back to the moment when the War Doctor—played by John Hurt—chose to press the button that would destroy the Time Lords and Daleks and end the Time War. While previously, the Time War had been spoken of as devastating because of the actions of both armies, the Time Lords being equally as responsible as the Daleks—as revealed in "The End of Time"—here, the Time Lords were portrayed as the innocent victims of an invading Dalek force. This made the Doctor's choice to destroy both of them much more reprehensible, as the Time Lords were clearly "not the bad guys." But the message of the special isn't pacifism. Rather, the message is: force should be wielded solely against one's enemies. In a twist that negated the Ninth Doctor's character arc, it's revealed that the War Doctor did not, in fact, destroy the Time Lords, he merely hid them.

During the special, as the Tenth and Eleventh Doctors try to convince the War Doctor not to press the button, they repeatedly inform him that he isn't a coward. They even construct his identity around this fact. He chose the name "the Doctor," we're told, as a promise to himself that he'd be "Never cruel or cowardly." In other words, the Doctor can't be the Doctor and remain a coward. It's impossible. The Ninth Doctor is wrong. Not only was he wrong about his cowardice and pacifism; he was also wrong about his guilt, since the Time Lords weren't destroyed, and his entire character arc no longer mattered. If the Time Lords had been destroyed then the Doctor's radical shift to pacifism and cowardice is a natural progression of understandable reactions to stress and grief. Without the death of the Time Lords and with the Doctor now a hero, the Ninth Doctor's arc of accepting his actions and learning to live again is pointless. The Time Lords were saved by the Doctor's incredible courage and moral decisiveness. The action hero Doctor was here to stay.

The Doctors Who Will Be

It's still too early to tell what sort of Doctor the Twelfth will ultimately turn out to be, but we do have indications that *Doctor Who* might be coming full circle. In the episode "Listen" (2014), Clara gives a monologue about fear to the Doctor himself as a child that seems to validate the Ninth Doctor's position on cowardice:

> Fear is a superpower. Fear can make you faster and cleverer and stronger . . . But that's okay, because if you're very wise and very strong fear doesn't have to make you cruel or cowardly. Fear can make you kind.

From the Ninth Doctor's insistence on the value of cowardice to an open refusal of it, the show and the Doctor changed a good deal in nine years. At the start, the Doctor seemed to be a representation of modern Britain as war-weary and covered in battle scars. He was afraid of the terrible things he'd done, and refused to do any more. As time went on, though, and global events continued to escalate, the Doctor grew less frightened, perhaps even a little eager to confront the enemies that frightened him before. He became, with Tennant's run, the "Oncoming Storm" and by Smith's tenure, the "Good Man Gone to War." The Doctor no longer ran, but now stayed to fight, sometimes going so far as to strike first. He changed. Did we?

The Doctor's transformation suggests a shift in the ideal man—no longer valuing the self-hating coward; we turn instead to the righteous man driven by purpose to defeat his enemies. It seems clear that the Tenth and Eleventh Doctors were influenced heavily by American action movies and the prevalent global desire for uncomplicated heroes. While it was all well and good for the Doctor to be a coward when the stakes were low, as the global situation became more intense and the focus of international politics came to rest more firmly, not on past failures, but on the importance of preventing future terrorist attacks, our cultural consciousness required a hero capable of preventing attacks proactively.

Cowards are fine in peacetime, but in times of crisis, we want a good man who will go to war.

2
How Time Lords Invented TV

Colin Dray

On the 23rd of November, 1963, an old man stepped out of a box many had dismissed as garbage, and casually remade the world. Appearing innocuous, both man and box bristled with depthless potential; and together, over the subsequent five decades, they would upend every expectation, every convention, every limitation that they faced.

The man was known only as "the Doctor." He was a contradiction, a conundrum; his name itself was a mystery. He looked like Ebenezer Scrooge but was a technical wizard, batting the laws of physics away like a tedious housefly. And his box—that magical, illogical box—the source of his magnificent powers? That allows him to traverse the stars and alter the very fabric of the universe? The box that can go anywhere and anywhen? That's bigger on the inside?

No, not the TARDIS. His *other* magical box—Television.

It's frequently observed that *Doctor Who* premiered the day after United States President John F. Kennedy was assassinated; less frequently acknowledged is that this was a period in which television was becoming the most influential medium in the Western world. For instance, programs like *The Andy Griffith Show*, *Coronation Street*, and *The Avengers* were becoming cultural touchstones, live reportage of Kennedy's assassination and funeral were some of the first global satellite broadcasts, Lee Harvey Oswald was murdered live on air, and in May of 1964, images filmed from the Faith 7 space capsule were screened on NBC. Able to reach into millions of homes, uniting them all with a shared experience, television was swiftly becoming the new campfire around which society could gather to hear its stories told.

The medium wasn't without its detractors, however. As early as 1961, Federal Communications Commission Chairman Newton Minow, in a speech to the National Association of Broadcasters, famously declared television a "vast wasteland":

> You will see a procession of game shows, formula comedies about totally unbelievable families, blood and thunder, mayhem, violence, sadism, murder, western bad men, western good men, private eyes, gangsters, more violence, and cartoons. And endlessly, commercials—many screaming, cajoling and offending.

The original version of Minow's speech read "a vast wasteland of junk," but he truncated the line on delivery. In hindsight, the edit is a shame, as for *Doctor Who*, it becomes curiously prescient. After all, it's literally from a junkyard that the Doctor and his fantastical box emerge, and yet the series would go on to articulate the most compelling argument for television, and the endlessly evolving audio-visual canvas it presents.

Let There Be Light . . .

The first episode of *Doctor Who*, "An Unearthly Child" (1963), is a marvelous expression of the show's central conceit, offering an arresting metaphor for the revolutionary imaginative journey about to take place. Playing out like an episode of *The Twilight Zone*, two high school teachers, Ian and Barbara— each representing the education that shapes young minds with facts and figures, one teaching history, the other science—are puzzled by the odd behavior of one of their students, Susan, and follow her home to a junkyard where she appears to be living. There they meet her grandfather, an extraordinary man who dislodges them from their rational, recognizable world, and delivers them to a new fantastical universe of wonder.

For the remainder of the episode, the Doctor—although begrudging and irascible in this first incarnation—acts as a Promethean figure for humanity. The narrative even travels back to the dawn of human civilization, where the Doctor grants fire to a tribe of squabbling cavemen, who are likewise trying to adapt to a new age of literal enlightenment—"With fire it is day." But it's with the Doctor's efforts to widen Ian and Barbara's perspective upon the universe that the narrative is truly concerned. This inscrutable Doctor and his impossible TARDIS introduce Ian, Barbara, and his audience to the infinite possibility of imagination that fuels all speculative fiction and that has remained at the heart of the *Doctor Who* mythos throughout the entirety of its run. Imagination is more powerful than fact. Don't accept anything at face value. Things are bigger on the inside.

"Run!" Keeping Up with the Doctor

"Upend expectation" became the mission statement for the program itself. If television was the junkyard Minow described, then instead of seeing this as a failing, *Doctor Who* exploited it as a boon. The show's plasticity allowed it to go anywhere, be anything. Like television itself, it could bounce from costume drama to high-concept sci-fi, adventure tales, parody, anti-utopian think-pieces and schlocky horror, thrillers, war fiction, political satire, broad fantasy, love stories, action, and farce. Its fictions re-appropriated an eclectic mix of source material: H.G. Wells, Sherlock Holmes, C.S. Lewis, Arthur C. Clarke, genre films, historical record, and myth.

One week the characters bumped up against Marco Polo ("Marco Polo," 1964), the next, they negotiated political struggles between moth people and telepathic ants ("The Web Planet," 1965). *Doctor Who* preludes the works of James Cameron's *Terminator* ("The War Machines," 1966), Ridley Scott's *Alien* ("The Ark in Space," 1975), and the Wachowskis' *The Matrix* ("The Deadly Assassin," 1976).

Despite being originally aimed at children, *Doctor Who* pitched concepts for all ages, utilizing its endlessly malleable form to play out myriad ideological and philosophical debates. In the wake of the Second World War, amidst Cold War paranoia, invasion stories and monster tales became commonplace: Daleks were squawking fascists and Cybermen personified an increasingly dehumanized, automated world. Totalitarianism, determinism, environmentalism, nuclear power, apartheid, even taxation, were all played out in expansive metaphors through which the Doctor, ever-curious, would ramble. With the rise of a more progressive view of women in society, companion characters like Sarah Jane Smith, Romana, Leela, and Ace helped break the tired damsel-in-distress mold of adventure tales. Diversity, sexuality, equality were respected; class divides, cruelty, intolerance were staunchly condemned.

The show was willing to innovate both on screen and off. Its producer, Verity Lambert, was the youngest and first female producer for a BBC drama series. Its theme music, an experimental wonder from composer Ron Grainer and the BBC Radiophonic Workshop, was the first to be made entirely from electronic distortion. Its title sequence was an optical illusion created by toying around with the cameras and monitors. It frequently invented otherworldly effects with lenses and perspective-shifted sets, and crafted unique design and costuming, evoking M.C. Escher drawings, sleek modern sterility, or Gothic decay. And throughout, it was a show that embraced its medium's limitations—most drastically when the ailing health of series star, William Hartnell, forced him to retire.

Television is replete with such production necessities—actors leave, plots get rewritten—but rather than trying to emulate Hartnell's characterization, as though swapping out Darrens in *Bewitched*, *Who*'s producers incorporated it into the DNA of the show. Embracing his alien nature, the Doctor regenerated into a whole new persona, one filled with his predecessor's experiences, but remade anew. Patrick Troughton presented a unique take on the same character—now a Chaplinesque figure, disguising his depthless wisdom with disarming foolery—and the result, continuing for each retirement of the principle actor, was a program elementally designed to evolve with the circumstances of its fiction and viewership. Beside a few inviolable personality traits—the Doctor arguably remains pacifist, moral, and altruistic—he could suddenly be anything: a dashing hero, a romantic Victorian, a Socratic trickster, a cowardly braggart, or a scruffy nonconformist. Each iteration draws upon those that preceded them while adding their own unique flair.

Thus, as television altered over the years, the show evolved ahead of it, winding the realities of its production into an organic part of the fiction. Cast members came and went. When the sets got too drab, the TARDIS redecorated itself. When color television emerged the Doctor's most sartorially vibrant persona appeared. Everyone in the universe speaks English because of a telepathic circuit in the TARDIS. Even when budget constraints impacted the show's ability to create alien environments, the Third Doctor was suddenly serving "Time Lord house arrest" on Earth (1970–73). And each time, these necessary concessions informed and enriched the fiction.

The show was never blind to criticisms of television, however—even to its own contribution to the medium. In the David Tennant episode, "Idiot's Lantern" (2006), the rise in television sales preceding the Queen's coronation is seen as a harbinger for social ruin. An alien living in the broadcast signal sucks people's identities away, literalizing the cliché that television rots the mind. Sylvester McCoy's Doctor in "The Greatest Show in the Galaxy" (1988) was forced into a gladiatorial arena for the entertainment of bloodthirsty pan-dimensional beasts, portrayed like a television-viewing family.

Christopher Eccleston's Doctor seemed to be a season-long interrogation of the media. In "The Long Game" (2005) a broadcasting hub called Satellite Five was manipulating the news to impede humanity's development, while in "Bad Wolf" (2005) murderous reality shows have overrun all television entertainment, leaving "fifteen minutes of fame" to be merely a temporary reprieve from death. In the mid-1980s *Who* even put itself on a meta-textual trail while under threat of cancellation. "The Trial of a Time Lord" (1986) was a season-long arc in which a series of loosely connected adventures depicted the Doctor being called to justify his very existence—those in the courtroom even watched his adventures on a "viewscreen."

And *Who* was alert to the intimacy television develops with its audience—the regularity with which it enters their homes. This was particularly true in the United Kingdom where it has predominantly remained a Saturday evening fixture, shared across generations: children cowering at their first sighting of a Cyberman; nostalgic parents watching their childhood adventures live on.

It's why fans speak of *"their"* Doctor distinct from his other personas, and why the Doctor's enemies enter the communal consciousness. Jonathan Bignell characterized the show as living in the minds of its audience in "Space for 'Quality': Negotiating with the Daleks." He states:

Doctor Who's mysterious fictional world and the lack of conventional closure in individual episodes or in series as a whole leaves room for sustained involvement, repeated viewing and intense attention . . . the persistence of memories of the Daleks in these different situations testifies to another kind of quality, measured by the enduring affect of television and its embedding in processes of identity-formation.

The audience grows with *Who*, giving life to it. And it was this interdependence that would allow the program to transcend its boundaries even further, when in 1989, the series was canceled.

A Postmodern Prometheus

For a character who defies death with transformation, it was fitting that the Doctor should survive cancellation by expanding into other media. As early as the first years of its original run, *Doctor Who* released supplementary comic books and short fiction, but when the series ended, the narrative leapt entirely into an ongoing series of novels, called *New Adventures*, that continued the journey of the inscrutable Seventh Doctor, Sylvester McCoy.

In 1996, an attempt was made to revive the series as an international coproduction between the BBC, Universal, and FOX networks. Sadly, the resulting pilot movie, *Doctor Who* (1996), was a promising but flawed mess. The plot was too bogged down in the show's history to be coherent to new viewers, while established fans were put off by its new action film sensibility: motorcycle chases, the Doctor's chaste flirtation with his companion, the Master inexplicably mutating into black goo.

It explored an intriguing *Frankenstein* motif and the TARDIS finally looked spectacular, but the only element universally praised was Paul McGann's performance of the Doctor. Unscathed by the melodramatic clutter surrounding him (Eric Roberts plays the Master as a cackling pantomime Dracula), McGann's Doctor was a charming Romantic. Consequentially, when the pilot failed, McGann's debonair Doctor nonetheless became the official Doctor of the expanding multimedia pantheon, adventuring across new comic series, novels, and radio plays. Other franchises have produced similar ancillary media—*Star Trek* cartoons, *Battlestar Galactica* novels—but

Doctor Who was the most remarkable example of how resilient a television fiction could be at evolving onward, even in the absence of the show itself.

It took another decade for *Who* to return to television screens; although when it did, it returned as a prestige program, and rather than completely rebooting itself, picked up where it had left off. Again reflecting the experience of its audience, the twenty-first century's first Doctor, the Ninth Doctor, was a man who—like Western civilization—had been rocked by bloodshed. Thematically evoking the shadow of terrorism and the emotional baggage of participating in an intractable war, this Doctor, played by Christopher Eccleston, was a profoundly altered man. Showrunner Russell T Davies chose to kill off the race of Time Lords in a conflict called the Time War. The Doctor was now a traumatized lone survivor, mourning the loss of his race and trying to outrun the horrors he'd seen, and inflicted, in battle. The man who had inspired so much hope in others over the years found his own profoundly shaken.

When Eccleston was replaced by the charismatic David Tennant, the Tenth Doctor became more of a heartbroken, wandering god, and the high, operatic tone of the show's serialized format was pushed to the forefront. Davies's scripts explored tragic love stories (Rose), heroic, sacrificial calls to action (Donna; Martha), fatalism and arbitrary evil ("The Waters of Mars," 2009 and "Midnight," 2008), and offered interconnected seasonal story arcs, like Bad Wolf, "he will knock four times," and the mystery of the stars going out, which all achieved the narrative unity unsuccessfully attempted in "The Trial of a Time Lord." Davies was also the first writer to seriously explore the ruinous effect that traveling with the Doctor could have upon companions and their families. Rose, heartbroken, is left stranded in an alternate universe. Martha's family was imprisoned and tortured by the Master. Donna had her memory, everything that she'd achieved and become in her time with the Doctor, erased. This was a man who, despite his good intentions, frequently left carnage in his wake.

Davies highlighted the operatic spectacle of televisual cheesiness. The color palate was striking—even garish—with fierce primary hues and high contrasts. Villains like the Slitheen were played for broad farce, farting over their horrid puns. Actors like John Simm were encouraged to chew the scenery. Finally, the Tenth Doctor's demise was punctuated by a soaring, choral Ood lament, echoing throughout space and time to sing him to rest.

When Steven Moffat became showrunner, he drew upon an even older source of iterative storytelling: *fairytales*—embracing the 'time' in 'Once upon a time . . .' His Eleventh Doctor, played by Matt Smith, was recast as a creature from folklore. A young girl, Amelia Pond—"a name in a fairytale . . ."—sees him fall like a shooting star and spends the rest of her adolescence wondering whether what she experienced was real, or just a dream. Over the course of this season, he grows from her imaginary friend—the "Raggedy Man," a Peter-Pan figure inviting her to come away with him on storybook adventures with vampires, cowboys, and the Whisper Men of nursery rhymes—into a legend told across the universe, a dangerous mythical trickster who must be stopped.

Pointedly, when the Doctor disappears only to return years later, Amelia's story becomes the most multi-layered meta-commentary on the audience-text relationship in the show's history. While young Amelia embodies the wish-fulfillment fantasy of a child dreaming of running off with the Doctor, Amy (as she calls herself in adulthood) represents a jaded adult outlook, measuring the Doctor against her memory, scrutinizing her nostalgic adoration.

Amy wasn't just another traveler caught in the Doctor's updraft—she was a fan. Delighted by the Doctor in her youth, she was heartbroken when he disappeared, even starting to lose faith that he would return. And so, in the "The Big Bang" (2010), when the universe was rebooted and the Doctor erased, the most powerful magic in all of space and time is revealed to be *belief*. Amy—like the Doctor's fans—literally willed him back into being by *believing* in him. She remembered his blue box (so vivid blue it was like something from a dream), and her investment in his story returns him to life.

A Doctor a Day . . .

Doctor Who used its Fiftieth Anniversary Special, "The Day of the Doctor" (2013), to once again indulge a feat it alone can exploit: having one character meet multiple versions of himself. Centering upon the unseen Time War between the Daleks and the Time Lords, Moffat used the return of two Doctors—David Tennant and the previously unknown form played by John Hurt—to revisit the Doctor's greatest regret: the act of genocide that decimated two races. Doing so, the show looks back upon its storied history, both as a fiction and a television institution.

There were nods to the first episode: the original title and theme tune; the sight of a policeman in Totter's Lane; the Doctor's current companion, Clara, being a teacher at Cole Hill Secondary School. There were self-aware allusions to "Reversing the polarity," the catchphrase of Jon Pertwee's Third Doctor—"*I'm* reversing it; *you're* reversing it back. We're *confusing* the polarity." There were also swipes at Tennant's fake British accent ("Brave words, Dick Van Dyke"), and even several grumpy asides from John Hurt's more traditional Doctor chastising the youthful antics of his latter selves— "*Timey Wimey*. Do you have to talk like children?" There's even the meta-textual gag of the Doctors traveling through time in a painting—the "television" of the past—to erupt back out through a shattering screen. There were the larger narrative references only possible in serialized television: the return of Classic *Who* enemies the Zygons and UNIT; depicting the infamous end of the Time War; and the show-stopping reveal of every one of the Doctor's incarnations circling Gallifrey.

It was a thunderous adventure, but at its heart lay a moment of introspection that the Doctor traditionally avoids. Locked (or *unlocked*) in a prison, unable to flee, he stared himself in the face and confronted his own actions. Moffat loads this self-assessment into the narrative at every level, inviting the viewer to explore their own relationship with this generational hero. It's why the Zygons, although not as iconic as Daleks or Cybermen, prove to be thematically resonant antagonists. In a fiction where the protagonist alters his face and is no longer sure who he is, shape-shifting alien frauds symbolize the perpetually fluctuating nature of the show itself, inviting us to question what exactly unites these disparate versions of "the Doctor."

And the answer, it seems, is hope.

Because the most significant thing Moffat does in this special is to restore the Doctor's fundamental optimism. Despite the narrative potential in Davies's decision to make the Doctor a war criminal, it had irreparably damaged him. He became the man who regrets; the man so burdened with countless sorrows that he welcomes the chance to forget. Returning to this point in his past, allowing him to remake his choice, Moffat legitimizes the Doctor's sacrifice, but rescues the character from his desolation. The man who inspires hope in others, is allowed to feel it again himself.

Having reaffirmed the Doctor's sense of self, the episode then projects into the show's future. After stealing a time machine and fleeing his planet, the Doctor finally has a restored faith in his homeland and himself; so much so that he commits himself to heading home. His quest is no longer one of escape, but restoration. After countless years of running, there's now somewhere to run to. For an alien over a millennia old—already a cantankerous grandfather before audiences met him—the Doctor is finally growing up.

Having started as a children's program, but swiftly compounding itself into a mythic institution, "The Day of the Doctor" celebrated what has made *Doctor Who* endure for generations—a legacy inextricably tied to what makes television such an appealing box through which to travel. The episode was a remembrance, a rebirth, a restatement of purpose, simulcast around the world to ninety-four countries; it returned us to that same fantastical character emerging from that same extraordinary box, in order to show just how far the show, the medium, and we the audience, have all evolved.

The Revolution Will Be Time-Lord-ized

Television has always embraced the irrational, the illogical. It asks us to believe in artificially serialized dramas; resolvable conflicts; families communicating in snappy witticisms while facing an invisible fourth wall. But years ago, stepping out of a junk pile, *Doctor Who* did something remarkable: rather than fight those limitations, or pretend them away, it embraced them, and exploited them.

Film and literature despite being elegant mediums, remain static. An audience can return to them and glean new meaning, but only the *viewer* has changed, not the text itself. *Doctor Who* reveals that television isn't constrained in such a manner—appropriately, as on ongoing series, it isn't a prisoner of time. Television shows return again next week and respond to audience feedback. Its characters grow, its genres merge and splinter, its plots can literally be rewritten, growing alongside its dedicated audience.

In the first episode, "An Unearthly Child" (1963), the TARDIS breaks. No longer able to disguise itself, it remains a big, blue anachronistic box—a magic portal, bigger on the inside. The TARDIS becomes television itself, a powerful symbol at the heart of a text that has consistently confronted limitation with ingenuity, cancelation with rebirth, constraint with transcendence. And for a program so enmeshed in the history of television, that speaks volumes about a medium once dismissed as a "wasteland," offending and dull.

The Doctor, his spacecraft, and the program itself, embody everything that makes the television medium such an adaptable, enduring canvas. The show's title is a question—Doctor *Who?*—and its genius is that it has never limited itself to an answer. The series never stops exploring the potentialities that arise when storytelling is unbounded, allowing the imagination to wander. *Doctor Who* just keeps inviting us off on new adventures, iterating, expanding, and exploring—showing us how the old can always be re-made anew.

3

The Mystical Alchemy of "Midnight"

KATHERINE SAS

When writer and producer Russell T Davies brought *Doctor Who* into the twenty-first century, he did so with the expressed intention of strengthening the emotional content in the story and the characters. In the DVD featurette "The Journey (So Far)," Davies explains that he

> wanted to create a story for the Doctor . . . That's the thing it's easy to miss on *Doctor Who.* You can just have the Doctor turn up and put all your energy into the aliens and the plot and the escapes and the chases and the explosions . . .

Instead, he wanted to create a story that "looked at a man with a past and with a history." In his vision for the New Series, Davies sought to craft believable and moving emotional arcs for the Doctor and his companions.

Literary Alchemy

One of the traditional toolboxes for depicting human change and transformation which writers have at their disposal is literary alchemy. Originating in the ancient and medieval practice of practical alchemy, this network of symbols gradually evolved into a useful framework for the depiction of the process of human change. This use of alchemical symbolism in fiction has become known as literary alchemy. As historian of literary alchemy Stanton Linden explained in his book *Darke Hierogliphicks*, "literary alchemy has the human condition as its prime concern, but it is the human condition as touched, or 'worked upon', by recognizable aspects of the theory and practice" of the art of alchemy. Historical alchemy itself is based on the literal process of change: the alchemist's transformation of lead into gold, mirrored sympathetically and symbolically by the purification of the alchemist's soul. The traditional maxim of alchemy—explained by Titus Burckhardt as "whatever is below resembles that which is above" in *Alchemy: Science of the Cosmos, Science of the Soul*—illustrates this symbiotic relationship between symbols and reality which characterizes alchemy. If, as Linden says, "alchemy is splendidly equipped to represent moral transformation and transmutation," then by invoking the symbolism of the alchemical process, a writer can represent figuratively the process of change in her characters, and by extension work that same change in the heart of sympathetic readers or viewers.

While scholars such as Linden and John Granger have shown that literary alchemy in this modern sense began in the Renaissance and early modern period with the dramas of Shakespeare and the poetry of John Donne and George Herbert, it has persisted quietly in highbrow literature since then, and recently it's experienced something of a pop-cultural revival. (See for instance Granger's account of alchemical imagery in *Harry Potter* in his book *How Harry Cast His Spell*). Likewise, alchemical symbolism has been part of *Doctor Who*'s scaffolding since its earliest conception. In his *TARDIS Eruditorum* series, Philip Sandifer has identified overt nods to alchemy throughout the Classic Series of *Doctor Who*. These nods were mostly derived from the show's first script editor David Whitaker who, as Sandifer puts it, is "the conscious author of *Doctor Who*'s weird legacy" and is "responsible for introducing a set of alchemical themes to *Doctor Who* that actively render the show mystical in its implications."

In particular, Sandifer notes that "both the Doctor and the TARDIS are clearly associated with mercury." The TARDIS because it, as established in the Classic Series episode "The Wheel in Space" (1968), runs on mercury; the Doctor for his playful and even chaotic qualities. As everything alchemical, mercury exists on several levels: as a planet, a god or a spirit, and as both a metal and element. Lyndy Abraham's *Dictionary of Alchemical Imagery* calls mercury (also Mercurius or "quicksilver") the "central symbol in alchemy . . . symbolizing the agent of transmutation . . . the transformative substance without which the opus"—the alchemical great work—"cannot be performed." In *The Discarded Image,* medieval scholar C.S. Lewis characterizes the conception of mercury in the Middle Ages as active, curious, eager, and bright. He advises the reader to take some real mercury in a saucer and play with it for a few minutes. *"That* is what 'Mercurial' means." By associating the Doctor and his time machine with this dominant alchemical figure, Whitaker and subsequent writers of the Classic Series identified the Doctor with this agent of alchemical change upon the world, marking him as the anarchic catalyst for the transformation of other peoples and worlds.

Alchemical Imagery in Davies's *Doctor Who*

While such use of alchemical symbolism shows that the New Series showrunner Russell T Davies didn't introduce alchemy to *Doctor Who*, it's also clear that Davies did initiate an unprecedented shift. As suggested by the earlier quote, Davies wanted to show the Doctor as not just triggering change in the outside world but being changed himself. While the Doctor has certainly always undergone the undeniably alchemical cyclical death and rebirth in the form of repeated regenerations, Davies wanted to take it a step further and show individual incarnations of the Doctor as undergoing a personal and interior journey.

The Ninth Doctor (played by Christopher Eccleston) underwent a journey towards redemption during Season One, but over the course of Seasons Two through Four chronicling the adventures of the longer-lived Tenth Doctor (played by David Tennant), Davies found the opportunity to carve an even more detailed, believable, and ultimately moving arc for the main character. While Davies hasn't publicly admitted to having studied alchemical imagery or using it consciously, these symbols have become such a pervasive part of art and culture (not to mention *Doctor Who* itself) that he used them intuitively and skillfully nonetheless—particularly in the Tenth Doctor's last season and in the special episode run-up to his symbolic death and regeneration.

Broadly speaking, the subject of the alchemical *magnum opus* travels through three stages on its way towards symbolic death and rebirth. First, in the nigredo (black) stage, the subject matter is broken down into its most basic form. Next, in the albedo (white) stage, the subject is cleansed and purified. Finally, in the rubedo (red) stage, the alchemical work is completed and the subject revealed in its reborn state. Towards the end of his life, the Tenth Doctor passes symbolically through all three stages and in the end—after achieving redemption through self-sacrifice for his companion Wilf—he regenerates and is reborn as a new man. Let's take a look at Davies's use of alchemical imagery in his Fourth Season episode "Midnight" (2008), which presents a harrowing depiction of the nigredo that kick-starts the alchemical process.

The Nigredo in "Midnight"

In Davies's episode "Midnight," the mood and imagery of the nigredo run rampant. The Doctor's current companion, Donna, stays behind to relax at a futuristic spa on a deadly diamond planet called Midnight, while the Doctor takes "a big space truck with a bunch of strangers" across its surface to visit its famed sapphire waterfall. In the Doctor's ominous and tongue-in-cheek words, "What could possibly go wrong?"

From the first, the title and setting of the episode indicate that the characters are in a dark and dangerous place, although the use of imagery isn't always obvious. Contrary to expectation, Davies subverts the light and dark imagery. The eponymous planet of Midnight on which the story takes place is, after all, remarkable for its brightness. It's a planet made of pure diamond which has been "poisoned" by deadly "Xtonic sunlight" that scorches it constantly. Strangely, Davies has created a world of a deadly midnight sun. Right away we're cued to question the nature of light and dark in this story, in which a world called Midnight can paradoxically be lethally bright and where sunlight, normally a source of warmth and life, can reduce a human body to dust. This environment is uniquely hostile to life itself and even seems to prevent new life from growing.

Despite the brightness of the setting, the concept of astronomical midnight is terribly important and sets the overall tone for the episode. Darkness is the most pervasive image associated with the nigredo. Jacqueline Simpson and Steve

Roud's *Dictionary of English Folklore* notes that in popular imagination "midnight represents the deepest point of negativity" and was broadly "applied to a period rather than a point of time." Thus midnight is less concerned with the hands of the clock and more with the phases of the sun, moon, and stars, signifying the dark of night when people are most vulnerable. That the planet is named 'Midnight' signifies that this period of vulnerability is never-ending in this place. Indeed, once the bus is stopped it's notable that the lights fail, the scene from then on is lit by emergency lights and flashlights, creating a harsh chiaroscuro effect that invokes the darkness of the episode's title. The Midnight Entity itself acknowledges this symbolic darkness when, despite the planet's brightness, it refers to having "waited so long . . . *in the dark* . . . and the cold . . . and the diamonds."

According to Simpson, traditional English folklore also considered midnight the time when "ghosts, demons, and all uncanny beings are most active" and "magic rituals and divinations" the most powerful. This notion has been popularly dubbed "the witching hour" or "witching time." Typically, paranormal beings in *Doctor Who* are explained away as just another type of alien—for example, witches as Carrionites in "The Shakespeare Code" (2007), vampires as Saturnynian in "The Vampires of Venice" (2010), and a werewolf as a Lupine Wavelength Haemovariform in "Tooth and Claw" (2006). But Davies pointedly never reveals the nameless Midnight Entity's true origin. Though technically an extraterrestrial, the Midnight Entity and its home-world seem to possess a more magical or supernatural nature than other *Doctor Who* monsters.

This is indicated by hints scattered throughout the episode. Driver Joe mentions the peculiarly occult-sounding "Winter Witch Canyon" as one of the tourist attractions the bus will pass, suggesting possible local legends lurking in the planet's background. Indeed, the very act of the Midnight Entity's possession of Sky and the Doctor, and the irrational fear, mistrust, and persecution it engenders, is strikingly reminiscent of the Salem witch-hunt, as portrayed in Arthur Miller's play *The Crucible*. Particularly similar are the scenes of escalating panic with the characters' dialogue overlapping in increasingly incomprehensible cacophony, even down to the eerily repeated dialogue. Compare the girls' repetitions of Abigail in *The Crucible*:

> **MARY:** Abby, you mustn't!
>
> **ABIGAIL:** [*Now all girls join, transfixed.*] Abby, you mustn't!
>
> **MARY:** [*To all girls, frantically*] I'm here, I'm here!
>
> **ABIGAIL:** [*With all girls*] I'm here, I'm here!

with Sky's repetitions of the passengers:

> **VAL:** Tell her to stop!
>
> **SKY:** Tell her to stop!
>
> **VAL:** She's driving me mad—
>
> **SKY:** She's driving me mad—
>
> **VAL:** Just make her STOP!!
>
> **SKY:** Just make her STOP!
>
> [*Sky raising her voice tips the room over the edge—rising panic.*]

The newly possessed Sky remains crouched on the ground, moving only in twitchy, jerking, unnatural movements and with the wild, staring eyes of a cornered animal. Dee Dee compares her to the goblin men from Christina Rossetti's "Goblin Market," quoting lines about the danger of eating goblin or fairy food and being put under a magical spell, an ancient and potent fairytale tradition. Rational scientific explanation or not, the Midnight Entity behaves like a devil out of a folk tale: grimacing and sneering demonically, sowing fear and discord among the passengers, and urging them to commit murder and suicide. In an ironic and eerie mockery of the passage of time evoked by the name Midnight, her power waxes as the Doctor's wanes. In a land where it's always midnight, it's always the witching hour. The Doctor recognizes this awful power when he suggests the settlers should "build their Leisure Palace somewhere else. Let this planet keep turning round an Xtonic star in silence." In a very rare moment of defeat, the Doctor admits that here, he's as powerless as everyone else, and he wants nothing more than to just leave.

When Midnight Isn't Dark

Considering that the midnight setting is integral to the story's premise, why then isn't the planet Midnight physically dark, as well? Why not only include sunlight but emphasize its ubiquity and peril? This is because the mechanics of the physical danger in this story are another invocation of alchemical imagery. The Xtonic sunlight can burn a body to ash and dust in mere seconds, which further links it to the nigredo that breaks down the alchemical substance into its most basic form. Abraham notes that ashes are the "remains after the calcination (conversion to a fine white powder through heat) of the base metal" that results from the process of the nigredo. The horror of the cremation suffered by Joe, Claude, the Hostess, and Sky is a literalization of the symbolic death and putrefaction that the Doctor and his fellow passengers endure.

Though all suffer aboard Crusader 50, the Doctor's experiences are most prevalent as he remains the central character whose journey is being charted. "Midnight," more than any other episode, shows the Doctor stripped of all his customary tools to his most basic form. In this way, "Midnight" becomes a piece of psychological horror in which the audience witnesses the result of the Doctor with all of the things that make him the Doctor forcibly taken away. Most obviously, he lacks his TARDIS, his magical machine that allows him to escape and slip in and out of worlds at will. His trademark gadget, the sonic screwdriver, seems pretty useless this time. Once the cockpit is lost, and since he can't use it to repair the vehicle, he's forced to wait for rescue with everyone else.

Most crucially, this episode is "Companion-lite," as companion Donna Noble (Catherine Tate) decides to stay behind and relax in the Leisure Palace. Absent Donna to back him up, the Doctor lacks the necessary support to calm the panicking passengers and gain their trust. Without a relatable human to convince the others of his competence and trustworthiness, the Doctor's normally reassuring confidence comes across as boastful and arrogant. His assertion that they should listen to him because he's "clever" offends the others, increasing their defensive positions and suspicion. His habitual egoism devolves into egotism.

The Doctor's arrogance in this instance leads to his eventual predicament. Simply put, it's difficult to imagine things getting

quite this out of control if Donna were there. The absence of a
companion is thus essential to this story. The Doctor's ego is
one of the things which must be destroyed in his journey
towards redemption and rebirth. Donna's absence also serves
as a chilling foreshadowing of the Doctor's painful loss of
Donna in "Journey's End" (2008), and the subsequent mistakes
across the Season Four specials that'll lead to his regeneration.

More subtly, the Doctor is also stripped of less tangible
assets over the course of the episode. As mentioned, without
Donna to defend him or convince the others, his authority
steadily erodes. While it may be slightly misleading to think of
the Doctor as needing a monster in any dualistic sense, nevertheless there's a sense in which the lack of any tangibly identi-
fiable monster in this episode similarly cripples the Doctor's
ability to function. The fact that the unnamed Midnight Entity
remains unknowable and ghostly plays a tangible role in
events. The passengers spend much of the episode quarreling
over whether Sky is possessed or just having a psychotic breakdown, while the Doctor (who certainly believes in the existence
of some alien intelligence possessing Sky) remains agnostic
about the creature's motivation until well into the episode. The
Doctor can't fight the monster when the issue of whether
there's a monster at all remains unsettled. Even in the end, the
Doctor and the audience are given virtually no information
about the creature's origins, powers, or motivations. Without a
monster to fight, the Doctor lacks purpose and becomes just
another frightened passenger aboard a stranded vessel.

The most terrifying loss, of course, is that of the Doctor's
voice. The most memorable and disturbing aspect of "Midnight"
is certainly the Midnight Entity's ability to mimic, then talk in
unison with, and then eventually anticipate the speech of the
human passengers. Though the Entity begins by applying its
weird power to the entire group, sowing paranoia among them,
it eventually focuses on the Doctor for special attention. For
every incarnation of the Doctor, the power of speech underlies
his mercurial wit and ability to talk his way out of sticky situations. For the Tenth Doctor, who began his life by remarking
on his impressive "gob" in "The Christmas Invasion" (2005),
this loss is further compounded. In "Midnight," Donna remarks
that she can't imagine the Doctor without a voice, stressing the
extent to which the Doctor is defined by his voice. Once the

Midnight Entity "steals" the Doctor's voice, he loses virtually all of what little power remained to him, capable only of barely holding himself together. He becomes literally immobilized, visibly terrified, and powerless to defend himself physically or verbally. The tension and panic in Tennant's performance convey a powerful internal struggle in which all of the Doctor's energy goes into an exhausting, futile resistance against an overwhelming invader. The helplessness and vulnerability of the normally confident Doctor account for "Midnight's" reputation as one of the show's most terrifying episodes.

All of these elements—the darkness and peril of the setting, the unusually paranormal aspects of the antagonist, the absence of the familiar trappings of a normal *Doctor Who* story, and the weakness and vulnerability of the Doctor—combine to create the mood of suffering and despair that characterizes the nigredo. This is one of the few adventures in which it's difficult to see how the Doctor will even survive, let alone triumph. Tellingly, there's no real triumph here. The villain is defeated by the Hostess's self-sacrifice, nodding to the necessary bloodshed in an almost ritualistic way. In her article on *"Doctor Who* and the Idea of Sacrificial Death," Melody Green argues that "Midnight" explicitly engages with the notion of ritual sacrificial death. In this way, the entire group becomes an example of humanity's basest urge to survive at any cost, transforming into a mindless mob that believes that only the death of the sacrificial victim (or scapegoat) will solve the perceived crisis.

There's the hint that this is an exorcism for the Doctor. When Sky becomes exposed to the burning Midnight sunlight, the Doctor screams in pain empathetically, and when Sky and the Hostess are sucked out, the Midnight Entity physically lets him go, propelling him forward with the force of its release. In this way, the scapegoat Sky and the self-sacrificial Hostess do act as literal substitutes, dying symbolically in place of the other characters. Similarly, the Doctor's privation and recovery of his assets serve as the symbolic death and rebirth required by the nigredo.

Once Sky and the Hostess are dead, and the Doctor restored, the passengers' fear and anger dissipate, replaced by shocked silence. Tension palpably leaves the room—the characters all collapse weakly to the ground, the murderous adrenaline driving them only seconds ago visibly gone. The Doctor lays exhaustedly on his back, repeatedly muttering "it's gone, it's gone, it's gone . . ." in relief. Davies's desire to use this episode to explore "humans at their worst"—as discussed in *The Writer's Tale*—and simultaneously the flaws and weaknesses of the Doctor combine to give the episode the despairing tone of the nigredo. Davies's description of the particularly difficult writing process mimics the language used to discuss the nigredo:

> The language is very stripped down, there are very few jokes or conversational riffs, all those things that I normally rely on. The characters haven't even got much backstory, which is odd, because Trapped People Dramas usually rely on that. But this one's about who they are now. Very bleak.

Very bleak, indeed.

It's Only the Beginning

The point of the nigredo, however, is that no matter how bleak it seems, it's only the first stage of the process. It's a painful but necessary step on the way towards healing, redemption, and regeneration. Death/Saturn/Father Time uses his scythe not only to reap souls for death but also clear the path for rebirth.

In a very alchemical passage of *Mere Christianity*, C.S. Lewis wrote that "nothing in you that has not died will ever be raised from the dead." The Doctor's symbolic death and painful dissolution on the planet Midnight are the first steps toward purification and ultimate redemption and regeneration. Despite the episode's bleakness and cynicism, there are hints of hope. The reunion of opposites between the masculine and feminine poles of the mercurial Doctor and the fiery Donna foreshadows the ultimate alchemical fusion of Doctor and Companion—the DoctorDonna. Donna's comforting hug at the end of "Midnight" reminds the Doctor that he doesn't have to be alone. The Doctor should've taken this as a sign. The Doctor without a companion is no true Doctor.

Though there are painful losses and lessons to come, "Midnight" begins the process of the Doctor coming to terms with his own failures and needs. Though the Tenth Doctor's fatal sin of becoming "the Time Lord Victorious" is still ahead of him, there at least he's saved by Adelaide Brooke's humanity and sacrifice ("The Waters of Mars," 2009). Things never again look quite as hopeless as they do in "Midnight," the episode which serves as the character's spiritual all-time low. From this point on, the Doctor begins the process of purification, which is signified by the many nominally watery characters he encounters—the wholesome cleansing with Jackson Lake and the more painful scouring with Adelaide Brooke bookended on either side by River Song and Amelia Pond.

The Doctor's dissolution and humbling on the planet Midnight enables him to be receptive to this transformative process. Though the process of regeneration is never easy, he eventually recognizes its need, admitting that he's "lived too long" and sacrificing himself for his friend Wilf ("The End of Time: Part 2," 2010). Without an episode like "Midnight," the Tenth Doctor's transformation would lack a fundamental step in his final journey towards new life. Davies's use of the imagery of the nigredo makes this abundantly clear, and contributes to the episode's enduring power and fascination with audiences.[1]

---

[1] I would like to thank my fellow Mythgard Institute students and Whovians Curtis Weyant, Kris Swank, and Kelly Orazi, who generously read this paper and made valuable critiques and suggestions. Special thanks to Curtis for first discussing "Midnight" and some of these ideas with me on our podcast (Kat and Curt's TV Review, Episode 53).

4

How Possible Is the Impossible Girl?

Donna Marie Smith

Imagine a girl, an ordinary girl, a schoolteacher living in twenty-first century London. Imagine if that same girl also lived during Victorian times as a barmaid and governess and also in the future as an alien being. How can such a girl exist? How is it possible for her to be the same person living at different times? Or is this girl an "Impossible Girl"?

Clara Oswald, as played by Jenna Coleman, is such a girl, and we first encounter her traveling with Matt Smith's incarnation of the Doctor during the Seventh Season of the new *Doctor Who*. She's a beautiful, clever woman whom the Doctor encounters during different time periods. When he first meets her, she's a Dalek living in a Dalek asylum at some time in the future. This Clara is named Oswin Oswald—the Doctor nicknames her "Soufflé Girl"—and has been captured by the Daleks and transformed into one of them. Next, the Doctor travels to the Victorian era and comes across a barmaid/governess named Clara Oswin Oswald. He then meets a woman called Clara Oswald who works as a nanny and a schoolteacher in present-day London.

Eventually, he deduces that the Victorian and twenty-first century Claras are the same person as Dalek Oswin. Although the Doctor has seen many strange and seemingly impossible things during his many journeys across time and space in his TARDIS, the Doctor is puzzled by her existence and can't figure out why he keeps on meeting different versions of her at different times. Even she's unaware that she has past and future selves. So just who is this "Impossible Girl," and how is it *possible* that multiple Claras exist across time and space?

The Impossible Girl

Showrunner Steven Moffat lays the groundwork for a fascinating mystery for the Doctor to solve throughout the course of the Seventh Season. Watching each episode is like looking through a kaleidoscope of Claras, seeing pieces of her swirling across time and space, with new clues coming into focus with every turn of the scope. Although Moffat cleverly left clues about Clara's identity within each episode, it wasn't until the end of "The Name of the Doctor" (2013) that we find out what happened to her. In attempting to save the Doctor and the universe from being destroyed by the Great Intelligence, she follows the villain into the Doctor's entombed timeline on Trenzalore—what the Doctor describes as the "scar tissue of his journey through the universe." When entering the "scar," a massive source of energy known as "time winds" splits Clara into a "million copies" of herself, which are then scattered across time and space.

While this resolves the mystery of the "Impossible Girl" within the fascinating storytelling of the sci-fi Whoniverse, it doesn't explain whether or not she's possible in our real-life universe. Further exploration of Clara and her many selves across time and space will show us that her identity has become an intrinsic part of the Doctor's own identity. Perhaps those copies of Clara are manifestations of the Doctor's own mind, living out different adventures within his subconscious? If so, then Clara wouldn't exist as a real flesh-and-blood human being. Yet, by drawing from the history of the philosophy of mind and learning about some of the theories of personal identity and self, we'll not only find out more about the Doctor and his "Impossible Girl," but we'll discover that an even greater mystery is afoot, one which philosophers have contemplated for over two thousand years—almost as long as the Doctor has lived. What it means to be a person and how we as individual beings exist across our own time and space are questions that Time Lords and humans alike have been pondering for millennia.

Soufflé Girl

To help us figure out the mystery of the "Impossible Girl," we need to understand the nature of this thing we call "self." For centuries, philosophers have grappled with the question of who we are and what the nature of the self is. Like the Doctor wanting to know how it's possible for all those Claras to exist, philosophers such as Aristotle (384–322 B.C.E.) have grappled with what it means to be a person and how that person exists in relation to time and the physical world. The area of philosophy that deals with this puzzle regarding the nature of reality is called metaphysics. While there are many areas of metaphysical study, some of the theories that explore the mind and what it means to have a mind—specifically the area of study known as the philosophy of mind—can help us solve our mystery.

When we first meet Clara in "Asylum of the Daleks" (2012) she's known as Oswin Oswald, the Junior Entertainment Manager of the starship *Alaska*. We, along with the Doctor, realize at the chilling conclusion of the story that she'd been converted into a Dalek. Here, we're faced with two puzzles. First, is Oswin the same person we'll come to know as Clara, even though she's a different person? Second, is Oswin still Oswin even though she's been changed into a Dalek by having her mind added to the Dalek form? Let's start with the first question.

Aristotle attempts to explain what it means to be a "being" in his work entitled *Categories*. He sets out to distinguish one thing from another based on their substance, and in turn, on those qualities that make one thing uniquely different from other things. Since Aristotle had not (as far as we know) met any alien life-forms like Time Lords and Daleks, he was trying to classify the differences between things in our world: people, animals, plants, rocks, and the like. Yet, in Aristotle's categories, humans and Daleks are essentially the same, but only in the broadest sense. They both have organic brains. Both are "thinking" or "sentient" beings. They each have a consciousness.

We know, though, that human beings and Daleks are two distinct races because they have different qualities. Humans have one heart and a brain that are protected by bones and flesh, and they are supported by self-sustaining internal organs. Daleks are genetically engineered, squid-like blobs with an external brain, and they are encased in a life-supporting metal machine. These are some of the properties that distinguish humans from Daleks. By these criteria, Oswin is no longer human. So how does she retain her human consciousness after the conversion?

Each human is a unique person, having his or her own thoughts, feelings, and experiences. Daleks also have individual brains. Each brain, though, shares a telepathic link or "pathweb" of information, much like a computer network ("Asylum of the Daleks"). Oswin's brain, then, has become linked to the pathweb. That's how she can "hack" into the Dalek systems to erase any trace of the Doctor from their memory banks, as well as to help the Doctor, Amy, and Rory escape from the asylum planet.

Yet, Oswin has no recollection of being converted into a Dalek. She's unaware that she's no longer human—at least not until the Doctor tells her at the end of the episode. Her brain is scrambled much like the soufflés she always thinks she's baking. She suppresses her memory of being captured by the Daleks and converted into one of them after her ship and crew crashed on the asylum planet. She creates an imaginary world where she's thwarting the insane Daleks, surviving on cleverness and imaginary soufflés alone. Her subconscious mind is protecting her from not only the bodily pain she suffered but from the horror of having her mind reprogrammed as a Dalek.

The Doctor explains to her what's been happening: "It's a dream, Oswin. You dreamed it for yourself because the truth was too terrible." Even after the Doctor reveals what she's become, Oswin fights off the Dalek nature inside of her and prevents herself from "exterminating" the Doctor. She rejects her "Dalek-ness" in order to help the Doctor escape the planet, telling the Doctor in what becomes a familiar refrain each time the Doctor encounters her: "Run! I am Oswin Oswald. I fought the Daleks, and I am human. Remember me. Run! Run you clever boy. And remember." This phrase becomes an important clue, a thread tying together all the other Claras whom we subsequently meet.

Interpretation of a Time Lord's Dreams

After the Doctor meets Oswin Oswald, he encounters a woman in Victorian England named Clara Oswin Oswald who's working as a barmaid and governess ("The Snowmen," 2012). The Doctor tries to save her and the two children in her charge from the nightmarish Great Intelligence—an alien who feeds off the minds of humans—except Clara dies. Her last words to the

Doctor were: "Run, you clever boy. And remember." The similarity between Clara's final words and the markings on her gravestone—"remember me, for we shall meet again"—is more than just a coincidence. The Doctor believes she might be the same person as Dalek Oswin. Yet, he remains puzzled as to how it's possible for these two people to be the same. Not until his impending death at Trenzalore in "The Name of the Doctor," does he realize that there's only one Clara, the nanny who lives in present-day England. The others were copies scattered throughout his personal timeline.

The Doctor's "scar tissue" that he encounters on Trenzalore is essentially the entirety of his experiences contained in his mind. So, after the real Clara enters his "scar," the copies of Clara become part of his subconscious mind. River Song explains to Clara after she resolves to sacrifice herself for the Doctor that "the time winds will tear you into a million pieces, a million versions of you, living and dying all over time and space . . . like echoes."

The works of Austrian psychiatrist Sigmund Freud (1856–1939), can help to explain why the copies of Clara are a manifestation of the Doctor's mind. Although he was a clinical psychiatrist—a scientist analyzing the behavior of people— Freud has significantly influenced how we think about ourselves and view the world. In fact, Freud's ground-breaking work in psychoanalysis, dream interpretation, and the concept of the unconscious being divided into an Id (instincts), Ego (reason), and Superego (conscience) has had, as Anthony Kenny explains in his overview of *Philosophy in the Modern World*, a lasting impact on Western philosophy in the twentieth century.

The Doctor's adventures with Clara's copies can be seen as his dreams, some even as nightmares, especially when he confronts the Great Intelligence. While the real Clara saves his life on Trenzalore, the copies also save him, but in an abstract, spiritual way—they act as his conscience, his Superego. Like many of the companions, especially the ones during the new-era *Doctor Who*, Clara keeps the Doctor on the moral path, helping him to choose good over evil. Even when given the chance to annihilate (once again) his life-long enemies, the Daleks, in "Into the Dalek" (2014), Peter Capaldi's Doctor trusts the judgment of this version of Clara, as she prompts him to help the sick Dalek remember the beauty and goodness it saw while suffering from radiation poisoning.

The Girl, the Leaf, and the Red Wardrobe

Swiss psychiatrist Carl Jung (1875-1961), who was a student of Freud's and was influenced by the Greek philosopher Plato (ca. 427–347 B.C.E.), would call all of the "impossible" copies of Clara archetypes, or common symbols, that we may encounter in our dreams via our collective unconscious. Where Freud thought dreams signified a person's underlying neurosis, most likely of a sexual nature, Jung saw dreams as tools to help a person understand more about himself, in order to achieve well-being. In his influential work, *Man and His Symbols*, Jung divided up the unconscious into an ego (the conscious part of the mind), a personal unconscious (the realm of dreams and suppressed memories), and a collective unconscious (the symbolic information about the world which we all know but of which we're unaware).

Jung would agree that the Doctor's "scar tissue" is his personal unconscious, with the tomb symbolizing his mind, or his soul. (Perhaps the Time Vortex that contains all the knowledge of past and future events—and to which the Doctor, his TARDIS, and all the other Time Lords have access—is the collective unconscious of the Time Lords?) Within his mind, the copies of Clara have been traveling across time and space, bounded by the Doctor's past and future.

Clara's name, her leaf, and her wardrobe all tell us something about what the Doctor needs in order to be a fully actualized person, or what Jung calls undergoing a "process of individuation." Basically, Clara—like many other companions—serves as the Doctor's conscience or moral compass, helping him to be a happy and healthy Time Lord, and not a "madman in a box," as Matt Smith's Doctor describes himself to Amy Pond in "The Eleventh Hour" (2008).

Names are an important part of our identity. While the Doctor's true name remains a mystery, Clara's name, which means "bright or clear" and suggests "clarity," reveals something about her personality and those qualities that the Doctor needs to help him be a good man. Clara, as his trusted companion, thus offers the Doctor clarity of purpose when faced with moral dilemmas. Capaldi's Doctor acknowledges this in "Into the Dalek" when he defines Clara as his "carer."

Clara's leaf is another important symbol that ties into both the real Clara and the Doctor's unconscious. The leaf, a symbol of life, death, and rebirth, is something that Clara describes in "The Rings of Akhaten" (2013) as "the most important leaf in human history, one full of stories, full of history." It represents the marriage of Clara's mom and dad and the birth of Clara, or as Plato would say, the leaf symbolizes Clara's soul. If a leaf hadn't blown into Clara's father's face causing him almost to be hit by Clara's mother's car, the birth of Clara would've never happened. And then, the Doctor would've never met Clara. Thus, the Great Intelligence would've destroyed the Doctor and all of creation.

Jung calls this "meaningful coincidence" of Clara's "blowing into the world on a leaf" and into the Doctor's life, "synchronicity." This type of coincidence can have metaphysical implications, essentially changing one's self. It wasn't a random coincidence each time the Doctor met Clara. All that the Doctor ever was or will be would've been wiped out by the Great Intelligence. All his memories, feelings, thoughts, and experiences would've been rewritten. He would no longer be the same person.

Her wardrobe also has symbolic significance and helps us to distinguish the "real" Clara from her copies. In "The Name of the Doctor," Clara attempts to save the Doctor from the nefarious Great Intelligence. In this episode she's wearing a blue dress. Blue is a color that evokes intelligence, strength, and steadfastness, all traits of which we can ascribe to Clara. Yet, blue also symbolizes purity, leading us to think that this is the original or "pure" Clara. In every episode prior to the season finale, Clara wore red clothes or accessories, such as a dress, a blouse, an umbrella, or a messenger bag. The color red is associated with sacrifice, death, and regeneration, and this suggests to us that the Clara in previous adventures, including Victorian Clara and Dalek Oswin, are the "copies."

Ceci N'est Pas un Soufflé

The soufflé isn't the soufflé. The soufflé is the recipe.

—Clara's mom, ELLIE OSWALD, "The Name of the Doctor"

What does Ellie Oswald mean by this, and how does it shed light on the possibility of the "Impossible Girl?"

As we saw in "Asylum of the Daleks," Oswin imagines she's baking soufflés as sustenance for herself, and so the Doctor calls her "Soufflé Girl." The real Clara bakes a soufflé prior to meeting up with the Doctor at his grave on Trenzalore, but the copies of Clara also like to bake soufflés. In saying "the soufflé isn't the soufflé; the soufflé is the recipe," Clara's mom means that this fluffy, puffed up cake is the sum of all its ingredients prepared in a certain way. To make a soufflé as opposed to the fish fingers and custard concoction that the Eleventh Doctor likes, Clara has to use a specific recipe with specific quantities of cheese, milk, flour, and so forth. Next, she has to mix up these ingredients and put them in a special baking dish to get the right shape of what we know a soufflé to be. Then she bakes the soufflé in an oven using a specific temperature for a specific amount of time. We call this finished product a "soufflé," which is the name for all those ingredients and directions listed on Clara's mom's recipe. We use the word 'soufflé' to designate a specific baked-good that some French chef created and named at one point, as well as to distinguish it from other foods like Jelly Babies and Jammie Dodgers.

A Clara by Any Other Name Is Still Clara

When the real Clara makes the decision to sacrifice herself in order to save the Doctor from the Great Intelligence, despite being warned by River Song that she'll break up into a million copies, she recalls her mom's saying about the soufflés. Even though the Claras will become "echoes" of her original self, she believes she'll keep all the essential ingredients of what makes Clara "Clara," whether or not she retains her human form. When the Doctor meets "different" Claras—Clara Oswald, Oswin Oswald, and Clara Oswin Oswald—he really only encounters the same Clara. Just like when we encounter "different" soufflés at the bakery, they're all considered the same— a soufflé. Like the soufflé, she's metaphysically the same person. Each Clara is physically different, yet each retains all of the original's essential feelings and thoughts, which means her inner nature retains its "Clara-ness."

Clara illustrates this idea each time she tries to make a soufflé, both real and imagined. Each time she bakes one, it never comes out quite right—they're always different. Hers are usually deflated and sunken in the middle instead of round and puffy like her mom's (or those of any respectable French chef!). Clara's soufflés are still soufflés, regardless of what they look like. The word 'soufflé' is still used for Clara's misshapen baked goods.

Philosophers and psychologists working in the field of social cognition—the study of how the brain processes information in relation to concepts and attributes we use to describe ourselves—suggest that we have within us more than one identity while retaining our essential nature. In their article "Self and Identity as Memory," psychologists John F. Kihlstrom, Jennifer S. Beer, and Stanley B. Klein state that we have multiple selves within our one self, and these different selves change over time and place. They don't mean that we have a mental illness such as multiple personality or dissociative identity disorder, but instead, we define ourselves in relation to other people and to the concepts or attributes we use to depict who we are. The different social situations in which we participate vary with our perceived attributes of ourselves. For example, at home, a woman may be a mother or daughter, and at work, she may be a schoolteacher like Clara. The attributes—or word labels, "mother," "daughter," and "schoolteacher"—convey our different roles in society. We also do different things at different times in our lives. Clara was a nanny to Angie and Artie before she became a schoolteacher at Coal Hill School. She's the Doctor's companion, but she was also fellow teacher Danny Pink's girlfriend. Even the Doctor himself provides us with a compelling illustration of this multiple-selves concept, with his many regenerations' different personality traits, behaviors, and relationships. We may have many different labels and play different roles throughout our lifetimes, but we're still the same person with the same essential nature. Therefore, if we consider that Clara is the same person regardless of her many named incarnations, or labels, then the "Impossible Girl" is possible.

A Kaleidoscope of Claras

While we enjoy seeing the adventures of the many Claras who live across time and space, we know that this is mainly possible because, as fans, we accept the "reality" of the Doctor's sci-fi world. In our real world, Clara would've died upon entering such a massive source of energy as the Doctor's "scar tissue." Her physical body would've been torn apart, and we have no proof that her mind would've survived her bodily death. Yet, some theories about the mind, self, personal identity, and social cognition offer possible explanations as to how the many Claras can exist across time and space.

Whether she resides within the Doctor's unconscious mind as a symbol of the Doctor's moral compass, through mental representations of the "idea" of Clara, or whether she's a real woman with different socially-construed identities, we can see how this seemingly impossible notion can be possible in our real world. Our imaginations are as vast and timeless as the universe the Doctor explores. Within the Whoniverse, anything is possible!

5

Every Lonely Monster
Needs a Companion

CHRISTOPHER GADSDEN

You see, this is what happens when you travel alone for too long.

—AMY POND, "A Town Called Mercy," 2012

Why does Tolkien's Gollum haunt our memories as one of the most pathetic characters in the canon of fantasy literature? He shows us the ruinous effects of protracted isolation.

Of course, the ring played a part in his ruin, but the ring could easily symbolize demons present in every heart, ever ready to consume us in our loneliness. Could a nobler being resist these forces—flourish in seclusion? Aristotle opines that only gods and beasts can live alone, because *all* sentient, mortal beings slowly unravel without society. But what about the Doctor? He's neither god, nor man (nor beast). Could he flourish in isolation?

Experienced Whovians will answer that question with a resounding *"No!"* The Doctor shouldn't travel alone. If you've watched a season or two, you know that the Doctor needs his companions in order to safeguard against emotional and moral meltdown. We witness this phenomenon multiple times each season, as far back as the Doctor's very first adventure. In "An Unearthly Child" (1963), Ian stops the Doctor from bashing in the skull of a wounded foe. And when the Time Lord dares to travel alone, the chances of an ethical train-wreck increase exponentially. Sometimes his companions explicitly scold him for putting himself in these situations, as did Amy Pond in "A Town Called Mercy" (2012).

The Doctor had been flying solo for ten months, but picked up the Ponds on his way to stop a space ship from crashing into the Earth ("Dinosaurs on a Spaceship," 2012). When it's discovered that the ship's hijacker, Solomon, murdered all the Silurians aboard, the Doctor obliquely executes him. In the subsequent adventure ("A Town Called Mercy"), the Doctor once again prepares to carry out the summary execution of an alien named Jex, perpetrator of unspeakable war-time atrocities. But Amy stops him. "You see," she says, "this is what happens when you travel alone for too long." The Doctor needed Amy to bring him back to his moral senses.

Nothing compares, however, to the meltdown in "The Waters of Mars" (2010). Here, the Doctor has once again been traveling alone for some time. When he visits the human colony on Mars, he realizes that he has arrived on the very day the colony will be destroyed—a fixed point in time. Nevertheless, he eventually defies the Laws of Time and rescues Captain Adelaide Brooke from the base, returning her to Earth. When Adelaide questions his actions, the Doctor declares himself "Time Lord Victorious," the sole authority of time. Adelaide retorts, "I don't care who you are; the Time Lord Victorious is wrong," and ends up taking her own life to restore order.

So it isn't a profound insight that the Doctor tends to morally and emotionally derail without companionship. But as D.I. Billy Shipton would say, "You're missing the big question." The *big* question is this: Exactly *why* can't the Doctor make it on his own? He's no mere human, after all, subject to all the natural human foibles. His wisdom, knowledge, and power are exponentially greater than ours. He has the perspective of nearly a thousand years of traveling among thousands of races and cultures. So precisely what does he so desperately need from his companions?

As a preliminary, let me say that I'm not suggesting that the Doctor's relationship to his companions is purely utilitarian. In many cases, a deep fondness (or even—gasp— romance) develops between the occupants of the TARDIS. But there must be a compelling reason why the Doctor always seems to have a companion, a reason that goes beyond the need for a conversation partner. Knowing the tremendous peril that he faces on a daily basis, why would he endanger a human by dragging them along? This is a bit like taking your four-year-old child along on a Colombian drug bust. It would be selfish and irresponsible for the Doctor to invite someone to travel with him into Dalek brains and death-trap trains if there weren't some vital reason. This raises another set of ethical worries, but we'll have to table those for the moment. Let's take a look at four potential answers to our big question.

Anti-Corruption Agent

John Emerich Edward Dalberg-Acton, 1st Baron Acton (a.k.a., Lord Acton) famously wrote that "power tends to corrupt, and absolute power corrupts absolutely." So perhaps a companion helps mitigate the corrupting influence of power. Russell T Davies said in a 2009 interview with *The Star-Ledger* that the Doctor "travels with a human because he needs a human. He's too powerful, and without that (human with him), he can become a dangerous man." Donna pointed that out to him in her very first story, "The Runaway Bride" (2006). Near the end of that episode, as the Doctor floods the lair of the Racnoss, he loses himself, relishing the spectacle of destruction. Donna has to call out to him, "Doctor! You can stop now!" Later, as the Doctor says his farewells, they have the following exchange:

> DONNA: Just promise me one thing. Find someone.
>
> DOCTOR: I don't need anyone.
>
> DONNA: Yes, you do. Because sometimes, I think you need someone to stop you.

So, perhaps the presence of a companion checks the corruption caused by the Doctor's immense power.

But there are at least two questions I have about this view. First, why should we think that power, in and of itself, would corrupt the Doctor? One possible answer is that immense power removes the only incentive to be just—the fear of dishonor and punishment. Time Lords with (nearly) unlimited power have little concern about retaliation.

In his *Republic*, Plato describes this idea in a conversation between Socrates and Glaucon. Glaucon tells the story of a man who happens upon a magical ring which renders the wearer invisible. The man discovers that, while wearing the ring, he can do almost anything he desires without fear of reprisal. Glaucon argues that a rational person with such power would seek out gain for himself without any consideration for justice. Once the fear of punishment and dishonor are removed, we disregard moral constraints.

Maybe the Doctor is like the man with the magic ring—there's almost no limit to what he can do and there's no one clever enough to stop him. But the maxim that *power corrupts* is by no means a proven fact. Recent research led by Katherine A. DeCelles, Professor of Business at the University of Toronto, seems to undermine this claim. She argues that people with "high moral-identity" understand how their actions affect others, and thus tend to use power carefully. Those with "low moral-identity" fail to consider others and are more careless in their use of power.

Thus, power doesn't corrupt; it only heightens pre-existing ethical tendencies. In a similar vein, Abraham Lincoln quipped that "If you want to discover just what there is in a man—give him power." So there's good reason to doubt that the Doctor's periodic moral missteps are caused by having too much power. They may simply be manifestations of something already present in the Doctor's hearts.

This leads to my second question about the power hypothesis. Even if the Doctor's power corrupted him, how could a companion possibly restrain him? If Glaucon is correct, then the only thing that could break the Doctor's moral fall would be the threat of reprisal or dishonor. But a human companion offers no real threat of reprisal. What of dishonor? Dishonor isn't guilt. Dishonor concerns your reputation in a community. I'm not sure a companion is well-placed to bring public shame or dishonor to the Doctor in his community—whatever his community is. It'd be far too easy for the Doctor to simply drop his companion off on some desolate rock and pick up a new one. The Doctor's *enemies* aren't even able to dishonor him—he could always find a way to destroy or discredit them. So, a powerful response to the Glaucon view would be this: if *power* is the source of corruption, then the presence of relatively powerless companions wouldn't constrain the Doctor's behavior. But somehow, companions make a difference. So, the Doctor's problem must be something other than, or more than power.

Empathetic Link

Another possible answer to the big question (Why does he need a companion?) is suggested by J.J. Sylvia in "Doctor, Who Cares?" Sylvia argues that the Doctor's ability to care for other beings and act in their best interests is grounded in his relationships to his companions. "Perhaps because the Doctor is able to develop these relationships with his companions in a one-on-one basis, he can apply that ethics of care . . . to the larger population and others in need." So, without the presence of a companion, the Doctor loses his empathetic link to humanity and thus his motivation to act in their best interests. This hypothesis would explain, for instance, the Doctor's preoccupation with the Earth—his (recent) companions are all human. This could also explain the Doctor's withdrawal from society and from "Doctoring" after he lost the Ponds. When we find him in "The Snowmen" (2012), something has changed inside him, something's missing. Only when he connects with Clara Oswin Oswald does he regain his desire to help humanity.

I think Sylvia is correct that the Doctor's relationship to his human companions explains (in part) his great compassion and care for the human race. But this won't fully answer the big question. The Doctor's link to say, Rose Tyler, doesn't explain his compassion for the Ood or other alien species. The Doctor seems perfectly capable of acting according to an "ethics of care" toward a species even without the one-on-one link. You might say that a humanoid companion provides a link to any (roughly) humanoid species. But then how do we explain his compassion for the great Star Whale in "The Beast Below" (2010), the Tritovores in "Planet of the Dead" (2009), or the Krafayis in "Vincent and the Doctor" (2010)? So, I think his companion is providing something more than an empathetic tie to the nameless masses.

Moral Vision

A third potential answer to the big question is that the Doctor's companion acts as a kind of moral seeing-eye dog. There's reason to think that due to his age and extensive travel through time and space, the Doctor suffers from a sort of moral myopia. Steven Moffat hints at this in an interview he did with "Doctor

Who TV" in 2012. "I thought about the Doctor traveling on his own and it always faintly depresses me. I'm not sure what he does on his own but I don't think it would be healthy. He's far too old and he's seen too much." There may be something that happens to a being who has lived for a millennium that's hard for us to grasp because our lives are so brief by comparison. Over centuries, as a Time Lord's knowledge of the universe and its workings grows, he can begin to see everything as commonplace and mechanical. The night sky and living things no longer seem beautiful and magical.

There's support for this view, though from technically non-canonical material. In a deleted scene from "Flesh and Stone" (2010), the Eleventh Doctor confesses to Amy exactly why he needs her.

> AMY: Then why am I here?
>
> DOCTOR: Because, because I can't see it anymore.
>
> AMY: See what?
>
> DOCTOR:**Doctor**: I'm 907. After a while you just can't see it.
>
> AMY: See what!?!
>
> DOCTOR: Everything! I look at a star and it's just a big ball of burning gas. I know how it began, I know how it ended, and I was probably there both times. After a while, everything is just stuff. That's the problem. You make all of time and space your backyard, and what do you have: a backyard. But you, you can see it, and when you see it, I see it.

What is the "it" that he can't see? It could be several things. It might be the *wonder* most of us experience when we look at the night sky, or a sunset, or a baby with its mother. Wonder is something we experience, but we don't exactly detect it with the five senses. You can't *literally see* wonder. But it may be something more. There are other things that we experience or perceive beyond our five senses, like beauty, value, and morality. Perhaps after a millennia of travel through all of time and space, the sense that allows a Time Lord to perceive such things deteriorates, just as a human eye can lose its ability to see.

From a philosophical point of view, the Doctor may be experiencing an acute case of what some people call the *fact-value split*. The eighteenth-century philosopher David Hume pointed out that there's a gap between the *physical (or observable) facts* of the universe and the values or *moral facts* of the universe. When we see a man steal from another man, we don't literally *see* the moral wrongness, because the moral features of the event aren't presented to our eyes or any other sense. Two physically identical events (two identical men tripping over the feet of two other, identical men) may be morally different (one was intentional, the other accidental). There's nothing about the *observed* physical facts that implies or entails any moral fact. Thus, we can never derive moral truths simply by observing matter in motion. So, it could be that the more knowledge and understanding the Doctor gains of the physical aspects of the universe, the more obscured the non-physical (moral, aesthetic) aspects become to him. Thus, a star ceases to be a breathtaking wonder and becomes just a "big ball of burning gas."

So, if the Doctor's moral perception is becoming clouded, this might lead him to revert to a purely calculating and rationalistic approach to moral decisions, or it might lead him to simply surrender to his emotions. I think we see both of these problems in "A Town Called Mercy." Once he realized who Jex was, all he could see was the magnitude of Jex's crimes and his own anger. What he missed, Amy saw: that meting out cold-blooded "justice" is wrong. "This is not how we roll, and you know it. What happened to you, Doctor? When did killing someone become an option?" If Amy hadn't seen this for him, he would've murdered Jex.

There are plenty of examples in which the Doctor seems to let his emotions dictate his actions in the absence of a companion. In "Dalek" (2005), the Ninth Doctor is ready to annihilate the last remaining Dalek, but is stopped by Rose. The Doctor's execution of Solomon in "Dinosaurs on a Spaceship" is similarly motivated, not by justice, but wrath. In "The Family of Blood" (2007), the Tenth Doctor has been practically companionless while hiding in human form. When he defeats the "Family," they experience the full "fury of a Time Lord." Driven by an unfettered rage, he condemns them each to horrific, eternal punishments. He acts alone, perhaps sensing that Martha would've stopped him.

I'm not claiming that the Doctor's moral character erodes, or that he somehow becomes bad, like a Jedi going over to the Dark Side. Instead, what we may have is a man who *loves* the good as much as ever, but simply can't *see* the good. He's like a man who loves mushrooms, but whose eyesight no longer enables him to clearly discern poisonous from non-poisonous ones. He hasn't lost his taste for compassion—he just can't see which actions are the compassionate ones.

So, I've suggested that a third possible answer to the big question (Why does the Doctor need a companion?) is this: because of his inhumanly long life span and vast knowledge, the Doctor gradually loses his ability to see beyond the physical facts of the universe to the moral realm. He can no longer see the forest for the trees. He needs companions with acute moral vision who can guide him through ethically treacherous situations.

Blind Spots

A fourth and final answer to the big question is that the Doctor needs a companion to reveal *blind spots* in his character and reasoning. This does sound similar to the third view, but unlike moral myopia, blind spots are common to all races (so far as I know) and all ages. They're a perfectly ordinary phenomenon. Blind spots don't need millennia to form, nor do they require unfathomable scientific knowledge. They're simply the product of psychological flaws inherent to sentient, emotional beings. On this view, the Doctor's moral perception is fine. His occasional ethical implosions happen when no one is there to remind him of the truth about himself.

We all have blind spots. Some of us tend to talk too loud and long without knowing it. Some of us are prone to awkward, unconscious bodily habits. The Doctor—he has a bit of a "god-complex" ("The God Complex," 2011). Because of his immense power and virtual immortality, he easily slips into thinking that ordinary rules (even moral rules) don't apply to him. It isn't that he can't discern right from wrong in these cases. Rather, he begins to see himself as god-like, and this dramatically alters your moral reasoning. What's wrong for a mortal may be just fine for a deity—for instance, taking life or intentionally altering history to suit one's desires. This hypothesis would explain very nicely the events in "The Waters of Mars," mentioned above. He doesn't necessarily make an error in moral reasoning—instead, he puts himself in the wrong starting point: that of a god-like figure.

So, the Doctor needs a companion to remind him that he's still bound by certain moral rules. Putting up a "Don't forget the moral rules!" poster in the TARDIS won't quite do it. Only a true *friend* can play this role effectively. In fact, Aristotle suggests in his *Nicomachean Ethics* that this is the primary value of friendship—that a friend reveals our blind spots to us. In the quest for true happiness, self-knowledge and self-understanding are absolutely necessary. But blind spots, problematic gaps in our moral self-understanding, will always exist. We need virtuous friends who act as mirrors that show us our true selves.

What's interesting about this answer to the big question is that it reveals the inadequacy of the term 'companion'. To protect us against our own blind spots, we need true friends, not mere companions, and 'friend' is a far richer concept. Friendships of virtue, as Aristotle calls them, aren't merely for utility or pleasure. They move both persons toward virtue and the good life. Moreover, friendships of virtue must be between persons who are *peers* on some level. The Doctor's companions aren't peers by age, knowledge or power, but the Doctor accepts them as moral peers—peers of virtue. This is the crucial aspect. Only a virtuous friend can show us the blind spots in our own moral framework.

Final Thoughts

So, what could justify the Doctor's repeatedly bringing a human into such dangerous circumstances? The first two options—anti-corruption protection and empathetic linking—seem inadequate to explain such actions. The third and fourth, however, could provide justification. Keeping himself from moral catastrophe, like violence or revenge, is of the utmost importance and the Doctor should do just about anything to ensure this. But the fourth view, that the Doctor needs someone who can show him his moral blind spots, has the advantage of helping to explain why the person flying around with the Doctor must be a true friend and not a mere companion.

In any case, we've four possible answers to our big question. Each has its merits; each tells us part of the story. Undoubtedly, the Doctor can't flourish, can't be *the Doctor* without the present friendship of another person. I suspect that this is true for all sentient, emotional beings and not just for Time Lords. But perhaps he, with this immense wisdom, simply understands this fact better than the rest of us. One more lesson we can all learn from the Doctor.[1]

---

[1] Thank you to my wife Kristin, my colleague and fellow Whovian Kenny Boyce, and to my eleventh-grade Introduction to Philosophy class at Heritage Academy.

SERIAL 2

Mind-Bending Impossibility-Shattering Jammie Dodgers

Dr. Scott Viguié (a.k.a. Doctor Geek)

TIME LORD PRESIDING

You're Fantastic!

DR. SCOTT VIGUIÉ (A.K.A. DOCTOR GEEK),
TIME LORD PRESIDING

For the entirety of the fiftieth anniversary year, we were focused on one question: Doctor Who? Quite simply, he's the Doctor. He's the one who makes us better, the one who reminds us of our untapped potential. Therein, I believe, lays the ultimate philosophy of *Doctor Who*: you're fantastic!

Ever since its beginnings, and especially since its rebirth in 2005, there's been a strong focus on how the Doctor brings out the best in individuals and challenges them to be better, smarter, and more compassionate than they ever thought they could be. He takes people yearning for something more and pushes them to be greater than they ever believed themselves capable of being.

It's this strong belief in us that in turn draws us to the Doctor. Given the chance, who amongst us would not walk the Earth, battle Daleks, or embrace the vortex itself if it could save the Doctor? While it's unlikely the BBC will ever offer me the role of the Doctor's companion, I still believe it's possible to answer the Doctor's call and live up to his expectations to be a proud member of what he called "an inventive, invincible, indomitable species" (Fourth Doctor, "Ark in Space," 1975).

Back in 2012, like Rose, Rory, or Donna, I was going nowhere fast. Sure, I had a decent job, but it was hardly the career I'd hoped for. The situation was soul-sucking to say the least. It was very easy to view life in the negative, to see only the obstacles in the way. Thankfully *Doctor Who*, one of my favorite shows, routinely presented an alternative. Rose, the shop girl, became the Bad Wolf, Rory—the man who lived in the Doctor's shadow—became the Last Centurion, and Donna the temp, became in a way, the Doctor herself. Week after week, the message was clear: if they could be fantastic, so could I.

No longer content with the status quo, and with no small amount of encouragement from my wife, I set out on my own adventure to discover my potential. As an archaeologist, I know how important science is to interpreting our past and preparing us for the future. To that end, I created *Doctor Geek's Laboratory of Applied Geekdom*, a science-fiction audio show, designed as STEM (Science, Technology, Engineering, and Math) outreach, with the intent of helping people get closer to those inventing the world of tomorrow. The unique blend of science and fiction resonated with so many that I created *Doctor Geek's Science Fair*, a full-day live event which, as the name suggests, combines a classic sci-fi convention with a science fair. I am proud of all of the accomplishments that developed during the first season of the show, but the one I'm most proud of is that many homeschooling parents have used the show as a supplement to their child's curriculum. Two seasons later, in a case of life imitating art, I routinely appear at conventions as Doctor Geek, where I encourage others to be fantastic. Together we can bring about the future.

That's what the Doctor is all about: the future. The future of the universe, the future of the human race, and the future of the individual are all-important. All those futures are bright if people just seize the moment, answer his call, and live up to their potential. By being the best of ourselves, we bring the spirit of the Doctor to life in our world. I've heard his call and answered. Have you? If so, what are you prepared to do about it? He's fantastic, and, you know what? So are we.

6
Weeping Angels and Many Worlds

PETER A. SUTTON

Philosophers usually make a lot of controversial, hard-to-prove claims. I'm no different, but just to vary things up a bit, I'll start off with the *least* controversial claim I can think of:

> The *Doctor Who* episode "Blink" (2007) is the best single episode of *Doctor Who* (or perhaps any show) ever.

If you're unsure of the truth of this claim because you've not seen "Blink" (2007). Go, do it now. I'll wait. If you've seen "Blink," but disagree with me, then I'm afraid I must ask you to leave. Please come back and finish this chapter when you've come to your senses.

If you're still reading, I'll assume you are a right-thinking person and agree with my uncontroversial claim above. Seriously, isn't "Blink" just the best? The Weeping Angels are one of the few *genuinely* scary monsters in the Whoniverse, and full of paradoxes: they're terrifying, but don't directly harm their victims (not in "Blink" anyway), and it's both trivially simple and almost impossible to stop them (just look at them, but don't blink!). And even apart from the Angels themselves, the episode is impeccably well done: the timing, the reveals, the crazy dialogue, the Doctor's coup at the end? Best. Episode. Ever.

Steven Moffat deserves to win the Nobel Prize for Literature for writing that episode, Hettie MacDonald should be beatified by the Papal Mainframe for directing it, and David Tennant should have an Emmy invented for him: "best performance by a lead actor in an episode in which his character barely appears." But I'm preaching to the choir here. Let's get on with the philosophy.

Philosophically, what sets "Blink" apart from almost every other episode of *Doctor Who* is that it *uses* time travel as a device to move the plot. Obviously, most episodes of *Doctor Who* involve time travel to some extent, but generally, the time travel is just what gets the Doctor and his companions *into* a situation that they then have to get out of using their wits. But in "Blink" the Doctor gets himself into a pickle and manages to get himself out of that pickle *by influencing the future*.

To recap the episode for those of you who didn't watch it last night (really? did you have something *better* to do with your time?), the story revolves around Sally Sparrow uncovering the mystery of the Weeping Angels. In the process, the Angels attack two of her friends, Kathy and Billy, sending them decades back in time to live out their lives in the past. Sally is aided in her investigation by hints given by those friends, by Kathy's brother Larry, and also by the Doctor, who's stuck in 1969 with Martha Jones. He needs Sally's help (in 2007) to get back his TARDIS. They're able to communicate because the Doctor hides his half of a conversation on DVDs that he knows Sally will buy. The Doctor knows Sally's side of the conversation because she gives him a transcript of it later on, when all the action of the story is over.

So we have a genuine causal circle. Sally's actions, in 2007, *cause* events in 1969, that *cause* events in the both the 1990s and 2000s that *cause* events in 2006 that *cause* Sally's actions in 2007. Take away any past event, and you remove its future effect. Take away any future event, and you remove its past effect. Neat.

The Problem of Freedom and Foreknowledge

Let's take it for granted that causal loops like this are possible. Their possibility has been defended perfectly well by William Eaton in *Doctor Who and Philosophy: Bigger on the Inside*. What I want to know is to what effect such causal loops have on the free will of the people involved in them. On the face of it, there's a conflict between knowing that somebody will perform an action and their being free with regard to that action. As the Doctor says, time can be rewritten, but "not once you've read it. Once you know it's coming, it's written in stone" ("Angels Take Manhattan," 2012).

By *free will,* I have in mind what's commonly called *libertarian* freedom (which isn't related to the Libertarian political party). To be free in this sense means that you could have done otherwise than you did. For example, you're currently reading this book. If you're reading it freely, that means that you didn't *have* to read it: you could have done something else with your time (but aren't you glad you didn't?). If, on the other hand, the laws of physics somehow forced you to read this book (whether you noticed yourself being forced or not), then you aren't really reading it freely. While there are other ways we might understand the concept of freedom—(for example, being the cause of our own actions, or acting in accord with our desires (see Gary Watson, *Free Will*)—it's libertarian freedom that's most obviously threatened by causal loops, and so that's where I'll focus my attention.

Here's the argument that I assume is behind the Doctor's claim in "Angels Take Manhattan": *Knowledge entails truth. If I know that you will do something, it follows that you will do it.* This may look like a good argument, but it isn't. Many of our actions are foreknown by various people. For example, my students knew I would be in class on Friday, my wife knew I would pick up our kids from daycare, and the clerk at the grocery store knew I would pay for my food rather than stealing it. And of course, I knew all these things about myself too.

This kind of ordinary foreknowledge has no bearing on libertarian freedom because even though these people knew what I would do, they in no way forced me to do it. I could easily have done differently, and if I had, they would've been wrong. Without me doing what I did, their foreknowledge would've been mere "forebelief" (which my spell checker tells me isn't a word, but that never stopped me before). You can have forebelief that someone will do something, but that only becomes fore*knowledge* if they actually *do* it. If I'm free, then other people's beliefs don't have power over me. Quite the reverse. I have power over them. I have the power to make them right or wrong.

The difficulty isn't in reconciling free will and foreknowledge in general, but rather free will and *infallible* foreknowledge. The causal loops we see in "Blink" and "The Day of the Doctor" (2013) don't involve "ordinary" foreknowledge. Since the Doctor already has solid evidence that the future actions have (or will have) happened, we can't say he has *mere* fore-belief. He really knows. And if he really knows what he'll do, and he knows that he knows, then how could he be free to do otherwise? Hence, his claim about the future being "written in stone."

The Solution: Many Worlds, Many Doctors

Even once you've read it, the future isn't written in stone, and it's at least possible (though by no means certain) that the Doctor (or anyone else) can have true libertarian freedom, even when stuck in causal loop. To start, let's assume that the Doctor and his companions usually have free will. (I can't prove that he—or anyone else—does, so we'll just have to take it for granted for the time being.) Then I'll try to make some sense of the Doctor's claim that the universe is a big ball of "wibbly-wobbly, timey-wimey . . . stuff."

Obviously he's being vague, both for comic effect and because the writers either can't or won't answer all the questions of time travel. And that's fine, because it's not their job. It's the job of philosophers and physicists. I bring up physicists at this point because this is a case where philosophy might borrow a theory from quantum physics to help make some sense of the Doctor's nonsense. Niels Bohr, along with many other physicists, tell us that subatomic particles (like electrons) behave differently when we observe them from when we don't observe them. If an electron has two possible paths it could travel, there's evidence (in the form of an interference effect) that it'll in fact travel along *both* paths simultaneously. But whenever we get a closer look at such an electron, we see that it definitely goes along either one path or another, not both. But in that case, we also lose the evidence that it went down both paths (the interference effect goes away). In other words, subatomic particles seem to behave very strangely: doing one thing when we observe them and doing lots of different things when we don't.

One of the theories that physicists have developed to account for the odd experimental data without having to say "electrons are magic" is Hugh Everett's *many worlds interpretation*. According to this account, whenever a particle has a number of different paths it can take, it does take all of them, but it does so in a number of different worlds. So, in one sense, subatomic particles like electrons are genuinely doing two different things at once; but when they do so, they've become two different electrons, so there really isn't a problem (at least from the standpoint of Newtonian physics). When we observe the particles, the "original" world has already split into two different worlds, one in which the electron took one path, and another in which it took the other path. The interaction effect we see in unobserved particles occurs when two parallel worlds "merge" back into one. As Lev Vaidman discusses, the resulting universe will retain features of each of the two universes from which it resulted, thus giving the appearance that the particles took both paths.

The many worlds interpretation deals with quantum phenomena, not free will, but it's pretty easy to adapt it to libertarian freedom. Whenever a free agent (say, Amy) makes a free choice between, say, choosing the green anchor and choosing the red waterfall, the free choice causes the universe to split into two universes: one in which Amy is sent to the "Kindness" facility and one in which she stays with Rory and the Doctor. The universes are different from that point on, but they still share the same history (indeed, they were the same universe), until the free choice was made. And when more free choices are made, those universes will split into many more (Peter Worley raises this possibility in the first *Doctor Who and Philosophy*). Metaphors and similes are dangerous in academic arguments, but I'll flirt with that danger by saying that the multiple worlds introduced by our free choices relate to each other like the branches of a tree. Two branches (worlds) of a tree come from the same trunk (past world) and then split off into many different sticks, twigs, and leaves (future worlds).

Let's look at another example of how this might work: in "The Angels Take Manhattan," Amy reads the Doctor a book from the future that tells him that he'll break River Song's wrist. (Actually, it merely records a dialogue, and makes no mention of wrists. But for purposes of my argument, let's imagine that it's more explicit.) Call the world they all start out in A (see diagram below). In A, the book was delivered to the Doctor and Amy reads the relevant passage. Later, while still in A, the Doctor is faced with a free choice: whether to break River's wrist (to save her) or not. He chooses not to break it, and at that moment, the universe splits into two universes, B1 and B2. In B1, he doesn't break her wrist—she winds up breaking it herself. In B2, he does break her wrist. Later on, in B2, River has a free choice to make: whether to write the book or not. This causes another split, into universes C1 (in which she writes the book) and C2 (in which she doesn't). At this point, there are three Rivers (which sounds like the name of a public park): B1-River, C1-River, and C2-River.

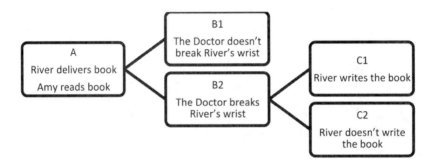

Later, in C1, she travels back in time to deliver the book to the Doctor. But remember that when C1-River travels back to her past (universe A), she's also traveling back to B1-River and C2-River's pasts, and what C1-River does in her past will affect *all* of her future selves, and all the parallel Doctors, Amys, Rorys, and Weeping Angels as well. All of them approached their decisions with knowledge of what was written in the book, and so she hasn't really changed anything, even though she did have an effect on all those possible universes.

This explains how there could be an accurate nonfiction book, sent from the far future, read by the Doctor in the present, saying he'll do something in the near future that he winds up not doing. The book honestly records one future, not all futures. This gels fairly well with Aristotle's account of "future contingent" propositions in Section 9 of his book *De Interpretatione*. Aristotle thought that all past- and present-tense statements were either true or false, but that future-tense contingent propositions lacked a definite truth-value. That holds true on this account as well. In world A, we can say that the book exists, but can't really say that the Doctor will break River's wrist, and we can't say he won't. It's indeterminate.

And now we see how the Doctor (or anyone else) could have genuine libertarian free will even when he's in the midst of a causal loop. Just because *some* future Doctor does something doesn't mean that *he* has to be that future Doctor. He can do what he wants, and some other future-him will take care of the causal loop. Problem solved.

I should take a moment to stave off a possible objection. I've not given, nor have I tried to give, any argument that the many-worlds interpretation of free will is definitely true, or even *likely* to be true. I'm only trying to show that there's (at least) one logically possible way of reconciling causal loops and libertarian freedom. As long as we can tell a coherent story according to which the Doctor is genuinely free, whether it's an actually true story or not, then the philosophical problem will be solved. We probably won't have much empirical evidence for or against the account until the physicists get off their rumps and build us a time machine. C'mon, physicists! What was that Large Hadron Collider for if it doesn't get us a time machine?

Free Will = Fatalism?

You might be thinking that my defense of free will is, at best, a Pyrrhic victory—one that sacrifices so much that it's really more like a defeat. This account of "timey-wimey" has it that every time I make a free choice, my future splits into two, one in which I do some particular thing and one in which I don't do that thing. But in that case, there really is no freedom at all. When confronted with a free choice, it turns out that I will do *both* things. When the Doctor decides not to break River's wrist, he splits the timeline into two, one in which he breaks the wrist and one in which he doesn't. That's not freedom, it's some obscene form of fatalism.

From an objective point of view, it does indeed seem strange to call this sort of thing "freedom." But maybe it's the objective view that's the problem. Perhaps that's why the Doctor gets so confused and confusing when he talks about the "non-subjective (that is, objective) viewpoint." We can't really make sense of our own lives *except* subjectively; and maybe that's okay. What matters isn't that there are a trillion different "me's" doing a trillion different things. What matters is this me, *my* me, the me I choose (or have chosen) to be.

Of course, if River jumps through time right back to C1 (assuming the TARDIS can hone in on specific futures), she won't be aware of any of the other possible Rivers, Doctors, and the rest of it. From her point of view, there's just the one time-line, the one that starts in A and ends in C1. And indeed, that's how good time-travel storytelling usually does things. The character winds up affecting the past, but nothing in the past has actually changed—consider *Harry Potter and the Prisoner of Azkaban*, *Bill and Ted's Excellent Adventure*, and *12 Monkeys*. But "Blink" raises an important question: what happens if the character goes back in time and *stays there*? Like Sally Sparrow's friends, Kathy and Billy.

In "Blink," both Kathy and Billy live out their lives in the past, but make provisions for Sally in the future. But if my interpretation is correct, and the future branches every time an agent makes a free choice, how could they be sure that they'd wind up in the same world as the future-Sally they knew and loved? After all, if humans are free, then there are presumably trillions of universe-splits every year, probably far more. Add to that all the free choices made by Daleks, Arachnos, Raxacoricofallapatorians, and even the Weeping Angels themselves, and you have quadrillions, quintillions, basically, pick an "illion," more universe-splits to deal with. So how do they know they'll wind up on the "right" branch, and that their messages will reach Sally? Answer: they don't. But they do know that at least one parallel "them" will succeed, which is enough to ensure the causal loop, even if all the others fail.

And here, perhaps, we find the answer to a final puzzle we weren't even thinking about: how is it that the Doctor is always so damned lucky? Answer: maybe he's not. Or rather, most "hims" are not. Most of the parallel Doctors died a long time ago ("Turn Left," 2008). But *one* of the Doctors happens to make the right choices, time and time again. That's the one the writers show us, because that's what makes for good television.[1]

---

[1] Thank you to Catherine Sutton for her helpful comments. Thank you also to Steven Moffat for "Blink." It was good enough that I can almost forgive you for what you did to the Angels in later seasons.

7

What the Doctor Can and Can't Change

Audrey Delamont

> I did come to Trenzalore, and nothing can change that now.
>
> —Twelfth Doctor ("The Time of the Doctor," 2013)

Could the Doctor have avoided Trenzalore? The Doctor changes things all of the time, and he had certainly heard of Trenzalore before arriving there. Given that it's the known place of his death, could he have simply avoided going there?

In the "The Wedding of River Song" (2011), Dorium Maldovar (more specifically Dorium's *head*) speaks the prophetic words that would echo throughout Season Seven: "On the Fields of Trenzalore, at the fall of the Eleventh, when no living creature can speak falsely or fail to answer, a question will be asked—a question that must never be answered: 'Doctor who?'" In "The Name of the Doctor" (2013) we learn from an imprisoned man, Clarence DeMarco, that the Doctor's grave has been discovered, and it's *on* Trenzalore—which just happens to be where the Dictor has gone to confront Dr. Simeon and his gang of Whisper Men.

Given that the Doctor was able to evade his own death at Lake Silencio, couldn't he also have avoided Trenzalore? He does have a TARDIS after all, couldn't he have just used time travel to avoid it?

Wibbles and Wobbles of Time Travel

People assume that time is a strict progression of cause to effect, but actually from a non-linear, non-subjective viewpoint, it's more like a big ball of wibbly-wobbly, timey-wimey stuff.

—TENTH DOCTOR ("Blink," 2007)

The rules of time travel are prodded, poked, bent, and pushed to their timey-wimey limits by the Doctor and his companions so often that you might not think there *are* any rules. But there are. Four of them, in fact.

Rule 1: Time can be re-written

Rule 2: Fixed points in time cannot be re-written

Rule 3: Knowledge of your future creates a fixed point

Rule 4: Changing your own timeline should be avoided

Case in point, Rules 1 and 2: In "The Waters of Mars" (2009) the Tenth Doctor stumbles upon Bowie Base One, the first human settlement on Mars. The Doctor knows that a mysterious explosion killed the entire crew of Bowie Base One. Since there were significant ramifications of that event throughout history, that explosion created a fixed point in time. So while the Doctor is forced to stay on the ship by the skeptical commander Adelaide Brooke, he resolves not to interfere with the outcome. However as the episode progresses, the Doctor can't help but do what the Doctor does. He uses the TARDIS to save the remaining crew, thereby changing a fixed point in time—or so he believes. The Doctor reasons that because he's the only remaining Time Lord he has dominion over all of space and time—the rules of time travel no longer apply to him.

- **Rule #1:** Time *can* be re-written. The Doctor, momentarily freed by the thought that he now has power to re-write time in such an unhindered way, finds his new-found optimism shattered by the sound of a gunshot. In his mind's eye, the Doctor watches newspaper articles that once depicted Adelaide as a hero, dissolved into a heartbreaking tale of disaster and suicide.

- **Rule #2:** Fixed points in time *cannot* be re-written. While the Doctor succeeded in changing a specific *moment* in time, the laws of time travel interfered, forcing events to occur more or less as they should have. While Adelaide and the two surviving crew didn't die due to the mysterious explosion on Mars, their impact on the world necessarily remained the same. Adelaide would be remembered as a tragic suicide, whose body was found on Earth, rather than lost amongst the stars. While her granddaughter *would* go on to travel into space as history had already foretold, she would be motivated by grief, rather than pride.

Rule #2 asserts itself in a number of other notable episodes as well, including "A Christmas Carol" (2010). There, we see Kazran turn out to be more or less the miser we see him depicted as at the beginning of the episode, despite the Doctor's attempts to change him. The laws of the universe seem to allow the Doctor to make small changes, so long as certain pivotal moments remain precisely as they are. If he attempts to change too much, the universe will correct the course for him. Here are some illustrations of some possible outcomes:

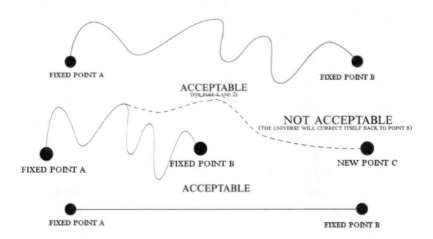

Together rules #1 and #2 demonstrate that while the Doctor is free to alter the course of history leading *up* to a fixed point, he can't actually change any fixed points in time. If he tries, the universe forcibly corrects itself.

Case in point, Rule 3—Knowledge of your future creates a fixed point: "The Angels Take Manhattan" (2012) most vividly depicts Rule #3, marking the final appearance of beloved companions Amy Pond and Rory Williams. The episode begins with the Doctor reading *Melody Malone: Private Detective in Old New York Town*. As the Doctor reads on, he realizes that Rory has become a character in the book and has been transported to 1930s Manhattan by a Weeping Angel. Taking the book, Amy reads ahead to try and find out where Rory is and what they ought to do next. The Doctor adamantly advises against this, explaining that reading ahead causes events to become fixed in time—like the TARDIS being unable to land, or River having to break her wrist to escape from the Angel's grip.

Throughout the episode, we see Rule #3 broken on a small scale, but it isn't until the end of the episode that the ramifications are demonstrated in full force. As Amy, Rory, River, and the Doctor return to the graveyard where the TARDIS is located, Rory notices a gravestone with his name on it and immediately vanishes. The very act of seeing his gravestone creates an unescapable fixed point in time (compare this to the Doctor seeing *his* gravestone on Trenzalore), and Rory is transported to a time and place that even the TARDIS can't reach Amy allows herself to be touched by the Angel who took Rory, causing her name to appear below his on the gravestone, fixing her death forever in time as well. This is the motivation for River's insistence that the Doctor remain ignorant of the events they see unfold at Lake Silencio in "The Impossible Astronaut" (2011).

The impact of Rule #4, changing your own timeline should be avoided, should seem like a fairly obvious consequence of Rules 1–3. If knowing your future creates fixed points in time, then surely traveling *back* along your own timeline is simply an instance of creating a fixed point. Throughout the series, we witness the effects of pushing the limits of Rule #4: the energy released by touching the same sonic screwdrivers together in "The Big Bang" (2010), the way the TARDIS malfunctions when both Amys try to board in "The Girl Who Waited" (2011), or the universe almost collapsing in "Father's Day" (2005). As the Doctor says to Martha Jones in "Smith and Jones" (2007), "Crossing into established events is strictly forbidden. Except for cheap tricks." Or more seriously to Clara in "Dark Water" (2014), "If I change the events that brought you here, you will never come here and ask me to change those events. Paradox loop. The timeline disintegrates. Your timeline."

What the Doctor Can and Can't Change

So why couldn't the Doctor have avoided Trenzalore? We've seen each of the four rules of time travel broken, so it certainly seems like in principle he could have. The answer as you might expect is fairly wibbly wobbly: yes and no.

In philosophy, we can distinguish loosely between three positions concerning the degree of control we have over our actions: Free Will, Determinism, and Fatalism. The Free Will Thesis says that at any time, the Doctor can do whatever he wants. He's free to choose and change his future. Fatalism says that the Doctor is and always has been fated to do exactly as he does; he can't do otherwise. Determinism says that all of the truths about the world, combined with the laws of nature, entail what the Doctor will or won't do.

The *Doctor Who* universe can't be a universe of unrestricted free action. Why? If it were, time travel Rules 2–4 wouldn't apply. If the Doctor could do whatever he wanted, he *would* be able to change the outcome of fixed points because there would be no constraints on the actions he could perform. However as we see in episodes such as "Father's Day," this isn't the case— recall how violently the universe corrects the Doctor and Rose's actions when Rose tries to save Pete's life. What we see is that the Doctor's, and everyone else's, actions are constrained in certain ways at certain times.

The Doctor isn't free to do everything he could possibly want, even if sometimes he thinks he is! However things aren't exactly *fated* to happen either, because we see the Doctor changing events that have already happened, like when he saves the Caecilius family in "Fires of Pompeii" (2008). So while we can see how events unfold, we can also see how they could have happened differently. This is precisely the result we get from Rules 1 and 2—time can change so long as certain key points are arrived at. So, if the Doctor is constrained in *some* timey-wimey ways by the laws of time travel, but unconstrained in other ways, what does that mean?

It means that the *Doctor Who* universe is ultimately *deterministic*. What does determinism mean? It's a philosophical concept that can be broken into two strains: soft determinism and hard determinism. Hard determinism is the doctrine that at any given time, a complete account of the way the world is (a collection of facts) together with all of the laws of nature entail all future truths. To understand this, imagine there are a thousand dominoes lined up in a pattern. The first domino is blue, and the last one is red. If we push the first domino down (and assuming we've set them up correctly!) they're going to fall a certain way, with the result of the red domino falling last. If I ask you, "Why did the red domino fall?" you'll respond, "Because the one before it fell and knocked it over." Now if I ask you what caused *that* domino to fall, you'll give me roughly the same answer—only in this case, you'll point to the domino two ahead of the red one, and say that when *that* one fell and hit the next one it caused the red one to fall. Every domino which falls has a preceding domino which caused *it* to fall (other than the first one of course). What that means is that as soon as the first blue domino falls, it's guaranteed that the red one will also fall. There's an unavoidable connection between the first cause (the blue domino falling) and the final result (the red domino falling). Hard determinism is also referred to as 'incompatibilism', because it's incompatible with the notion of free will.

Soft determinism, on the other hand, is the denial of incompatibilism. Although actions might be causally determined, so long as they're the result of our own choices and desires (and aren't caused by external forces) we can still be free.

So, what does this have to do with the Doctor arriving on Trenzalore? If "arriving on Trenzalore" is the last red domino, in order to know if it can be avoided, we first must look at all of the proceeding dominos that led to the event. The way in which those events occurred will tell us if the Doctor's universe is bound by hard or soft determinism. Hard determinism will mean the Doctor couldn't have avoided Trenzalore, whereas soft determinism yields the result the timey wimey result that he could have.

From There to Here and Here to There

In "The Time of the Doctor," the Doctor is drawn to an unknown planet by an incomprehensible message that is broadcasting throughout space and time. The Doctor learns from "Handles" a decaying Cyberman-head that the message is Gallifreyan in origin, and subsequently boards the Church of the Papal Mainframe to speak to Mother Superious, Tasha Lem. The

Doctor and Clara are sent down to the planet to investigate the source of the message, and find themselves in a town called Christmas. At this point, the prophecy discussed for nearly two seasons comes to fruition as the Doctor learns two crucial pieces of information: 1. The town of Christmas is surrounded by a truth-field, and 2. the question, broadcast through the cracks in space and time, is "Doctor *who*?" The Time Lords, having been stowed away in a pocket universe in "The Day of the Doctor" (2013) now seek to verify that they've found the correct crack to come through by posing a question that only the Doctor can answer, in a location in which he can't lie.

Tasha Lem can't allow this question to be answered. Charged as peacekeepers, the Church of the Papal Mainframe realizes that should the Doctor speak his name, the Time Lords would return and the Time War would begin anew. She tells the Doctor as much, who then asks one final question: What is the name of the planet? Tasha reveals that it's called Trenzalore—which, as we know from "The Name of the Doctor," is where the Doctor is buried. Understanding the scope of the situation, the Doctor resolves to stay on Trenzalore to defend it against his enemies, without answering the broadcast question. The Church undergoes an unscheduled change of faith, resolving itself to a single purpose that has been echoed throughout the previous season: Silence will fall.

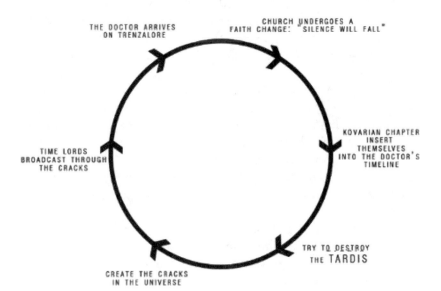

THE DOCTOR ARRIVES ON TRENZALORE

CHURCH UNDERGOES A FAITH CHANGE: "SILENCE WILL FALL"

KOVARIAN CHAPTER INSERT THEMSELVES INTO THE DOCTOR'S TIMELINE

TIME LORDS BROADCAST THROUGH THE CRACKS

TRY TO DESTROY THE TARDIS

CREATE THE CRACKS IN THE UNIVERSE

Now that we know what our red domino is, in order to understand if the Doctor could've avoided Trenzalore, we must look at all of the dominoes (that is, events) that caused the Doctor to arrive in the first place.

In order to prevent the Doctor from ever reaching Trenzalore, the Kovarian Chapter of the Church of the Papal Mainframe—led by Madame Kovarian—attempts to kill the Doctor by inserting themselves into his past. For example, the Silence try to kill the Doctor at Lake Silencio in "The Impossible Astronaut," but in order to do this, they needed to create his murderer, which involves stealing Amy's baby (a.k.a. River). These events go back to "The Impossible Astronaut," "Day of the Moon" (2011), "The Curse of the Black Spot" (2011), "A Good Man Goes to War" (2011), and "Closing Time" (2011). Even earlier, in "The Pandorica Opens" (2010) and "The Big Bang" (2010), the Alliance tricks the Doctor into coming to Stonehenge where the Pandorica is opening. Prophesied by Vincent Van Gogh's painting entitled "The Pandorica Opens" which reveals an exploding TARDIS that ends the universe, the Alliance locks the Doctor away, believing that because only he can fly the TARDIS, imprisoning him will prevent the explosion ("The Pandorica will open . . . Silence will fall"). However, River's involvement and ability to fly the TARDIS thwarts this effort, and the entrapment of the Doctor is precisely what leads to the TARDIS exploding. Although Silence does fall, it only does so because the cracks created by the exploding TARDIS swallow up everything except the Earth and the Moon.

Between Seasons Seven and Eight, during "The Day of the Doctor," we see all twelve Doctors seal away the Time Lords in a pocket universe to prevent the annihilation of Gallifrey during the Time War. Trying to escape this universe, the Time Lords broadcast a question that only the Doctor can answer in order to ensure that they've found the right universe to return to. However it's only because the crack in the universe exists that they're able to do so. And it's only because of this broadcast message that the Doctor arrives on Trenzalore in the first place.

Does this sequence of events support hard or soft determinism? Time travel muddies the philosophical waters here quite considerably. The Doctor's actions are clearly constrained by the four rules of time travel and as such fail to be unencumbered by external forces the way that soft determinism requires. In "Dark Water" Clara says to the Doctor, "I have seen you change time, I have seen you break any rule you want." To which the Doctor replies, "I know when I can, I know when I can't." This suggests that the *Doctor Who* universe is governed by hard determinism. However, because the Doctor has the ability to travel backwards in time, our definition of hard determinism will need to be amended. At any given time, a complete conjunction of all given facts at that time, combined with the laws of nature *and the laws of time travel*, entail all future truths.

Therefore, in order to change the outcome of an event, the Doctor would need to go back far enough in time and change enough facts about the universe to alter the future truths that would be entailed. So we know that once the dominos begin to fall, the Doctor can't do anything to stop them. In that sense, the answer to our original question is *No*. The Doctor couldn't have avoided Trenzalore. But that isn't the *whole* story as we all know, because time can be wibbly-wobbly as well as timey-wimey. Just how far back would we have to go to stop the original domino from falling? That is, what facts about the universe would need to be changed in order to avoid the truth of the Doctor reaching Trenzalore?

Well, we know that if the cracks had never appeared on Amelia Pond's wall—first revealed in "The Eleventh Hour" (2010), the Doctor would never have met Amy, who would never have conceived River, who would never have grown up to try and kill the Doctor or learn to fly the TARDIS. But in order for *that* to never have happened, the Doctor couldn't have ever locked the Time Lords away in a pocket universe (for if he hadn't, they wouldn't be broadcasting out of the cracks, which would necessitate the Silence creating the cracks in the first place). But the only reason that the Time Lords were displaced was because of the Time War.

What initiated the Time War? That isn't exactly clear. We know that the Fourth Doctor attempted to stop the creation of the Dalek species in "Genesis of the Daleks" (1975), and that tension between the Daleks and the Time Lords escalated from that point onwards. It seems that in order for the Doctor to avoid Trenzalore altogether, we'd have to eliminate the histories of Doctors Four through Twelve, and try to alter things *before* the initial conflict between Time Lords and Daleks. Imagine going back from the red domino, and trying to change the pattern from the very beginning so that it never falls. Just how far back would you have to go?

Thus, the timey-wimey answer to the original question is also *yes* (in a wibbly-wobbly sort of way). The Doctor *could* have avoided Trenzalore. But if the *Doctor Who* universe is deterministic in this way, that would require changing the initial starting conditions of the universe itself, which would mean *eliminating* the Doctor from history all together. And as the Doctor says in "Time of the Doctor," "*You can't change history if you're part of it.*"

8

Could the Doctor Have Avoided Trenzalore?

Massimo Pigliucci

The Eleventh Doctor famously took his last stand on the planet Trenzalore. Twice, as it turns out. Two diverging timelines ended in very different outcomes: in one the Doctor dies, the TARDIS becomes his tomb, and the planet is destroyed ("The Name of the Doctor," 2013); in the other, the Doctor is granted an additional regeneration by the Time Lords, and both the TARDIS and Trenzalore itself can look forward to many more adventures in time and space ("The Time of the Doctor," 2013).

Which, of course, raises a host of both philosophical and scientific questions. Could the Doctor have avoided Trenzalore? Well, which version? Or do we mean to ask whether he was fated to take a stand (last or not) on that planet, regardless of his choices?

One way to look at the issue concerns the perennial and thorny philosophical conundrum of free will: do we, as sentient, conscious beings—be it Time Lords or humans—have the ability to make different choices from the ones we actually do make? Classically, there are three ways of looking at this issue in philosophy: compatibilism (for which the answer is yes, sort of), deterministic incompatibilism (the answer is a resounding no), and libertarian incompatibilism (the answer is hell, yes).

Now, during "The Time of the Doctor" we witness this exchange:

> DOCTOR: A split in the skin of reality. A tiny sliver of the 26th of June, 2010. The day the universe blew up.

CLARA: Missed that.

How can Clara have missed the fact that the universe blew up? I mean, just how absent-minded is the girl, anyway? Of course she missed it because it happened in a different timeline, as a result of a different decision made by the Time Lords. Mark one in favor of libertarian incompatibilists, it appears.

A second way to consider the issue, however, seems natural in situations where we get the sense that the Doctor is *fated* to do certain things, no matter which decision he makes. And I'm not just talking about quips like "Every ship I go on, they just shoot at me"; I'm referring rather to a deeper and more mysterious observation made by our time-wandering hero: "the Destiny Trap. You can't change history if you're part of it" ("The Time of the Doctor"). Is that true, even if you try *really* hard?

In the following we'll explore these questions, taking a look at what, if anything, certain interpretations of quantum mechanics (yes, of course this has to do with quantum mechanics!) can tell us about Trenzalore. It's going to be fun in a number of unexpected ways since, as the Ninth Doctor famously put it in "The Long Game" (2006): "The thing is, time travel is like visiting Paris. You can't just read the guide book. You've got to throw yourself in, eat the food, use the wrong verbs, get charged double and end up kissing complete strangers—or is that just me?"

What's a Timeline Anyway?

All of the adventures in which our good Doctor finds himself to be the protagonist are, of course, based on the idea that time travel is both logically and physically possible. This is far from a settled matter in contemporary—Earth—physics, with most scientists being rather skeptical. Apparently, though, we'll have to wait for a complete theory of quantum gravity to decide the issue, and that's nowhere to be found at the moment. (Depending on whom you ask, the prospects look rather dire: see Jim Baggott's "The Evidence Crisis.") However, in the *Doctor Who* universe, Time Lord–physics has been successful in mastering time travel. Given this, what sense may we make of the fact that the Doctor died on Trenzalore in one timeline, yet managed to get a whole new regeneration cycle in an alternate timeline?

One way to think about this is to see that we're really con-templating a case of what in the sci-fi literature is known as "allohistory," which allows us to explore how events unfold under two possible scenarios. It's an *if . . . then* thought experiment, of the type in which philosophers engage all the time (and refer to with the rather pompous term of "counterfactual think-ing"). As it turns out, the idea of writing allohistorical stories is pretty old; the first known example being the Roman poet Livy, who in his *History of Rome* (written around the end of the first century B.C.E.), imagined what would've happened if, three centuries earlier, Alexander the Great had sought to expand his empire westward rather than eastward. Naturally, he con-cluded that the Romans would've defeated him, thus giving rise to their empire anyway.

Maybe it's for similar reasons that the Kovarian Chapter failed to kill the Doctor when they went back up his timeline to make sure he'd never even reach Trenzalore, as it gradually transpired from "The Impossible Astronaut" (2011), "Let's Kill Hitler" (2011), "Closing Time" (2011) and, of course, "The Wedding of River Song" (2011). Indeed, in a classic example of a potentially paradox-generating causal loop, it was this very attempt by the Chapter that ended up causing the crack in time that they were trying to prevent. (I know, time travel makes your head spin!)

The pivotal decision—the one switching the course of events from one timeline to the other—was, obviously, made by the Time Lords. In one case, as we see in "The Name of the Doctor," they apparently (for rather mysterious reasons) don't grant a new regeneration cycle, and as a result, the Doctor dies on Trenzalore, which itself is reduced to rubble. In the other case, which played out in "The Time of the Doctor," they do grant Clara's request for help, and the rest is (alternate) history.

But how's this possible? What does it mean for the Time Lords to make one decision in one timeline and a different deci-sion in another timeline? A number of sci-fi writers have explored "paratime" situations before, beginning with the clas-sic stories by Sam Merwin Jr., Andre Norton, and H. Beam Piper in the 1940s and 1950s. But their accounts of paratime plots relied on vaguely hinted-at "higher dimensions," or, worse, on the scientifically questionable writings of the Russian esotericist Peter D. Ouspensky. Beginning in 1957, however, science has given us a better option: the Everettian (named after physicist Hugh Everett III) interpretation of quantum mechanics, better known as Many Worlds.

Many Worlds and Time Lords

Quantum mechanics is the most successful scientific theory currently on offer, in terms of its ability to predict experimental results in fundamental physics to very, *very* high degrees of accuracy. It also provides us with a notoriously strange view of the world, populated by things that behave either as waves or as particles, depending on the circumstances, as well as by cats that are neither dead nor alive until someone looks at them. Oddly for a scientific theory, it comes with a number of "interpretations." (I mean, have you ever heard of different interpretations of, say, the theory of evolution, or of continental drift?) These include the early Copenhagen interpretation, many-worlds, Bohmian mechanics, quantum Bayesianism, information-based models, consistent histories, and even something called "quantum Darwinism," among others.

Tom Siegfried has even compiled a "top ten" list of interpretations of quantum mechanics! Still, not all interpretations are equally popular amongst those in the know: Maximilian Schlosshauer and colleagues ran a poll according to which 42 percent of physicists prefer the Copenhagen version, 24 percent go for information-based models, 18 percent for many-worlds and a scatter of others for the rest. Cosmologist Sean Carroll has summarized the somewhat embarrassing situation at his blog, in a nice graph that ought to encourage some degree of humility among physicists the world over.

An interpretation of quantum mechanics is a semantic account of the equations of the theory—it's a way for human beings to wrap their limited cognitive functions around what the theory is saying in precise mathematical language. I wonder whether Time Lords, too, have different interpretations of quantum mechanics. Some physicists—who refer to themselves as belonging to the "Shut up and calculate" school of thought—simply refuse to engage in the interpretation game: give me the equations and I'll crunch the numbers. But philosophically (and, really, for any genuinely curious scientist as well), one just can't do without semantic explanations of what the theory actually tells us about the fundamental nature of the world.

Partly because I find it fascinating, partly because the above mentioned Sean Carroll (who is a physicist and no dummy) endorses it, and partly because it fits well with the Doctor's adventures, here I'm going with the Everettian interpretation, also known as the many-worlds version of quantum mechanics. This is the basic idea: a fundamental problem in quantum mechanics—and one on which the differences between "interpretations" actually hinge—is the so-called measurement problem; that is, what happens when a "measurement" is carried out.

A "measurement" in quantum mechanics can be an interaction between a scientific tool and a given object of study (say, the slits through which you send a beam of electrons), but it can also be any interaction between physical systems, regardless of whether one of them includes, or is made by, a human being. Consider the box inside which the famous Schrödinger's cat is being housed. The Copenhagen interpretation says that until we open the box the cat is *neither* alive *nor* dead, as counterintuitive as that surely sounds. When we open the box, however, something called the wave function—the mathematical description of the quantum states of a given system (like the cat)—"collapses," meaning that the system goes from an undetermined state (alive/dead) to a determined one (either alive or dead). Many-worlds quantum mechanics, instead, says that when the measurement (that is, the opening of the box) happens *both* outcomes occur, just in different worlds: the universe splits at the moment of measurement, and from then on, one universe features a dead cat, the other a live cat. (Fun fact: you can create other universes through quantum-based random decision-making using the Universe Splitter app <http://goo.gl/2moGes>.)

There are good and not-so-good objections to many-worlds quantum mechanics, but it would take us too far afield to consider them here. Suffice to say that the obvious one—that it multiplies entities (or universes) needlessly—appears to be one of the bad objections, since quantum-mechanical theory already comes with the (mathematical) capacity to describe a very, very large number of universes by deploying something called a Hilbert space, a generalization of Euclidean space where wave functions "live" (yes, I know, sounds complicated, and it is!).

Why is this relevant to our concerns about Trenzalore? Because many-worlds quantum mechanics has been by far the best bet of any writer in recent times who wishes to engage us with paratime stories, such as the one that originates from the Time Lords' decision (or not, in a different Everettian world) to grant the Doctor a new cycle of regenerations.

And it gets better. Remember Clara's puzzlement at the revelation that the world had ended on June 26th, 2010? ("Missed that," she says rather flippantly.) That raises the question of why we focus on the one timeline (where the Doctor saves Trenzalore and gets extra regenerations) rather than the other one (where the Doctor dies and Trenzalore is destroyed). Well, I mean other than for obvious reasons of continued production of the television series we all love. It turns out that there's a similar question affecting the many-worlds interpretation. In fact, two related questions: why do universe splits give origin to only certain states and not others, and why are those outcomes described by certain probability distributions? There are good technical reasons for both, but I like the answer given by physicist (and strong supporter of Everettian quantum mechanics) David Deutsch, quoted in Marcus Chown's "Taming the Multiverse":

> By making good choices, doing the right thing, we thicken the stack of universes in which versions of us live reasonable lives. When you succeed, all the copies of you who made the same decision succeed too. What you do for the better increases the portion of the multiverse where good things happen.

So that's what the Time Lords did in responding to Clara's plea for help: they made a good choice, which disproportionally affected the quantum multiverse. (Incidentally, you may have been wondering all along whether EQM's many-worlds are related to the idea of a multiverse in cosmology. *Prima facie*, they aren't. But Sean Carroll—again—is intrigued by the possibility, based on his readings of recent theoretical research into the relationship between the two concepts.)

Back to Free Will

So much for quantum physics and timelines. But we still haven't answered the question posed by the title of this chapter: could the Doctor (or the Time Lords, or someone else) have avoided Trenzalore altogether? Is there a timeline in which our favorite time traveler doesn't blow up the universe, doesn't die on Trenzalore, and doesn't even have to become old there in order to stave off an interstellar war?

Actually, in part we have—implicitly—answered the question: it depends on how much the Doctor's (and others') choices influence the evolution of the multiverse, as seen in the quote by Deutsch above. But the very idea of "choice" inevitably (ah!) leads us to entertain the notion of free will, a much contested idea in philosophy and even neuroscience.

I don't actually like the term "free will" at all. It traces back to a theological concept of contra-causal (that is, independent of any cause) ability to make decisions, which supposedly is the get-out-of-jail-free card available to theologians who are embarrassed by the Problem of Evil and how to reconcile it with the alleged existence of an all-powerful, all-knowing, and all-good god. I'm a scientist and naturalist philosopher, so I think the idea of contra-causal anything is just plain silly. I think that a much better way to talk about the subject at hand is by using the preferred term among cognitive scientists: volition, the ability of human beings (and possibly other animals) to make autonomous (*not* contra-causal!) decisions exercising their agency. And just to be clear, here's what I mean by autonomous: if you decide to raise your arm and follow through with the actual action, that's volition at work; if someone else forcibly raises your arm against your will, that's not volition.

Whatever vocabulary we wish to use, it's time to look at the three fundamental ways to think about free will and volition from a philosophical perspective. As I mentioned before, these positions are usually labelled compatibilism, deterministic incompatibilism, and libertarian incompatibilism. Each comes in a variety of flavors, but we'll stick to the fundamentals. Beginning with the second one, deterministic incompatibilism is the idea that—since the universe is deterministic (meaning, it behaves according to the laws of physics, without exceptions)—then humans aren't "free" to do anything at all. We have the mistaken *impression* that we make autonomous decisions, but that's just an illusion. There are neither free lunches nor free will. The Doctor clearly disagrees, since he's always talking about the consequences of his choices, and occasionally even attempting to redress them by going back in time and making different ones. We can safely conclude that Time Lords, at the least, have decided that deterministic incompatibilism isn't the way to go.

Libertarian incompatibilism has nothing to do with the political meaning of the term "libertarianism." Rather, it affirms our sense that we're agents capable of autonomous decision making, and concludes that if this is incompatible with determinism, so much the worse for determinism. (As it turns out, incidentally, even if the laws of nature were irreducibly stochastic—as in some interpretations of quantum mechanics—one still couldn't have free will independently of such laws). Relatively few philosophers, and even fewer scientists, accept this bold position, because it seems to flatly contradict much of what we've learned from science about how the world works. And I think the Doctor would agree that the laws of physics can't be ignored: Time Lords, after all, can do what they do because of their mastery of such laws, not because they're magicians capable of transcending them.

Which leaves us with compatibilism. This is the idea that we can have our cake and eat it too, although only in a pretty specific sense of "having" and "eating." Compatibilists accept that the universe is a deterministic system. (In case you're wondering, quantum mechanics is a deterministic theory—it's the measurement problem that introduces the randomness of processes such as atomic decay. Here's one way to put it, from correspondence with my friend Sean Carroll: in Everettian quantum mechanics, the full wave function describing all the worlds evolves deterministically, but the single world to which any given observer has access exhibits random jumps. That is, the world splits deterministically, but we have no way of knowing in which world we happen to be.) But compatibilists also agree that human beings are agents with the ability of making their own decisions. How is this possible?

Think of your brain, at the least in part, as a type of evolved biological machinery to make good enough decisions about your survival and reproduction. A functional human brain makes better decisions than a less functional one (for instance, like compulsive gamblers, or people with different types of severe neurological damage). It also makes better decisions than the less sophisticated brains of other species, largely because we seem to be unique (on this planet) in our ability—under ideal circumstances—to reflect on the available options before actually taking a particular course of action. Presumably, Time-Lord brains evolved in a similar manner, and are even better-equipped to consider various possibilities and act accordingly. So I'm betting that the good Doctor is, philosophically speaking, a compatibilist about volition.

If compatibilism (and therefore determinism) is true, how is it that the Time Lords can make one decision in one timeline and another in a different timeline? We've seen that from the point of view of many-worlds quantum mechanics, every decision leads to a split in the multiverse, thereby generating new timelines. The decision, however, doesn't have to be the result of some kind of contra-causal "free will." It can simply be the outcome of a slightly different random (see measurement problem above!) interaction of the decision-making system (the Time Lords' brains, or the "apparatus" in quantum-mechanics parlance) with the surrounding environment. This makes sense of the different outcomes on Trenzalore. Though if I understand the physics correctly, there's no way for anyone from a given timeline to visit a different timeline—so the Doctor and the Great Intelligence couldn't possibly have found out about the TARDIS-as-tomb if they belonged to the timeline where that outcome was, thankfully, avoided.

Fate and Set Points in Time

Remember "Cold Blood" (2010)? In that episode, the Eleventh Doctor had to solve a tricky little problem with the Silurians which could've led to a war or to peaceful co-operation between humans and Silurians. The Doctor explains to Amy that this is a real choice because:

> There are fixed points throughout time where things must stay exactly the way they are. This is not one of them. This is an opportunity! Whatever happens here will create its own timeline, its own reality, a temporal tipping point. The future revolves around you, here, now, so do good!

So, apparently, there are such things as "fixed points in time," which in fact appear repeatedly across the *Doctor Who* series, for instance in "The Fires of Pompeii" (2008), when the Tenth Doctor and Donna Noble actually cause—and can't avoid—the devastation imposed by an exploding volcano on the Roman city. (Interestingly, of course, they do manage to save a single Roman family, whose patriarch is played by a certain Peter Capaldi . . .)

The idea of fixed points on the timeline (for which, as far as I know, Earth science has found no evidence) is interesting because it allows us to make a crucial distinction between the free will-volition issue just discussed and the concept of fate. Fate concerns situations in which human beings (or Time Lords) can, in fact, do different things, taking different courses of action, but these different paths all lead to the same (inevitable, fated) outcome.

It's an ancient Greek idea, best exemplified in the tragic story of Oedipus. The hero was told of a prophecy according to which he'd end up killing his father and marrying his mother. In order to avoid such a horrible fate, he leaves town and begins wandering. But he ends up doing exactly those things anyway, by apparent accident (and he feels somehow morally responsible for them too, which leads him to blind himself with two pins from his mother's dress, after she's committed suicide).

Putting everything together, then, we could conclude that the Doctor was fated to be at Trenzalore, because his last stand against the assembled forces of many races who seek revenge against the Time Lords is a fixed point in time. But the specific outcome of the siege depended on a choice made by the Time Lords trapped in a pocket universe nearby, with their choice splitting the multiverse and creating two timelines, the second one of which gives us the regeneration that results in Peter Capaldi, the Twelfth Doctor. At least, this is my story. And as the Doctor himself said in "The Big Bang," 2010: "We're all stories, in the end. Just make it a good one, eh?"

9
How the Doctor Knows

Paula Smithka

> **Doctor:** You know what the big problem is, in telling fantasy and reality apart?
>
> **Ashley:** What?
>
> **Doctor:** They're both ridiculous. ("Last Christmas," 2014)

Could we be dreaming now? Perhaps the world that we think is real is nothing but a dream state induced by Dream Crabs while our brains are being devoured ("Last Christmas").

Philosophers call this type of thought experiment "a brain in a vat." Maybe I am, and maybe you are, just brains in a vat of life-preserving fluid hooked up to an elaborate computer system that creates for us a virtual reality which we believe is "real." A program provides us with all of the experiences with which we're so familiar—a planet filled with trees, birds, other humans, the sun, the moon, and the stars, a job as a temp in Chiswick (perhaps) or a school teacher, fish fingers and custard, Jammie Dodgers, and even a TV that airs a brilliant show called *Doctor Who*. (Check out John Pollock's short story, "Brain in a Vat." Pollock doesn't give *Doctor Who* examples, though.) If I'm a brain in a vat, none of my world is real. But how could I *know* that it's *not* real?

The Doctor, Amy, and Rory find themselves in a similar "dream pickle" in "Amy's Choice" (2010). The Dream Lord has presented them with two worlds, Leadworth in 2015 and the TARDIS world. The Dream Lord states, "Here's your challenge: Two worlds—here, in the time machine; there, in the village that time forgot. One is real, one is fake." They need to determine which world is real; and the Doctor asks, "But which is which?" They don't *know*. After all, if you *know* something, you have to be *certain* about it. No mistakes allowed. There's no saying about what you *know* that "I had a wobble—a big wobble" (Clara, "Mummy on the Orient Express," 2014). When I say, "I *know* my keys are on the table," that means the keys are there and I'm aware of my belief that they're there. But what if I don't find my keys on the table despite having claimed that I knew they were there? Well, you'd clearly say, "She *thought* the keys were on the table"—drawing the distinction between what I *merely thought* to be the case and what I *knew*. You can't be mistaken about what you know. Right? Or, *can* knowledge be a bit wibbly-wobbly, and maybe even a little timey-wimey?

Let's Go Poke It with a Stick

The Doctor trusts his senses, as well as his reliable sonic screwdriver to give him even more empirical information about his surroundings in order to solve the problem *du jour*. The Doctor tells us to trust science; but in order to have scientific knowledge, scientists need to be able make generalizations, predictions, and form hypotheses; and if knowledge entails certainty, we can't do any of that, as we'll see. In order for the Doctor to figure things out, like what's in the shadows ("Silence in the Library," 2008), or how the *Starship UK* remains in flight even though there are no engines ("The Beast Below," 2010), or which world is the real world in "Amy's Choice," he's got to use empirical evidence and a reliable sonic screwdriver to give him even more information. When the Doctor asks Amy and Rory in "Amy's Choice," about what they inform him is the old folks' home in Leadworth, he says, "You said everyone here lives into their nineties. There's something that doesn't make sense. Let's go poke it with a stick!" How empirical is that?

So, what's the big deal about empirical evidence contributing to knowledge; doesn't everybody grant that? No, because 'empirical' means what our senses tell us and what our senses tell us can't be one-hundred percent positively certain—and certainty is what's required for knowledge, at least for some philosophers like René Descartes (1596–1650). I mean, can *you* be so *certain* there's not a Dream Crab on your face responsible for your "reality"?

Knowledge . . . What?

The ancient Greek philosopher Plato provides us with the most commonly accepted view of knowledge in his dialogue, the *Theaetetus*. A bit of knowledge is a justified, true belief.

Knowledge has to be more than mere belief because people can believe false things. Some people seem to believe that humans have never landed on the moon, despite the fact we have moon rocks. The Doctor *believed* that the Daleks were wiped out in the Time War. One can't *know* false things. In the case of a true belief, something has to be added to shore up that belief to make it knowledge.

Your belief can't merely be accidentally true; it needs justification. Justification provides evidence for the true belief. Consider a lucky guess; we wouldn't call it knowledge, because there's no evidence to support the belief. I might believe that horse #4 will win the race; after all, horse #4 is a good-looking animal. (Aren't all racehorses good-looking animals?) It turns out that horse #4 did win the race; but I had no good reason to believe that he would win since I didn't know horse #4's track record or the jockey's success record. I just got lucky. Clearly, I didn't *know* horse #4 would win. So, in order to know something, you must have evidence which supports the true belief.

Knowledge is a justified, true belief. Settled? Not quite. Philosophers argue about what counts as adequate justification: reason alone or can senses do the job?

Strong Foundationalism: No Wobbles!

René Descartes in his *Meditations on First Philosophy* provides us with the original dream-world problem in his quest to settle this question of knowledge. Since we can't be wrong about what we know, we must be certain. Well, of what can we be certain? That's the question.

Descartes reasons that if something can be doubted, it's not certain and won't serve as the foundation for knowledge. So what can be doubted? Just about everything, it turns out. Descartes argues that our senses can deceive us. Just look up in the sky at the sun or the moon. They appear to be rather small in size. You've done that pencil-in-the-water experiment. It appears to be bent.

That's Descartes's point—you can't trust your senses. In fact, there could be some God or Evil Genius (or Dream Lord in the Whoniverse) who constantly deceives us into thinking that there's a world, a sun, a moon, (a star burning cold), or that we have a body. (Descartes doesn't think God would deceive us, so if we're deceived in this way, it must be by an Evil Genius.) According to Descartes, no sensory information is, or can be, certain. Since I can't trust my senses, I must be skeptical about the physical world in which I live. (Which one is the dream world?)

It turns out, says Descartes, that the only thing we can be certain of is our own existence. If I say, "I think I don't exist," then surely I'm contradicting myself. I need to exist in order to think. So, Descartes's famous axiom is: *Cogito ergo sum*—I think, therefore I am. That's the foundation on which all of human knowledge is based. Descartes developed analytic geometry so he's fond of axioms and the process of deduction (that is, if all the premises or evidence given in the argument are true, the conclusion must be true).

Since I can't trust my senses, I must use *reason* to provide me with evidence for the existence of the physical world. Descartes is a "rationalist" and a rationalist says that reason is our best source for knowledge. Now, Descartes doesn't deny that there's a mind-independent physical world, it's just that I can't know it by using my untrustworthy senses; I must *deduce* the existence of the world.

According to Descartes, I believe the world exists and I have a body, but it's only by using my reason together with "evidence" in the form of other beliefs, namely, that God exists (he's allegedly proved that, too, using reason) and that God is no deceiver—that's the justification part—that I can conclude that what my senses tell me is the way the world is. So, I know, I am certain, that is, I've a justified, true belief, that the physical world exists and that I have a body. I *know* that I know this because without me being able to reflect on whether I know something and can provide a deductive proof for something's existence, I could never be sure. I know the physical world only *indirectly* via my ideas and not *directly* with my senses. Philosophers call this position in epistemology "strong foundationalism." All knowledge rests either on basic beliefs that are innate (those I am born with) like "I exist" or they're self-evident (they're obviously true to my reason) like "triangles have three angles."

Is the Doctor a rationalist and a strong foundationalist in his knowledge of the external world? Just imagine the Doctor questioning the reliability of his senses as a Cyberman approaches him and Clara ("Death in Heaven," 2014). According to Descartes's model, the Twelfth Doctor would have to reason this way: I've an idea of a Cyberman, my idea must be caused, God exists and is no deceiver (at least for Descartes), and that therefore (finally!) there *is* indeed a Cyberman approaching . . . now, *run!* Not likely. And, in "Amy's Choice," the Doctor instructs Amy and Rory to question what their senses tell them in the context of the Dream Lord's two worlds scenario—one real, one fake—but also to use their senses to find clues that would distinguish between the "worlds." He says, "Trust nothing we see, or hear, or feel. Look around you; examine everything. Look for the details that don't ring true." Rory points out however, "What rings true isn't so simple." (They're in a time machine with a bow-tie-wearing alien, after all.) But, the Doctor's instruction isn't a dismissal of sensory information as being untrustworthy, unlike Descartes. Instead, it embraces sensory information to find clues.

Descartes's approach preserves the notion that knowledge must entail certainty and it does answer the problem that our senses *can* deceive us sometimes—really, are we dreaming now? But I think this view tosses the baby out with the bathwater. Just because the senses *can* deceive us at some time or other doesn't mean that they always do, or do so most of the time. They're much more reliable than that. Contrary to Descartes, justification can come in the form of empirical evidence; and the Doctor agrees.

Reliabilism: Justification Comes in a Causal Chain

Reliabilism in epistemology takes a very different approach than that of Descartes. Reliabilists tend to focus on the belief-forming process. They assume that beliefs are formed via causal relationships with the world. If the causal process is reliable in actual situations, then true beliefs are automatically formed in us. The justification for the true belief is packed into the causal relationship. A true belief wouldn't be formed if the person didn't stand in the right causal chain with the object of the belief. Perception, according to this approach, unlike Descartes's, is considered to be a reliable belief-forming process, along with good reasoning. So, when I say, "I know my *Disappearing TARDIS* coffee cup is on the table," my belief is formed because I see the cup on the table and vision is a perceptual process that tends to be reliable in actual situations and will usually produce the same belief in similar situations.

According to reliabilists, "seeing is believing," at least in normal situations. If I'm in some unusual situation, my beliefs may not be reliably formed, like when I'm told there are two worlds, one real and one fake, by the Dream Lord. If it's 1960s London and I'm walking around the city, the belief that I see a blue police box (that's a closed phone booth used at that time by British police) is reliably formed. However, if I'm walking around London today and I see a blue police box, my belief that it's a genuine *police box* is suspect, since police boxes aren't used anymore. (They must be filming an episode of *Doctor Who*!) Knowing that police boxes aren't used anymore defeats my belief that I'm actually seeing a genuine *police box*. This is called a "relevant alternative." (But don't we just love being in those relative alternative situations, like funhouses at carnivals or the Haunted Mansion at Disney World where we see the ghost riding in the car with us?! We expect our perceptions to be misled and *that's* what makes it fun!)

Alvin Goldman gives three criteria for perceptual knowledge in his "Discrimination and Perceptual Knowledge": 1. The belief is the result of a reliable belief-forming process; 2. There should be no perceptual equivalents (the blue police box in London today) in the relevant alternatives that could lead to a false belief; and 3. The belief is true. (This less formal presentation of Goldman's position is by Jack Crumley.)

This view is attractive because it fits really well with our common-sense notions of perceptual knowledge. We can have knowledge without needing to have reasons in the form of other beliefs that serve as the justification for our claim to knowledge. I don't have to spell out *why* I know my *Disappearing TARDIS* coffee cup is on the table (though perhaps I could); I'm standing in the right causal chain and that's enough to *be justified* in my belief that my *Disappearing TARDIS* coffee cup is on the table. Having reasons isn't a necessary condition for justification. I might, in fact, *be justified*, but can't give a reason.

Reliabilism opens the door to having direct perceptual knowledge that's much more basic than the kind of knowledge Descartes and other rationalists defend. It's definitely time to climb out of the skeptic's hole of doubt regarding the physical world and trust those reliable senses of ours—scientists do, and so does the Doctor.

Somewhat Wobbly Knowledge

Descartes champions deductive reasoning patterns (like those in analytic geometry for example)—if all of the premises in your argument are true, they guarantee the truth of the conclusion, and that provides certainty. All well and good—deduction is a fine reasoning pattern, Sherlock claims to use it all the time—but it's limited in what it can do for us. Scientists do use deduction, but they don't *only* use deduction. Scientists, and other people, like you, me, and philosophers, make generalizations, predictions, and formulate hypotheses (called inferences to the best explanation), whether we call them that or not. In order to do this, we use *inductive* reasoning patterns. Charles Sanders Peirce (1839–1914) broke out "inference to the best explanation" from the category of induction and called it "abduction" (though not of the alien variety—of course, if it's the Doctor coming to call, that sort of abduction is perfectly fine by us!) In order to engage in inductive or abductive reasoning, we need evidence, which usually comes in the form of empirical evidence.

Consider a scientist, like Davros, working in a lab on a new and perfect killing machine that's a "living, thinking, self-supporting creature"—his Mark III Travel Machine, later dubbed "Dalek." Although we might consider Davros's work "immoral and evil" as did the scientist Ronson and some of the other scientists, we must acknowledge that he employs sound reasoning principles ("Genesis of the Daleks," 1975). Once the killing machine is developed (this is, of course, after many chemical experiments on animals and ultimately on the Kaleds to produce the "ultimate creature"), Davros first needs to test his creation.

He calls the scientists together to demonstrate his work on the voice-recognition program and the new "death ray gun" weapon.

The new Dalek performs splendidly! It recognizes that the Doctor and Harry aren't the kind of life-forms found on Skaro, and we hear the now infamous, "EX-TER-MIN-ATE" as the Dalek raises its newly installed gun to carry out the extermination. After having thwarted the Dalek's kill-attempt and Davros's experiment (to Davros's displeasure), Ronson congratulates Davros on having come up with the perfect weapon. "Brilliant, not perfect . . . yet," Davros responds. Davros then sends the scientists away to work on improving the Dalek's optical systems and sensory circuits (and later has Gharman remove compassion and pity from the ones he's created).

All of the data recorded from the many tests of the Dalek-killing-machines forms a sample. Davros and the scientists trust what their senses tell them about the effectiveness of the Daleks' systems. Standing in the right perceptual causal chain, Davros is justified in believing his creation is a brilliant weapon system. Based on the sample, he predicts that the next Dalek he creates will be an effective weapon. After many successful trials, he may generalize his claim: all of the Daleks I create will be effective killing machines!

You can't reason this way using deduction; because even if one Dalek was an effective killing machine, we can't be *certain* that the next Dalek created will be, or that all Daleks will be perfect "ex-ter-min-a-tors." Predictions or generalizations could turn out to be false even when all the evidence suggests they're true. (In our own Earth world, some doctor's prediction that a tried-and-true antibiotic would kill a bacterial infection in a patient turned out to be false in the case of some "superbugs.") But, if the sample size is large enough and it's an unbiased sample, it's certainly *reasonable* to conclude that Daleks will be effective killing machines, even if we don't have certainty.

Now, consider abductive reasoning. Gregor Mendel (1822–1884) was the Moravian scientist and Augustinian monk who's famous for crossing pea plants—tall with short, red with white, and wrinkled with smooth. Today we call him the father of modern genetics, though the term 'gene' wouldn't be coined until 1909 by the Danish botanist Wilhelm

Johannsen. Mendel crosses his pea plants over and over and finds that he gets (fairly) consistent results in the proportions of red, pink, and white pea plants in the second generation and so on with tall and short, smooth and wrinkled.

Mendel hypothesized that there must be "hereditary factors" being passed along from parent to offspring—today, we call them 'genes'. That was the *best explanation* to account for the regularity in his empirical data. This is the sort of reasoning that CSIs use in a crime scene investigation, too. Collect data and come up with the best explanation to account for the data. The CSIs put together the best competing whodunit hypothesis based on the evidence. They could be wrong in their hypothesis about who committed the crime, but they formulate a reasonable hypothesis on the basis of the empirical evidence. Sherlock does this, too, but he claims he's doing deduction, not abduction. Perhaps because *he* is *Sherlock*, he may have access to more alternative competing hypotheses than we (normal folk) would as CSIs and maybe *he's* deducing the guilty party, but *we're* using abduction to come up with our hypothesis. You use abduction when you try to come up with the best explanation for why your keys aren't on the table, where you thought they were. Where *are* those keys?

Induction and abduction are reasoning patterns used by scientists and others and, together with their reliance on empirical evidence, serve as the basis for much of what we call "scientific knowledge," even if that knowledge is a little wibbly-wobbly. It might even be a little timey-wimey too, since what once counted as "scientific knowledge" might change over time and in the face of new evidence. Scientists used to think that microbes could just suddenly appear from non-living matter—spontaneous generation or abiogenesis (the latter term was coined by Thomas Henry Huxley). Experiments were conducted to show this, for example by John Needham in 1745. Needham boiled chicken broth, let it cool and microbes grew. He claimed it showed spontaneous generation. However, Louis Pasteur settled the matter in 1864 with his published results disproving spontaneous generation. He wrote, *"La génération spontanée est une chimère"* ("Spontaneous generation is a mythical beast"). He's credited with the Law of Biogenesis which states: *Omne vivum ex vivo*, or "all life comes from life."

A Reliable-ist Doctor

The Doctor is a reliabilist. He trusts his senses, as well as his reliable sonic screwdriver to give him more empirical information about things in his environment; and in his adventures, he employs inductive and abductive (and even sometimes deductive) reasoning patterns to solve the crisis at hand.

Consider the puzzle in "The Beast Below." After hearing children cry, the Doctor and Amy board *Starship UK*. Right away, he notices that something's amiss. He does "the thing." He puts a glass of water on the floor of the ship. No ripples. He's immediately justified in his belief that there are no ripples. He's standing in the right perceptual causal chain. He goes to the engine room only to find electrical boxes with wires that aren't hooked up. Again, he doesn't doubt his perceptual knowledge. He draws his first conclusion based on the empirical evidence he collects: the best explanation is that there are no engines on the ship.

New question: what, then, moves the ship? After further investigation and learning from the video that it's a Star Whale propelling the ship, the Doctor doesn't doubt that his reliable sonic screwdriver will make it possible for Liz 10, Mandy, Amy, and the others to hear the cries of pain by the Star Whale. Does he (or the others for that matter) question the reliability of their senses when they hear the cries? Not at all. He predicts that his altering the controlling device directing the Star Whale will render it brain dead. Of course, in this episode, it's Amy's inference to the best explanation that saves the day: the Star Whale came willingly to help. No need to keep torturing the creature!

In "Silence in the Library," the Doctor, Donna, Professor River Song, and her crew have to contend with some unusual deaths of their comrades. What's the best explanation that accounts for how Miss Evangelista and Dave died? The Doctor and the others aren't skeptical of the sensory information they have about the existence of the skeletal remains of Miss Evangelista and Dave. They don't wonder *whether* their comrades are dead—could this be a dream?

They do wonder about the cause of the unusual deaths; they trust their perceptions that they've lost two in the party. The Doctor conducts an empirical experiment—he tosses a chicken leg into the shadows. The chicken leg is consumed. He counts the shadows and tells the others to do so. This evidence is used to support his hypothesis that the Vashta Nerada are the cause of the deaths. Even though the Vashta Nerada aren't able to be observed directly, in the way their colleagues' skeletal remains can be observed directly, the empirical evidence he gathers, together with his knowledge of the many species across worlds, forms the best explanation to account for the phenomena: it's the Vashta Nerada, "Piranhas of the air . . . shadows that melt the flesh."

In "Amy's Choice," after the Dream Lord has declared himself defeated and taken his leave, and Amy and Rory are satisfied that the TARDIS world is the real one, the Doctor informs them that he's planning to blow up the TARDIS. They're shocked. But the Doctor reflects upon all the information he's gathered as they've moved between the Leadworth and TARDIS "worlds," like when he opened the door to the TARDIS and they (the Doctor, Amy, and Rory) looked out at the "cold star." Amy notes that "stars burn hot." The Doctor says, "It is hot; it's just burning cold." And now, based on sensory evidence like that, he concludes that both "worlds" are dreams. He tells Amy and Rory:

> DOCTOR: Notice how helpful the Dream Lord was. There was misinformation, Red Herrings, malice, and I could've done without the limerick, but he was always very keen on making us choose between dream and reality. Star burning cold. . . . Do me a favor!

Telling fantasy from reality? They're both ridiculous!

The Doctor doesn't believe he lives in a dream world. He's no Cartesian skeptic about what his senses tell him, that is, unless he realizes he's in one of those unusual perceptual contexts like that presented by the Dream Lord. If we know we're in a *non-normal* situation, then we're right to question whether our beliefs have been reliably formed. But this doesn't happen often for us or for the Doctor. Perception is generally a reliable belief-forming process. The Doctor uses induction and abduction, (as well as deduction), to get to the heart of the problem he's faced with.

The Doctor's a reliabilist when it comes to knowledge. Standing in the right causal chain with the physical world is the thing; it's all the justification he needs to warrant his perceptual knowledge. That's a good thing for us humans, because when we're threatened by Daleks or Cybermen, Silurians or the Atraxi ("The Eleventh Hour," 2010) or any other beings bent on our destruction, our Doctor is reliable.

CLARA: What are we to you?

DOCTOR: You are the only mystery worth solving. ("Hide," 2013)

Aren't we lucky!

10

One Good, Solid Hope— the Impossible Girl

CHARLENE ELSBY AND ROB LUZECKY

Clara is the biggest mystery of Season Seven, going by the various names of Clara Oswald, Clara Oswin Oswald, and Oswin Oswald. The Doctor first knows Clara as "Soufflé Girl," when he meets a girl who spends her time making soufflés in the Dalek Asylum—but where does she get the milk?

During a different incarnation, she compares herself to a soufflé, to explain how she can exist across time in different incarnations—like cooking from the same recipe over and over. In other words, what Clara is, ultimately, isn't any one of her particular incarnations, but she's that which remains consistent between her incarnations, just as multiple soufflés are all made from the same recipe.

She's the "Impossible Girl," because she seems to do the impossible—she lives in multiple timelines, through different times and in different places, but always and in all places somehow the same. Throughout the season, the Doctor looks for some indication that Clara is special in order to explain her "impossibility." She's also called "the Impossible Girl" because she appears at different points in the Doctor's timeline, physically the same person, but with no memory of her other selves despite eerie similarities between them. For instance, Clara gives her Wi-Fi password the mnemonic device of her Victorian self's dying words: "Run, You Clever Boy, And Remember."

In "The Name of the Doctor" (2013), Clara Oswald (the "real" one) steps into the Doctor's timeline in order to prevent the damage just done to it by the Great Intelligence. This event is meant to explain how she's appeared as other incarnations throughout the season—Oswin Oswald, the reluctant Dalek, and Clara Oswin Oswald, the Victorian governess. River Song explains that though the "real" Clara Oswald will die in the process, "echoes" will be created throughout the Doctor's time-line capable of helping him out of sticky situations. But Clara doesn't die by stepping into the Doctor's timeline. He follows her and brings her back. Clara just keeps doing impossible thing after impossible thing. But "impossible," in the *Doctor Who* universe, is a relative term. Some things only apparently impossible come to be possible when they're, in fact, done.

If we can figure out what it is that remains consistent between Clara's incarnations, we can figure out her "essence." In other words, what does it mean to be Clara, at any point in time and space? Clara's nicknames, "Soufflé Girl" and the "Impossible Girl" provide clues.

The Soufflé Isn't the Soufflé; the Soufflé Is the Recipe

Clara uses this axiom a couple of times in the series. In "The Name of the Doctor," one of the children asks Clara how it's possible that she's making her *mother's* soufflé. Clara isn't her mother, therefore, she must be making her own soufflé. Clara responds that the soufflé isn't the soufflé, the soufflé is the recipe. So anyone working from the same recipe must be making Clara's mother's soufflé.

She uses the same response, in the same episode, to explain how it's actually she who's going to be dispersed throughout the Doctor's timeline. We see first, when the Great Intelligence hops into the Doctor's temporal scar—a tear in space and time that resulted from the Doctor's life of traveling—inside his tomb at Trenzalore, that this results in the Great Intelligence being able to change any or all of the events in the Doctor's history to have more dire conclusions: stars disappear from the sky, people die, friendships never occur.

Clara's plan is to reverse the damage done by the Great Intelligence by hopping in after him and helping the Doctor out at key points in time. Her actions will result in there being "echoes" of Clara throughout the Doctor's timeline, and the echoes of Clara will follow the same basic "recipe" as that of the girl we'd like to call the "real" Clara—like soufflés made from the same recipe, which are almost identical, yet not exactly the same.

The temporal scar is essentially making copies of Clara throughout time, but what's the nature of these copies? Are the echoes more like duplicates printed from the same file, or more like a bad photocopy of an artistic masterpiece? What the echoes have in common is that they look the same as Clara, and they have the singular purpose of saving the Doctor. But to what extent are these echoes actually "Clara"?

Before we can answer how Clara can be Clara over and over again, it might be helpful to answer a simpler question. How's it possible that the sophisticated and refined individual you've become is the same person as that stupid little kid you used to be, who didn't even know how to tie their shoes? How is any one thing "identical" to itself at different points in time?

There are a couple of popular notions to work with: one is that something is identical if it is *exactly the same in all respects* over time. On this line of thinking, the fact that you change a little bit from second to second means that you're, in fact, a different person at each second. If this is true, we might as well throw out a concept of identity, or define it as something transient and unreliable. Contrary to this view is the idea that while we certainly change over time, there must be something that preserves our identity. That is, over and above all of the individual little changes, there's something more basic, more essential, which ties all the little things together into the single, unified awesomeness that is distinctly *you.*

UnLocke-ing the Recipe

John Locke (1632–1704) came up with what seems like a very convenient answer to the question of *physical* identity for living beings in his *Essay Concerning Human Understanding*, which is that your current majestic physical self and the one who cowered behind the sofa during *Doctor Who* are one and the same by virtue of being a continuation of one and the same life. The continuation of one and the same life means that that life continues not only in the sense of events that happen, but continues with the body as well. But the body expels and replaces its material, so it continually changes, which is why Locke doesn't think *personal* identity consists in the matter alone.

Throughout, personal identity maintains a kind of unity, namely the same life, and for Locke, the identity of the *person*, that is, what makes you *the same person* over time is your consciousness as it extends backwards in time. It's a type of psychological unity that results from your ability to remember doing things in the past. So, if you remember hiding behind the sofa, then you're the same person who did in fact hide behind the couch.

If we're opposed to Locke, we might say that personal identity is tied to some material aspect, like her body. There's an old thought experiment attributed to Plutarch that asks about the identity of the Ship of Theseus and goes something like this: If Theseus's ship has to be repaired over time when the boards rot, and eventually all of the boards come to be replaced, is it still *the same* ship? The Doctor makes the same argument in "Deep Breath" (2014), except he uses the example of a broom—"Is it the same? . . . of course it isn't."

It seems, then, that if we want to say that it's the same ship, there's something else besides the boards that make the thing distinctly Theseus's ship. The thought experiment extends to the human body as well, since its cells die off and are replaced by new ones, just like the Clockwork Man. Thus, there must be something more that makes the person than merely the matter which composes the body. The answer given by many prominent philosophers in the history of Western philosophy is that there has to be something immaterial, like a soul.

Though Locke was concerned with issues regarding the soul, Locke's concept of the unity of the same life overcomes the need for religion and metaphysics. What Locke's account suggests is that what's important about identity isn't that the material parts are the same, or that there's a single unified soul that makes the thing identical to itself over time, but just the fact that the thing partakes in the same psychological continuity—in other words, memory.

But Clara seems to defy all of the traditional theories of identity for the reason that she has neither a continuation of the same material parts, nor a continuation of life, nor of psychological continuity, since she can't remember being any other Clara. Clara's echoes have different (though similar-looking) bodies and different minds than the "real" Clara; and the "real" Clara has no recollection of the lives of Oswin Oswald or Clara

Oswin Oswald. If we go by the soufflé theory of identity, then we lose something important about what it means to be the same person over (and for Clara, across) time.

One of the fundamental facts of life we seem to be most attached to is the idea that "there's only one of me. I'm special. Look at me go." But in Clara's case, that just isn't true. There are several Claras. What it is to be Clara is like what it is to be a recipe. You can make the same soufflé over and over again, but in some sense it's always different. You can perform the same song again and again, but it'll be a different song, at different times, in different places. Even if you play the song from the same recording, the sounds produced exist at different times, and possibly different places, every time you play it. If what it is to be Clara is more like a recipe than a particular soufflé, then she's defying traditional distinctions between what philosophers call "particulars" and "universals," the difference between being a "one" and a "many." For instance, we tend to think of individual people as particulars. We say things like, "There'll never be another one like him!" We want to say that Clara, too, is a particular individual, but because there are many of her, Clara is more properly a universal than she is a particular.

The Soufflé Is the Soufflé

What it is to be Clara is more like what it is to be a species (a universal thing, something that describes a "many"), than what it is to be one particular thing existing over time, because there's something that all of the Claras share; there's not just one particular Clara existing at a particular time. The difference between the species as a universal thing and the particular thing is the difference between what it is to be a kind of thing, say, a squirrel and what it is to be *that* particular squirrel, say, Bob. Bob the squirrel is a particular instance of the kind squirrel. What Bob and other particular squirrels have in common is that they're all squirrels. The concept 'squirrel' applies to Bob and his friends.

While some philosophers might object that there is no such a "thing" as a universal, we think that there's something real that's being referred to when we say "Bob is a squirrel." The concept of being a squirrel is part of Bob's "essence." When we recognize one of the particular Clara incarnations, we recognize her as part of the general concept of Clara. So, in a way, there's the "species" of Clara. Each particular Clara shares the Clara-concept with all the other particular Clara incarnations. For this to be true, there must be an "essence" of Clara; that is, there's something which makes each Clara, Clara. But if what it is to be Clara is a species as opposed to an individual, then what it is to be Clara isn't something unique to the particular incarnations. What is the thing that we point to in *all* of her incarnations in order to say, "Yep, that's a Clara all right," Clara Oswald, Clara Oswin Oswald, and Oswin Oswald, are all made from the Clara recipe, and are all "Claras" in the same sense that the concept "squirrel" applies to all particular squirrels; or that the concept of soufflé applies to this fallen soufflé even though this soufflé is an imperfect one.

To say there's an "essence" of Clara, what we need is a "real" Clara that serves as the "template" for all other Claras. We should reject the idea that there's only one Clara. The Doctor makes this mistake in "The Snowmen" (2012), when he says, "The same woman, twice. And she died both times. The same woman!" This is only impossible if the Doctor assumes that there's only one Clara in the first place who's somehow splintered across time and space. Instead, we should distinguish between a "real" Clara, the one who steps into the Doctor's "scar," and the echoes that pervade the rest of time and space.

But does that mean that the echoes are somehow not real or less than real? How real are they? Real enough to save the Doctor. Does this make Clara's echoes real people, on the same level of being as Clara herself? If so, then why is the "real" Clara any more real than any of the other ones? The fact that they're called "echoes" gives us a hint as to the answer, and the stories we see in "The Rings of Akhaten" (2013) and "The Name of the Doctor" are origin stories. Clara Oswald is the "real" Clara (so the theory goes) because she's the one who got the whole Clara-echo thing started in the first place. In non-linear time, Clara Oswald from modern-day London is the first of all the other Claras whose existence depends on that original Clara's action of stepping into the Doctor's timeline. We can't say that Clara is *only* a bundle of echoes, because echoes don't exist without a cause.

We don't really know for certain how Clara's echoes pop up through time. Are they born into families, or do they just pop up at convenient times, with memories and jobs and full wardrobes? We don't know. But we do know that they wouldn't be there if it weren't for that "real" Clara jumping into Doctor's time stream to eliminate the damage wrought by the Great Intelligence. In that respect, the modern-day London Clara is responsible for all of the other Claras; she's the "real" one.

Hope and the Essential Impossibility of Clara

Maybe Clara isn't "real," at least not in the way we have been talking about, where reality is either something material or some vague concept of a continuing life, memory or soul. What Clara is, is the girl who saves the Doctor, and she's saved the Doctor many times over. Since real effects have real causes, the saving of the Doctor, a real effect, was caused by real Claras. So we need the sense of a "real" Clara whose impossibility has nothing to do with whether it's possible to exist across time with many bodies and many minds.

Maybe Clara's reality has nothing to do with her material incarnations, and everything to do with her impossibility. Clara's multiple existences begin with her saving the Doctor, and the result of her choice to step into his timeline results in her helping the Doctor many times over. Wherever Clara is, there's hope. We can't say that wherever she is, there are some identical particles to an original Clara, nor can we say that wherever Clara is, there's the mind of some original Clara persisting. The only thing consistent between Clara's existences is that wherever she is, hope exists. In essence, *what* Clara is, in all of her incarnations, is hope. She's hope for the Doctor, and for the rest of the world. Remember "Rings of Akhaten," when a parasite-god was feeding off the population who were willing to sacrifice their children to save themselves. What stopped the parasite from consuming the planet? What saved the little girl? There were three things. First, the Doctor offered all of his memories (the memories of the birth and death of the universe, and of the last great Time War). Second, there was the girl leading the people in song. Third, and most of all, there was Clara. The Doctor had given his all, but the parasite still demanded more, still needed more, and what was that more that the parasite needed? What was that thing that stopped the parasite? It was "the most important leaf in human history." That leaf *is*, Clara says, a whole future that never happened, an infinity; all of her mum's days that never came. For Clara, those days have and will come; in her multiple incarnations, she's an infinity of potentialities, a future and a past, all of the days of all of her lives, and what she *is for* all of those days is hope.

The *real* Clara (in all of her incarnations) is defined by one trait above all others, and, in philosophical terms, we call this her "essence." As long as that essence remains, Clara remains. This essence is the "real" Clara, and it's indicated by what Clara does. Clara refuses to walk away. She refused to walk away from the children in London, she refused to walk away from the Doctor when he was already spent on Akhaten, and she refused to walk away when his timeline was being torn apart by the Great Intelligence. When Clara refuses to walk away, what we understand is this: there's still hope. Walking away is the action of someone who has given up hope, and this is precisely what Clara *does not do*.

Remember in "The Snowmen" when the Doctor went and hid up there among the clouds. He'd given up his wanderings through space and time, and he'd given up protecting the humans. He drew into himself up there in the sky and grew a beard. At the start of the episode, he'd already lost too much from life, and was wearied by the battles against the Daleks, the Cybermen, the Master, and the Weeping Angels. So he hung out in the TARDIS and read books, losing himself in the words, and forgetting what those words were about. Who brought him down out of the clouds? Who gave him hope? It was Clara. She found an invisible ladder in a park and climbed to the stars to track down someone who might not even exist. And what was she when she did this but the living, breathing, embodiment of hope? It was Clara that brought the Doctor down from the clouds, and she was able to do this because she is hope.

She tells the Doctor to run, and keep running toward the future, toward the past, towards everything that can be or might be, and she's willing to give up her "real" self to do this time and time again. What's really being sacrificed in that moment when she steps into the Doctor's time-stream? Everyone including the Doctor tells her not to do it. Everybody gives her every reason to fear doing it. But she does it anyway. The thing she's sacrificing isn't her life, but the fear of attempting the *impossible* task of saving the Doctor when the Great Intelligence has already won. She does this because she *is* hope. Hope is her essence, hope is what makes her leap into the unknown, and she persists through time and space as hope.

Perhaps Clara's greatest moment is in "The Time of the Doctor." The Daleks were coming for their final victory. The Doctor had no more regenerations left, he had nothing "up his sleeve" until Clara convinced the Time Lords to give him another cycle of regenerations. This is what hope does: it tells us that in the darkest of nights at the fall of Trenzalore there's still something to believe in, there's still something that urges us up the steps to face those pesky Daleks, it gives us the power to regenerate and take our lives in a new path.

Clara can't be defined according to traditional definitions of what it is to be a particular human, because she's neither traditional, nor a particular human. Clara isn't just a symbol of hope, but hope itself. All other definitions fail, and all we're left with is a sense of the impossible, instantiating itself throughout time.

11
What the Soufflé Girl Could Teach Descartes

HJÖRDIS BECKER-LINDENTHAL

DOCTOR: Trust nothing you see, hear or feel.

Rory: But we are awake now.

DOCTOR: You thought you were awake in the TARDIS, too.

—"Amy's Choice," 2010

In "Amy's Choice," the Doctor's instruction to doubt everything is an echo of a question that has haunted philosophers for thousands of years: is the external world what we perceive it to be? This skepticism, including the suspicion that we might not be able to distinguish between dream and reality, dates back to antiquity, but it was the French philosopher René Descartes, who in the seventeenth century became famous for his methodology of doubt.

In his *Meditations on First Philosophy*, Descartes describes a malignant genie or demon, who bears striking similarities with the Dream Lord in the episode "Amy's Choice": he puts all his energies into creating a dream that resembles reality to the utmost. Descartes's encounter with this genie is an exact description of what happens to the Doctor and his companions when they meet the Dream Lord. As Descartes says:

> I shall think that the heavens, the air, the earth, colors, figures, sounds and all external things are nothing other than the playful deceptions of dreams by means of which the malignant genie [the Dream Lord!] has set traps for my credulity.

Whereas Descartes pointed out that the rational *I* is the basis we can always rely on, the case with the Doctor and his companions is a bit more complicated: their adventures revolve around the fact that the source for deception is the "I" itself. The power of *self-delusion*, dismissed by Descartes rather easily, advances to its full potential in "Amy's Choice" and in "Asylum of the Daleks" (2012).

Something Is Overriding My Controls

The episode "Amy's Choice" takes us to Leadworth, a quiet little town, where Amy and Rory have a surprisingly "normal" life. Everything looks like a Fifties advertisement for domesticity—well, except for Rory's haircut that takes Eighties chic to a new level: they own a beautiful house with roses in the front yard, and Rory is the sole breadwinner, while Amy is a pregnant housewife baking cakes in a sunbathed kitchen. If it weren't for the Doctor, who lands his whooshing TARDIS in one of their neatly arranged flowerbeds, they could've lived happily ever after. Or so it seems.

When Amy and Rory give the Doctor a tour through their new hometown and take a rest on a bench, all three fall asleep to the lulling chirping of birds and wake up in the TARDIS. There, Rory doesn't sport the mullet, and Amy isn't pregnant: they're "awake." They're convinced that *now* they're back to real life, but before they can even debate whether they shared a nightmare or a dream, they're alarmed to hear the same birds—in the TARDIS!—and drift off yet again; only to find themselves in Leadworth once more. They repeatedly fall asleep in one world and wake up in the other, and wherever they open their eyes, in the TARDIS or in Leadworth, they're convinced that *this* is reality.

The see-saw is upset further when the Dream Lord, a smirking little man dressed in the same attire as the Doctor, emerges from nothing and announces his game: the Doctor and his companions will wander between Leadworth and the TARDIS, and they need to decide which one is a dream and which one is reality. In both worlds, they'll face a deadly danger—an attack of hostile aliens in Leadworth, and drifting towards a cold sun in the TARDIS. So, which is which?

Maybe even more fascinating than the Eknodine, a species that hides inside senior citizens, now and then peeking out of their mouths with one eye and discharging lethal gas, is the psychoanalytic persiflage of the Doctor, Amy, and Rory. The events provide us with textbook examples for dream interpretations according to Sigmund Freud's *Interpretation of Dreams*. In the sleepy village, the Doctor and his companions act on unfulfilled wishes, repressed desires, primal instincts, and they experience their deepest fears. This is most obvious in Rory's case.

In Leadworth, Rory isn't a nurse, but a well-respected doctor, and he clearly enjoys the fact that the pensioners regard the Doctor as *his* companion; namely, as a junior doctor under his supervision. The "elephant in the room," the usually subliminal rivalry between Rory and the Doctor regarding Amy, becomes explicit, including multiple sexual innuendos. The Doctor suggests to Amy that they should cut off Rory's *ponytail*—what a feast for Freudians! "You hold him down, I'll cut it off!" The assassination on Rory's manhood becomes obsolete, because a bit later, Rory cuts his hair himself—for Amy, he says. But there's not only "self-castration." Rory even dies, giving way for his competitor. Viewed from a Freudian perspective, Rory's death is the Doctor's deepest wish: the Time Lord's *alter ego* wants Amy all for himself.

However, this *alter ego* gets a separate voice—the Doctor is the Dream Lord, as we learn at the end of the episode—come on, who else wears a bowtie? He's the result of a speck of psychic pollen heated up in the time rotor. Similar to the "vapor of black bile" described in Descartes's *Meditations*, the fumes of this pollen cause hallucinations. Psychic pollen are a kind of mind parasite that feed on "everything dark inside you, gives it a voice and turns it against you." Since the Doctor has accumulated more darkness than Amy and Rory during his nine-hundred-and-something years of experience, his *alter ego* materialized as the Dream Lord, which isn't odd at all, considering the Doctor's many bodies.

The whole Freudian dream issue spills over to the TARDIS, where the Dream Lord forces Amy to stay awake with him, while Rory and the Doctor drift off back to Leadworth. "Spooky old, not to be trusted me," he says, lasciviously lolling in a bath gown, "anything could happen." But it doesn't, because Amy's *alter ego* isn't as dark as the Doctor's. Instead, it reveals her kind, soft side. In Leadworth, she's confronted with the fear of not reconnecting with the Doctor, of losing and abandoning him. But when Rory dies, Amy's choice is pretty clear: she doesn't want to live either. Freudians would say that she gives in to *Thanatos*, the death drive.

Until the very end, the Doctor and his companions can't make out any criteria to decide which world is real and which world is the dream. Amy's decision to crash the van and to "kill" herself and the Doctor first seems to be yet another song praising the power of love that can overcome everything. But when the Doctor, Amy, and Rory wake up in the TARDIS, covered in ice, and drifting towards the cold sun, the Dream Lord's riddle isn't solved at all. In order to distinguish reality from a dream and to regain the Cartesian certainty of the *ego*, the Doctor first needs to admit what he's suspected all along: that he himself is the Dream Lord. When the TARDIS powered down, it was his suppressed *alter ego* who was overriding the controls. He himself orchestrated the dreams—yes, plural, the frozen TARDIS is dreamed also, he finally realizes, because the Dream Lord as the Time Lord's *alter ego* can only appear in dreams. By crashing the TARDIS into the cold sun, the Doctor ends both dreams and lets his superego take the reins again.

At the very end, we shortly see the Dream Lord as a reflection of the Doctor in the TARDIS's control panel. The Doctor literally faces his *alter ego* and reminds us that the deceiver isn't an external malignant genie, but rather within us. But does self-delusion always need to be overcome? The later episode, "Asylum of the Daleks," provides a different view.

Making Soufflés with Self-Delusion and Self-Formation

In "Asylum of the Daleks," the Doctor, Amy, and Rory are kidnapped by Dalek puppets and brought to the Daleks' spaceship. We're familiar with the Daleks' attempts to create chimeras—recall for instance the slave pigs or the Dalek-human hybrids in "Daleks in Manhattan" (2007), but this time, they seem to have succeeded. The Daleks whom the Doctor and his companions now encounter, are human bodies with human voices. The scary thing isn't that once in a while a blue Dalek stereoscope breaks through the skin of people's foreheads, but the fact that their minds have been wiped and reprogrammed.

When the Doctor asks the Dalek puppet Darla whether she remembers who she was before the Daleks "emptied" her out and turned her into their puppet, she answers: "My memories are only activated if they are required to facilitate deep cover or disguise." The Doctor, aghast: "You have a daughter." Darla responds, "I know, I've read my file." Clearly, any feelings, together with her individual identity, have been deleted. Despite her human appearance, Darla is Dalek.

You would think that after this success in their hybridization experiment, the Daleks should thrive. Yet they kidnap the Doctor and demand that he "save" them (the Daleks' own words!). But save them from what? In the "asylum"—the planet used by the Daleks as dumping-ground for malfunctioning "individuals" of their species—someone is hacking into the Dalek audio and control system. The Doctor and his companions immediately witness this "threat." Suddenly they hear Bizet's *Carmen*, which makes the Daleks panic hilariously: "What is the noiiiiise?" When the Doctor traces back the signal, and calls out for the sender, he hears a young woman's voice answer excitedly: "Are you real? Are you actually, properly real?!"

The Doctor is just as perplexed. He's totally swept off his feet when he hears that Oswin Oswald, former junior entertainment manager of the starship *Alaska*, is the only survivor after the ship crashed on the asylum planet; and even more, has managed to stay healthy and even joyful on Dalek territory for a whole year. The Doctor demands to know how she protects herself from the Daleks. Her answer: "Making soufflés." Unfortunately, there isn't time to learn more about this interesting survival strategy. The Doctor, Amy, and Rory are fired to the asylum planet with orders to take its force field down, so the Daleks can eliminate it. After some scary encounters with the crew of the crashed starship *Alaska*, all turned into Dalek puppets by the nanocloud of molecular robots, the Doctor and his companions fight for their survival in the underground arches. Oswin guides them through the tunnels via electronic interface.

Oswin seems to be a genius, and she claims to be able to take down the planet's force field. But before she agrees to help the Doctor accomplish his task, she demands to be picked up, so she can also leave the planet. However, when the Doctor arrives at Oswin's barricade, he stares into the blue diode eye of a Dalek. Only then do we learn that Oswin isn't the pretty girl we thought she was. The former junior entertainment manager of starship *Alaska* has been "fully converted." Yet out of the metal shell it clinks: "I am not a Dalek, I am human." What do we do with this?

As audience, we've been fooled by Oswin's own illusions. We've watched a miniature girl inside a Dalek—notice she looks out of her hiding place through a huge bull's eye: the Dalek stereoscope. The *homunculus* (Latin: "small human") is a classic depiction of the relation between mind and body, with mind being the sole source of personality (the true "I"), totally independent of the body. This *ghost-in-the-machine* argument has been strongly rejected in the contemporary philosophy of mind, most prominently by Gilbert Ryle in his book *The Concept of Mind*. Today, we commonly understand body and mind as an interdependent whole. However, the case of Oswin provides a different view. Despite the drastic bodily change of her warm flesh to Dalek-hardware, Oswin seems to have remained the same person. Parts of the episode are narrated from Oswin's point of view, so the audience "sees" her self-perception, which is a compassionate, energetic girl who commemorates her dead mother by baking soufflés. Whether we agree with Descartes or not, we have to admit that Oswin's body is distinct from her mind. Her true "I" isn't dependent on a body.

In Oswin, we don't only encounter a fully-fledged Cartesian dualism between mind and body, but she also provides us with a thought-provoking modification of the so-called *brain-in-a-vat* argument, which is a modern version of Descartes's dream scenario. In the book *Reason, Truth and History*, Hilary Putnam replaced Descartes's deceptive genius with an evil scientist, who manipulates pickled brains and makes them "think" they're persons with thoughts, feelings and bodily experiences.

Technically, Oswin's brain is in the same situation as the brain-in-a-vat. In both cases, "the nerve endings have been connected to a super-scientific computer," and the person whose brain it is has "the illusion that everything is perfectly normal." However, there's one crucial difference between the classic brain-in-a-vat and this brain-in-a-Dalek-shell. Whereas the brain-in-a-vat experiences exactly what the evil scientist wants it to experience, the Oswin-Dalek follows its own agenda.

Oswin has hacked the Dalek program that usually lets the Daleks perceive everything according to Dalek categories, namely, with no emotional reaction but hate, and without any sense of individuality or aesthetic appreciation. A Dalek's action is determined by its genetically engineered obedience, and by the impulse to *exterminate* everything that's non-Dalek. Yet, Oswin doesn't think or act like a Dalek. She converts the sense-data according to her own program and thus creates the illusion that she still is the *girl* Oswin, hiding from the Daleks. She translates the input from reality into a world where she can stay human. For instance, she perceives the cries of other Daleks as the enemy's battle cries, not as the noise made by fellow inmates in the asylum's "intensive care."

We could also say that she distracts herself by *imagining* baking soufflés—in fact, Oswin says so herself in the beginning of the episode! She keeps herself busy with the construction of a fantasy world, and it's through self-deception that she can protect her "I" from becoming a Dalek on the "inside" as well. According to neuroscientist Antonio Damasio, the neural basis for the self sojourns "with the continuous reactivation" of two sets of representations: representations of key events in an individual's autobiography, "on the basis of which a notion of identity can be reconstructed repeatedly," and "primordial representations of an individual's body."

Oswin manages to stay "herself" by focusing on what's been important in her former life: her mother, music, baking soufflés . . . Sure, she doesn't have a human body to remind her who she is, but by simulating bodily impressions, she keeps her human coenesthesia—the totality of sensations arising from bodily organs through which she perceives her own body. Oswin saves her "real self" by an illusion. Any doubt would turn this self into a Dalek.

Eggs . . . Eggs . . . Eggsterminate!

Sadly, the Doctor initiates such doubt in Oswin when he meets her face to face. "Does it look real to you . . . where you are right now?" he asks. Oswin's answer: "It is real." He replies: "It is a dream Oswin . . . You dreamed it for yourself because the truth was too terrible." What follows, is one of the most disappointing moments I've seen in the Whoniverse so far: with the words

"I am so sorry, but you are a Dalek," the Doctor turns away from her. It's clear that he won't take a Dalek with him on the teleport. Oswin's bodily appearance isn't the only criterion the Doctor uses to decide that Oswin *is* a Dalek. Already when he was talking to Oswin on the radio, he performed the *Turing Test*, a test suggested by the British mathematician Alan Turing in "Computing Machinery and Intelligence," to "decide" whether a computer is "thinking" or "conscious."

In Turing's test setting, a human person—"the judge"—has a written conversation with both a human person, whom he doesn't know, and with a computer. If the judge can't decide which is which, the computer is regarded as "conscious." The test may sound weird at first, but consider this: How do we assume that our fellow humans are conscious? Basically, we simply infer from their speech and behavior to their consciousness. If they speak and act in a way that is similar to ours, and since we regard ourselves as conscious, we consider them conscious, too.

Putnam adapted the Turing Test in order to explore the notion of reference. The point Putnam makes is that computers can't truly refer to anything external when they talk to us, because our "talk of apples and fields is intimately connected with our *nonverbal* transactions with apples and fields." The Doctor is philosophically up-to-date, and according to him, Oswin doesn't pass Putnam's *Turing test of reference*. Paradoxically, the Doctor tries to *explain* this to her, reminding her that she talked about baking soufflés when she couldn't possibly get the ingredients on the asylum planet: "The milk and the eggs . . . where did it all come from?" After one year, all the stocks of the crashed starship *Alaska* must have been used up. The Doctor applies exactly the same criteria as described by Putnam, who points out that "the machine is utterly insensitive to the *continued* existence of apples, fields, steeples, etc. [and milk and eggs!] Even if all these things *ceased* to exist, the machine would still discourse just as happily in the same way."

Well, "happy" wouldn't be the right word to describe Oswin's situation, and the Doctor is far from doing so. Still, he refuses to take Oswin with him. One could argue that he's right in his decision—after all, the word 'eggs' triggers the Dalek program, and Oswin starts to act upon the "exterminate" impulse, closing in on the Doctor. However, she doesn't continue. No deadly rays are fired at the Time Lord, and Oswin dismisses him with the famous words, "Run you clever boy, and remember." She takes down the force field and stays in the asylum, which then gets eliminated by Dalek missiles.

This ultimately demonstrates that Oswin isn't the "prisoner who perhaps enjoys an imaginary freedom in a dream," as described in Descartes's *Meditations*. Oswin's self-deception hasn't simply been an escape. It worked as a type of self-formation that turned a Dalek puppet into a human Dalek. By means of self-deception, Oswin kept her free will and, as we know, her free will had important effects on reality—it saved the universe.

12
How to Build a TARDIS

Doctor Benjamin K. Tippett and
Doctor David Tsang

This is an explanation of Doctor Tippett and Doctor Tsang's proposed TARDIS time machine, written for laypeople who are interested in time travel, but have no technical knowledge of Einstein's Theory of General Relativity. So, grab ahold of a TARDIS rail, it's going to be one heck of a ride!

The first part of this chapter is an introduction to the pertinent ideas from Einstein's theory of curved spacetime, followed with a review of other popular time machine spacetimes. The fundamental concepts of curvature and lightcones are introduced, and then we explain the Alcubierre Warp Drive, the Morris-Thorne wormhole, and the Tipler cylinder.

The second part of this chapter describes the Traversable Achronal Retrograde Domain in Spacetime (TARDIS), and explains some of its general properties. Our TARDIS is a bubble of spacetime curvature which travels along a closed loop in space and time. A person traveling within the bubble will feel the effects of a constant forwards acceleration. A person outside the TARDIS will see two bubbles: one which is evolving forwards in time, and one which is evolving backwards in time, moving in the opposite direction. We then discuss the physical limitations which may prevent us from ever constructing a TARDIS.

Finally, we conclude with a proposal for a method through which a TARDIS can be used to travel between arbitrary points in space and time, and the possible dangers involved with exiting a TARDIS from the wrong side.

Before we begin, would you like a Jelly Baby? Seriously, have a Jelly Baby. They're great! Or a Banana. Bananas are fantastic!

The Background of General Relativity

Spacetime tells matter how to move; matter tells spacetime how to curve.

—John Archibald Wheeler

Let's begin by introducing Albert Einstein's greatest achievement: the Theory of General Relativity. According to his theory, the three spatial dimensions aren't formally separate from the dimension of time. Rather, the four directions (left-right, up-down, forward-backward, and future-past) comprise a four-dimensional surface, across which the stars and planets and all the rest of the matter in the universe tumble. We interpret the effects of this curvature on the trajectories of these objects as the force of gravity.

Imagine an old quarry, the uneven floor of which is covered in smooth lips and bumps and bowls. Suppose that one were to ask your robot dog to drive through the quarry, and to do so with its steering wheels in the forward pointing position. Over flat ground, according to these instructions, the tin dog would move along a straight line. In contrast, the curved floor of the quarry will cause your companion's path to bend and twist and skew (Figure 1).

Similarly, in Einstein's theory of gravity, the curved orbits of the planets are accounted for by the curvature of the underlying spacetime. In a "flat" spacetime, devoid of any gravity, planets and stars would move along straight lines. In the vicinity of a massive star the spacetime geometry becomes curved, and the trajectories of nearby planets will bend into elliptical orbits around the star.

Unlike the geometry of the floor of the quarry, in Einstein's theory, the curvature is dynamic. Both the degree to which the spacetime is curved and the character of the curvature depend upon the quantity and character of the matter present. The mathematical relationship between the curvature and the matter is called the *Einstein Equation*.

There are two different strategies which are used to "solve" the Einstein Equation.

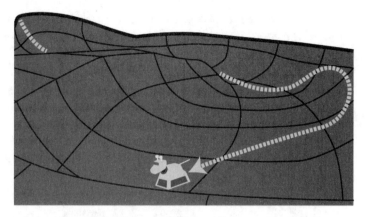

FIGURE 1. We ask K9 to steer straight-ahead as he moves over the curved ground of an old quarry in Wales. The curvature of the surface is manifested by causing the tin dog's path to bend and skew.

We could begin by focusing on the matter in the spacetime. A physicist could choose a type of matter and an initial three-dimensional configuration, and then will use a computer to simulate the evolution of the geometry and the matter. The computationally generated history of the three-dimensional system then comprises the dynamical four-dimensional spacetime.

Alternatively, we could focus on the geometry of the spacetime. A physicist could define the four-dimensional geometry in its entirety and then use the Einstein Equation to determine the distribution and character of matter required to bend the spacetime into this shape. It's important to analyze the qualities of this matter skeptically, since many geometries require types of matter which have never been observed.

Unfortunately, there are more possible types of curvature than there are types of matter in our universe. The most popular criteria for judging physicality are called the *Classical Energy Conditions*. These conditions require that matter be gravitationally attractive and that matter may never travel faster than the speed of light. Any matter which doesn't satisfy the Classical Energy Conditions is referred to as *unphysical* matter or as *exotic* matter.

Causal Structure

The fundamental insight underlying Einstein's theory of relativity is that the universe has a speed limit: massive objects must travel slower than the speed of light. In Figure 2 Captain Jack and River Song are Dalek hunting: Jack is armed with a revolver and River with a laser pistol. They've come upon a pair of Daleks, and they pull the triggers of their guns simultaneously. Since Jack's bullets have mass, they must always travel slower than the speed of light, and thus slower than the massless photons in River's laser pulse.

Therefore, no matter how awesome Jack's gun might be, River's laser pulse will always reach the Dalek ahead of Jack's bullet.

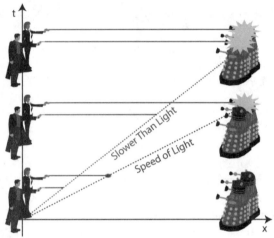

FIGURE 2. Nothing which possesses mass can move faster than the speed of light. The two companions pull their triggers at the same time. Captain Jack's lead bullet, no matter how awesome his gun is, will never beat River Song's laser to the Dalek. This is an example of a *spacetime diagram*, with space on the horizontal axis and time on the vertical axis. The dashed lines are the respective trajectories of the bullet and the laser pulse. The laser pulse has a shallower slope than the bullet because it is moving faster than the bullet.

Figure 2 is an example of a *spacetime* diagram: it plots how the positions of objects change in time. Since Jack and River aren't moving, their trajectories will be a vertical line. The trajectories of faster-moving objects will have shallower slopes. Note also that since the laser pulse travels at the speed of light, no massive object's trajectory may have a shallower slope than the laser's.

In Figure 3, River has two lasers, and shoots one pulse to the left and one to the right. (It's ironic that a woman who dislikes Silents this much should spend so much time in a library. SPOILERS!) The trajectories of the two laser pulses will trace the *boundary* in spacetime between the points which can be reached at slower-than-light velocities and those which can't (starting from the point where River pulls the triggers). We call such a boundary a *lightcone*.

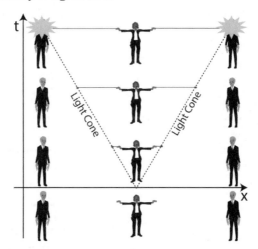

FIGURE 3. Oh, dear! River finds herself facing down two Silents, one on either side. Luckily, she's wonderfully adept at using her laser pistols, and immediately shoots a stream of deadly photons in both directions.
By plotting the trajectories of photons emitted in all possible directions from one point, we generate a *lightcone*. A lightcone divides spacetime into two regions. If a point lies within the lightcone, it can be reached at a velocity slower than the speed of light *starting from* the point when River pulled her triggers. Conversely, if a point lies outside the lightcone, it's inaccessible for a massive object starting from tip of the lightcone.

We can draw a lightcone originating from any point in the spacetime, and sometimes it's useful to draw a series of light-cones to illustrate where massive objects are allowed to travel. For example, the simplest justification for why a person can't ordinarily move *backwards* in time is because a looping path in spacetime would cross the lightcone wall, indicating a require-ment for faster-than-light speeds.

Lightcones are incredibly powerful tools for visualizing spacetime curvature, since spacetime curvature causes light-cones to *tip* relative to one another. Mapping out the orienta-tions of the lightcones in a spacetime can illustrate the paths along which a massive object may travel.

As an example, let's consider a black hole. It's widely known that once you fall into a black hole, you may never emerge. The simplest explanation for this fact involves illustrating the orientations of nearby lightcones (Figure 4). Near the middle of the black hole, the lightcones are tipped entirely towards the central singularity. Thus, massive objects are corralled by the lightcone walls towards the center of the black hole. Alternatively put, escaping a black hole requires faster-than-light speeds.

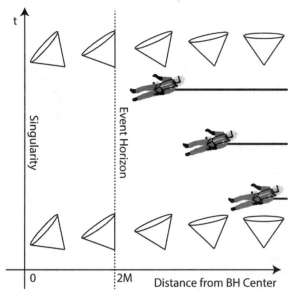

FIGURE 4. Light cones gradually tip inwards, the closer to the center of a black hole you look. Within the *Event Horizon*, the lightcones tip entirely towards the center. Thus, once you've fallen inside a black hole, the orientation of the lightcones will not permit you to climb out again.

The Alcubierre Warp Drive

Miguel Alcubierre has proposed a way for a massive object to travel *faster* than the speed of light: the Warp Drive. This spacetime geometry can be described as having a bubble configuration: a shell of curvature containing a flat vacuum interior. Spacetime expands and contracts around the edges of the bubble in a manner which allows it to scuttle across the surrounding spacetime at faster-than-light speeds. Lightcones contained within the bubble are tilted in whichever direction the bubble

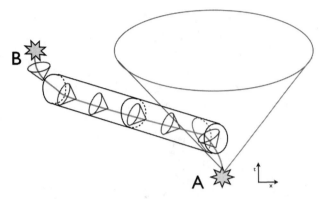

FIGURE 5. The Alcubierre Warp Drive can be used to carry massive objects through spacetime at superluminal velocities.

is headed, thus massive objects can be carried through spacetime at superluminal speeds (Figure 5).

The reason we can't ordinarily travel backwards in time to interact with our former selves is because doing so requires that we cross the lightcone, and this would require speeds which exceed the speed of light. It follows that, through a judiciously chosen sequence of Alcubierre warp bubbles, a traveler may end up moving backwards through time to interact with their past self, as A.E. Everett suggests in "Warp Drive and Causality."

How *realistic* is the Warp Drive? Recall that any curvature in spacetime is accompanied by a specific distribution of matter: the "source" of the curvature. When we apply Einstein's Equation to the geometry of the Alcubierre Warp Drive, we discover that the matter required to generate it will violates the classical energy conditions. Thus, no material which humankind has ever discovered can curve spacetime in the way required to build a Warp Drive.

Wormholes

An alternative way to travel into the past was proposed by Michael Morris and Kip Thorne in "Wormholes, Time Machines, and the Weak Energy Condition," and takes advantage of an exotic object called a *wormhole*. The simplest way to imagine a wormhole is as a pair of spheres which are actually the same sphere in two places. (Not very simple to imagine, is it? Silly mathematicians. I still have some Jelly Babies, if you'd like one.) If we drive a robot dog into one of the spheres, as it crosses the surface of the first sphere it'll instantly emerge from the second one. We refer to the two spheres as the *mouths* of the wormhole (Fig. 6), and the mouths of the wormhole connect two places across space *and time*.

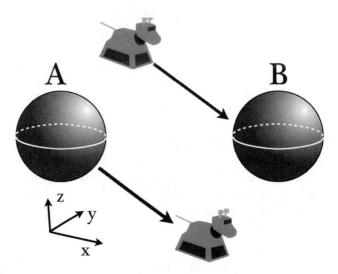

FIGURE 6. A wormhole is drawn as having two mouths (A and B). If your second best friend enters one mouth, it'll emerge from the other.

Suppose we were to take the two wormhole mouths and pack them into boxes, and then give the two boxes to a pair of twins. One of the twins is a space explorer and the other is a gardener. Our first twin sets off in a rocket, visits a distant star, and then returns to Earth. The story of the twin paradox is familiar: the space twin experiences less time over the course of his journey than his sibling does on Earth. (The simple reason for this is that the space twin endures a lot of acceleration in his rocket, and when you accelerate, time passes at a slower rate. For a better explanation, listen to "The Titanium Physicists Podcast," episode 29.) Thus, upon their reunion, the space explorer will be younger than his gardener sister.

Let's tell the reunited twins to open their boxes. Just like the twins, the wormhole mouth which journeyed in space will be younger than the mouth which stayed at home. If you were to throw a baseball at the astronaut's wormhole's mouth, it would emerge from the gardener's wormhole mouth at a time when the gardener's wormhole was the same age as the astronaut's *currently* is. So, the astronaut's wormhole mouth can be thought of as a door to a *past* time, and the gardener's wormhole mouth as a door to a *future* time.

As seen in "Billiard Balls in Wormhole Spacetimes with Closed Timelike Curves," Morris and Thorne used this type of time machine to perform fascinating thought experiments. What if a billiard ball traveled back in time only to bump into itself, ultimately preventing a younger version of itself from entering the wormhole in the first place?) Billiard balls are good for this thought experiment because they're simple and we're under no illusions about free will affecting their behavior.) This series of events would be causally inconsistent with itself. These scenarios are collectively referred to as the *Grandfather Paradox*, referring to the possibility that a time traveler could kill her grandfather before he has sired her father, which can be found in Daniel Streetmentioner's *Time Traveler's Handbook of 1001 Tense Formations*, Volume 1. The episode "Father's Day" (2005) is concerned with such a paradox.

The Grandfather Paradox doesn't pre-empt an object from interacting with its past self. Consider a billiard ball which travels backwards in time in order to collide with itself, and knock its past self into the wormhole (Figure 7). Unlike the previous scenario, this self-interaction would be historically self-consistent.

Clearly, whenever time travel is possible, the traditional way of describing cause and effect becomes skewed. Consider,

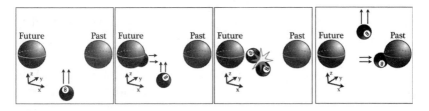

FIGURE 7. A possible way that an object can interact with its past self in a self-consistent way. The two wormhole mouths don't sync up in time, one (light gray) is older than the other (dark gray) and can be used to travel into the past.

for example, how in "Smith and Jones" (2007) the Tenth Doctor travels backwards in time to take off his necktie in front of Martha. In these cases, we must think of causality in terms of actions and consequences over the entirety of a four-dimensional spacetime: the future can interact with the past so long as the past isn't modified. This "law of nature" is referred to as *Novikov's Self-Consistency Condition.*

Suppose the Doctor were to travel to the planet Skaro and attempt to prevent the creation of the Daleks. Novikov's self-consistency condition dictates that all of his efforts would fail, since his motivation for pre-empting the Daleks will have depended upon the Daleks having existed at some future time. (If you have trouble imagining it, watch "The Genesis of the Daleks," 1975. It has Davros in it. Do you think he can see out of his big blue forehead eyeball? Gross.)

Although Morris and Thorne's model of time travel is both wonderful and simple, constructing this geometry is even more difficult than the Warp Drive. One problem is that we must build a wormhole. Physicists aren't sure how to even begin punching two holes in the universe and sewing them together—we do what we must, because we can. Another problem is that the wormhole must be traversable. If any massive object were to attempt to cross through a wormhole, it would cause the wormhole to collapse and pinch off into a pair of black holes.

As J. Friedman, K. Schleich, and D. Witt show in "Topological Censorship," holding the wormhole open requires a type of unphysical matter which is gravitationally repulsive.

Tipler Cylinder

Unphysical and exotic matter isn't always required to build a geometry which permits time travel. All you need is an infinite amount of spinning matter! Formulated by F.J. Tipler, in "Rotating Cylinders and the Possibility of Global Causality Violation," the Tipler cylinder is a very popular method for explaining the possibility of using spacetime curvature to permit time travel, requiring only an infinitely long, massive rod, which is spinning on its axis.

Spinning mass has an interesting effect on spacetime: like twirling a spoon in a glass of water, the spacetime swirls around with the object in its direction of rotation. This effect is called *frame dragging* and it causes lightcones to tip slightly in the direction of the spin. The effect increases with the angular momentum, and with the proximity to the object. The frame-dragging effect generated by the Earth is subtle, but as seen in C.W.F. Everitt *et al.*'s "Gravity Probe b," it's been detected by satellites!

In the case of an infinitely long cylinder, the frame dragging effect becomes quite potent. Near the cylinder surface, the lightcones tip *all the way* over, allowing us to travel backwards in time by circling the cylinder (Figure 8).

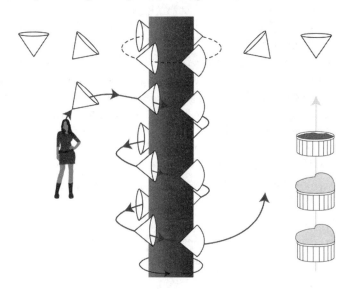

FIGURE 8. Clara discovers that the secret to a fluffy soufflé is *timing*! Light cones near the edge of the Tipler cylinder tip towards the direction of rotation. By repeatedly circumnavigating the cylinder, Clara can move into the past and reach her soufflé before it fell." See Daniel Streetmentioner, *Time Traveler's Handbook of 1001 Tense Formations*, Volume 1.

TARDIS Geometry

Our TARDIS geometry can be described as a bubble of spacetime geometry which carries its contents backwards and forwards through space and time as it endlessly tours a large circular path in space and time. The inside and outside of the bubble are a flat vacuum, and the two regions are separated with a boundary of spacetime curvature.

In this case, TARDIS stands for Traversable Achronal Retrograde Domain In Spacetime. The name refers to a bubble (a *Domain*) which moves through the spacetime at speeds greater than the speed of light (it's *Achronal*); it moves backwards in time (*Retrograde* to the arrow of time outside the bubble); and finally, it can transport massive objects (it's *Traversable*). You might be asking "Why aren't you concentrating on making it bigger on the inside?" The short answer is that it's very easy to make a spacetime which is curved so that a very large volume sits inside a very small box. You can even use curved spacetime geometries to make very large objects appear very, very small! Long story short: Bigger on the inside is too easy to bother with.

Figure 9 is a spacetime diagram which shows the orientation of lightcones inside and outside of the TARDIS bubble. Outside of the bubble, the lightcones are all oriented upwards, pushing everyone steadily towards the future. Inside the bubble, lightcones tip and turn, allowing massive objects to move along a closed circle in spacetime. If a person were to be transported within the bubble, she'd be moving alternatively forwards, sideways, and even backwards in time!

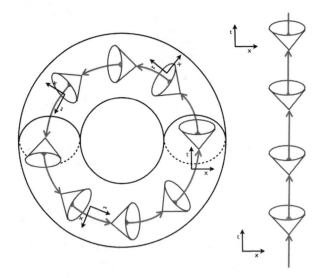

FIGURE 9. This spacetime diagram illustrates how lightcones will be oriented around the TARDIS geometry. Outside of the TARDIS, time is aligned in the vertical direction. Inside of the bubble, lightcones tip along a circular loop, and massive objects can travel backwards in time.

A person traveling within the TARDIS would describe it as a room which is constantly accelerating. Furthermore, any events which occur inside of the TARDIS bubble must satisfy Novikov's self-consistency condition. The Doctor and Romana were stuck in a loop of repeating events in the "Meglos" (1980). The episode also involved a cactus as the villain, so . . .

A person outside the bubble would describe an entirely different scene (see Figure 10). Due to its closed trajectory, there'll be a time *before* the bubble (and its contents) exists. Abruptly, we'd see a bubble appear and split into two, the two boxes moving away from one another. Initially, they'll be moving at superluminal speeds, but they'll decelerate to a stand-still. The pair of boxes will then begin accelerating towards one another until they merge and disappear. Mysteriously, the contents of one bubble will appear to evolve forwards in time, while the other will evolve backwards.

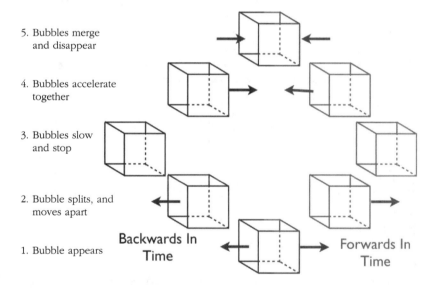

5. Bubbles merge and disappear

4. Bubbles accelerate together

3. Bubbles slow and stop

2. Bubble splits, and moves apart

1. Bubble appears

Backwards In Time

Forwards In Time

FIGURE 10. An external observer will see two bubbles suddenly emerge from one another, one whose contents appear to move backwards in time.

To illustrate how time is experienced inside and outside of the bubble, imagine that there are two people in our spacetime: Amy, who's traveling inside the bubble; and Barbara, who's been left behind. Suppose that the two women are holding

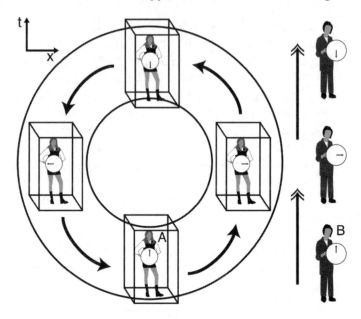

FIGURE 11. This is a schematic of the trajectory of the TARDIS bubble as it travels through spacetime. Arrows denote the locally defined "arrow of time." Life inside the bubble is sexy and fun. Life outside the bubble is drab, and everyone dresses like a school teacher from the 1960s.

large clocks, and that the walls of the bubble are transparent, so that the two women can see one another (See Figure 11).

Amy will only ever see the hands of her own clock move in a clockwise direction. When she looks out at Barbara, she'll see the hands of Barbara's clock moving clockwise at some times and counterclockwise at others, depending on where Amy is along her circular trajectory.

Barbara, on the other hand, will see the hands of her own clock moving clockwise. She'll see two bubbles, each one containing an Amy. In one of them, the hands of Amy's clock will be moving clockwise; in the other, counterclockwise.

To consider the matter in more detail, we've plotted the trajectory of light rays as they cross the spacetime (See Figure 12). Most of the curvature is located at the walls of the bubble, so we see most of the bending of the light occurring near the walls. This type of diagram is helpful because it shows us which parts of the spacetime will be visible to other parts, and also because it details the orientation of lightcones. Based on

Figure 12, Amy may also be able to (occasionally) catch glimpses of herself in the past and future. The Doctor and Jo Grant met and interacted with future ghosts of themselves when the Doctor was trying to fix the TARDIS in the episode "Day of the Daleks" (1972).

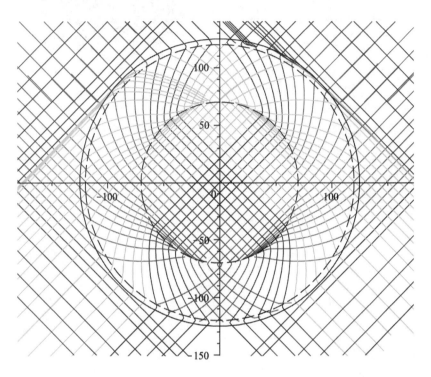

FIGURE 12. This is a computer-generated spacetime diagram of how rays of light will travel through the TARDIS geometry. The thick dashed circles represent the boundaries of the bubble. Rays of light end up getting strongly diffracted whenever they encounter these edges.

We should add that traveling inside the TARDIS bubble comes at a price. Travelers within the bubble will feel a persistent acceleration: the narrower the circle traced in spacetime, the larger the acceleration required. It seems that larger jaunts through space and time are easier on the body than short hops.

Could a TARDIS time machine ever be constructed?

As we've discussed, we use the Einstein Equation to determine the matter's character and distribution (see Figure 13). Unfortunately, just like the Alcubierre Warp Drive, generating

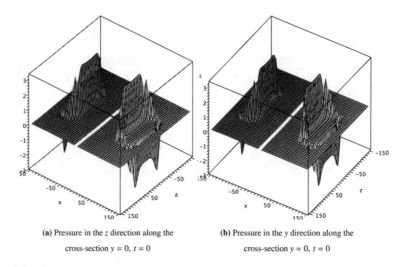

(a) Pressure in the z direction along the cross-section $y = 0$, $t = 0$

(b) Pressure in the y direction along the cross-section $y = 0$, $t = 0$

FIGURE 13. To build a TARDIS we require matter which has strange and unphysical properties. These graphs demonstrate that this matter must have negative pressure.

the TARDIS geometry would require exotic matter (violating the classical energy conditions). This matter would be gravitationally repulsive and would need to move faster than light.

In addition, the geometry contains a few *curvature singularities*: places where the spacetime is pointy. It's not clear whether these singularities have come about from the fact that our model is too simple, or if they're somehow generic to these types of geometries.

Traveling through Time and Space

Even if we could construct the TARDIS geometry, in the form we have presented, it would be of limited value to explorers. Who wants to go in a circle? Circles are boring.

The true power of the TARDIS geometry is unlocked through the use of another clever technique: the spacetime equivalent of scissors and glue. Segments of different spacetime geometries can be mathematically cut up and then spliced together to create novel composite geometries.

Suppose I find myself at one point in spacetime (A), and I want to explore another point (B) which lies outside my lightcone. By cutting and splicing a series of TARDIS bubble sections together, I could travel to the recent past of point (B) (See Figure 14).

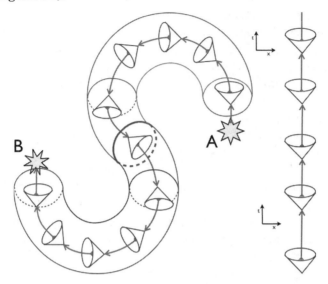

FIGURE 14. Sections of different TARDIS geometries (the top and bottom half) can be spliced together (along the dark and dotted line in the middle) in order to put any point (A) in the immediate causal past of any other point (B).

An alternative way to use the aforementioned technique involves cutting a TARDIS geometry in half, resulting in an open-ended U-shape (Figure 15). Travelers who enter the

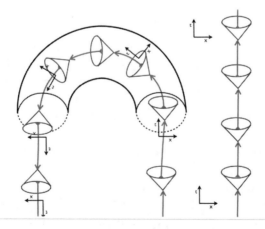

FIGURE 15. An object which enters a TARDIS half-pipe will emerge the mirror image of itself, moving backwards in time. This could be considered antimatter.

geometry on one side would exit the other moving *backwards in time* with their right and left directions switched.

This is notable because the physical laws of our universe are time-symmetric in a specific way (called CPT symmetry: Charge, Parity, Time). If you take a particle and then switch the direction of the arrow of time, and then switch left-and-right, the equations which govern it will look the same as if we had switched the sign of the electric charge. Simply put: antimatter is just regular matter moving backwards in time. If you think that this idea is fun, look up the one-electron universe hypothesis.

Thus, it's possible that a traveler who has passed through a half-TARDIS geometry will end up (by virtue of its moving backwards in time) being made of antimatter. Alternatively, from the traveler's perspective, she'll emerge into a universe made of antimatter. In "The Three Doctors" (1973), the ancient Time Lord Omega converts the Second and Third Doctors, as well as their companions, into antimatter. Perhaps his mastery of TARDIS geometries allowed this to occur? Of course, if you were standing outside the TARDIS, you'd see two bubble chambers, with antimatter entering one end, and regular matter entering the other, and then you'd see the two chambers move together and disappear. The half-TARDIS will then resemble the process of Annihilation between matter and antimatter from quantum field theory.

Full Circle

We began with a brief explanation of Einstein's theory of curved spacetime: General Relativity. We discussed the light-cone as a means of illustrating the causal structure and curvature of a spacetime geometry. We then explained other proposed methods for using curved spacetime geometry to travel backwards in time.

We introduced the basic properties of our TARDIS spacetime geometry. TARDIS is an acronym which stands for Traversable Achronal Retrograde Domains In Spacetime. Our TARDIS is a hollow bubble which allows its contents to travel along a closed, circular path in space and time. Travelers within the bubble will feel a persistent acceleration. People outside the TARDIS will see *two* bubble chambers: within one, time is evolving forwards; within the other, time evolves backwards.

Building the TARDIS bubble geometry would require an exotic type of matter which violates the classical energy conditions. We couldn't generate the required spacetime curvature using normal matter.

Finally, we discussed other ways the TARDIS geometry could be used. By cutting up different TARDIS tubes and joining them together, the new geometry could transport a traveler between any two points in space and time. If a TARDIS geometry is cut in half, a traveler who enters one end may emerge into a universe made of antimatter. If this ever happens to you, say "Hello" to Omega!

SERIAL 3

Values in the Time Vortex

Ken Spivey
TIME LORD PRESIDING

The *Doctor Who* Masculine Romantic Ideal

KEN SPIVEY, TIME LORD PRESIDING

Last year, the improbable happened. I was awarded the title "Sexiest Man in Tampa Bay" by *Creative Loafing*, a Tampa Bay periodical.

I would never have dreamed of receiving such adulation from the opposite sex. I was a bookish academic, accustomed to being often overlooked by attractive women in high school and college. It's no coincidence then that my professional career skyrocketed, once I turned from traditional music forms to Gallifrey-inspired rock. My regeneration from geek to chic is now complete, thanks in part to the fact that, as a "Time Lord Rock" musician, I'm seen to share qualities in common with the Doctor. My experience as a professional authority on all things *Who* has given me the opportunity to interact with many aspects of *Doctor Who* fandom. Be it from the stage or more intimately one-on-one, one thing is clear, many fans view the Doctor to be their "ideal male."

So, let me see what sort of characteristics the Doctor has that I share with him.

The Doctor has a set of desirable characteristics which appeal to many women who enjoy the increasingly popular *Doctor Who* series. Here I'm only looking at female to male attraction, yet I hope this will open the door to a dialogue between the parallels along the various pairings possible in the endless spectrum of gender.

Furthermore, a portion of the Doctor's appeal, through association, is transferable to others in the fandom. I'm a recipient of this transference. From my academic background in Interpersonal Communication, with a focus on male-female relations, I've developed a working model to which these women are attracted, and I call it "The Doctor Who Masculine Romantic Ideal."

Once I became conscious of the characteristics associated with the Last Time Lord, I was able to apply that lens to myself. In seeing more clearly how being associated with the Doctor potentially affected the way in which women perceive me, I also recognize how I'm changed by those perceptions. Thus, to be more attractive to women who are fans of the Doctor, I've striven to accentuate the characteristics I already share with the Doctor to better appeal to the female audience. Through positive reinforcement, those aspects of my character which best fit "The Doctor Who Masculine Romantic Ideal" continue to be enhanced, both in my public persona and in my personal life. This ideal type is characterized by a keen sense of humor, a lively intellect, and the appearance of "being broken while unattainable."

When faced with incredible odds or a foe of unspeakable power, the Doctor rarely reaches for a firearm or brandishes a menacing word. Instead, he wraps a tie around his head, invents the banana daiquiri, and makes life-or-death situations comedic and manageable. The Doctor frequently uses humor with devastating effect. He gets what he wants with a smile. Female fans of *Doctor Who* are exposed to the possibility that a "funny guy" may be an interesting, strong lord, worth their time. From that perspective, a lighthearted nature such as mine, actually becomes an advantage when attracting women, as opposed to being a mere novelty.

The Doctor is, as his title suggests, educated and brilliant. Intellect is the pistol the Doctor draws whenever his sense of humor can't properly disarm his adversary. Intellect allows the (alleged) Last Son of Gallifrey to win seemingly unwinnable battles. His brilliance continues to draw companions to view him in a romantic light. *Doctor Who*, the series, may influence women to see "bookish" men, such as myself, as having potential solutions to the hardships of life, something which they may not have previously considered.

Finally, the Doctor has a past which is often alluded to, but never fully explained. We're privy to the knowledge that he has loved and lost more than he's willing, or able to, admit. In like manner, many men, me included, have pasts which haunt them and wounds which time may not heal. My emotional scars keep me, at times, distant from the women in my life. Similar scars have also kept the Doctor aloof from the amorous embrace of those companions who romantically loved him. Whether I remain "broken" or could be "saved" by a Rose Tyler depends on whether I may be able to find someone to mend a post-Time-War-torn heart. Many women, who associate men with this aforementioned ideal, may also associate men of this variety as those in need of a companion's salvation. The need to save another is a powerful opiate, which is a plausible cause for companions to be attracted and addicted to the Doctor, and may draw women to men with whom they see parallels.

Doctor Who has given a great gift to jovial and scholarly men everywhere. These cool savants are often overlooked by women in favor of our less articulate male rivals, perceived followers of more obviously traditional masculine ideals. "The Doctor Who Masculine Romantic Ideal" gives men, such as myself, hope.

13

Should the Doctor Eat His Companions?

GREG LITTMANN

> I'm a human being. Maybe not the stuff of legend but every bit as important as Time Lords, thank you.
>
> —DONNA NOBLE, "The Stolen Earth," 2008

Have you ever noticed that the Doctor never puts his humans on a leash? How many times over the years would he have been spared from having to perform a perilous rescue just by taking this simple precaution? In fact, he never seems to chain them up at all, or even lock them in their bedroom at night. All in all, it's a strange way to treat an animal.

Like the relationships we humans have with other animals on Earth, the relationships the Doctor has with his human companions are unequal. He's a millennium-old genius from a race of geniuses, with technology able to do anything the script requires, while we are, well, merely human. As the Peter Capaldi Doctor puts it in "Deep Breath" (2014), from his perspective, Earth is "the planet of the pudding-brains." The Doctor's intellect and capability easily outshine even the most brilliant humans, like the Patrick Troughton Doctor's companion, the astrophysicist Zoe, and the Jon Pertwee Doctor's companion, Liz, who has "degrees in medicine, physics and a dozen other subjects."

In recognition of this unequal relationship, the Doctor often makes decisions on behalf of his human companions, as if they were pets of his. In "The End of the World" (2005), Rose protests to the Christopher Eccleston Doctor about the way he let the

TARDIS link to her telepathically to translate unknown languages: "Your machine gets inside my head. It gets inside and it changes my mind, and you didn't even ask?" Likewise, in "Day of the Moon" (2011), the Matt Smith Doctor doesn't ask before implanting telepathic nanorecorders into Amy, Rory, and River so that they can record the Silence. Later in the same episode, the Doctor learns that something strange is going on inside Amy's body, possibly involving pregnancy, but doesn't tell her about it, preferring to explore the mystery alone.

Given his superiority in intellect and education, perhaps the Doctor should give his companions even less freedom to make decisions on their own behalf, for the sake of their own safety. Pets have to be looked after! The Smith Doctor recognizes the problem in "The God Complex" (2011), explaining that he has a special duty to save Amy and Rory because "I brought them here. They'd say it was their choice, but offer a child a suitcase full of sweets and they'll take it." And if the likes of Amy and Rory don't really understand the risks, how much less are those risks understood by the Troughton Doctor's companions, the nineteenth-century Londoner Victoria and eighteenth-century highlander Jamie, or the Tom Baker Doctor's companion, Leela, the savage "primitive" human from the distant future? In "The Eleventh Hour" (2010), the Smith Doctor even invites an eight year old Amelia Pond to come adventuring with him. If he'd succeeded, she presumably would've been slaughtered by the Weeping Angels ten minutes into "The Time of the Angels" (2010).

Of course, the amount of self-determination the Doctor allows to his humans is far from the only difference between the way he treats us and the way we treat the animal species in our power. Most striking is the difference between the value the Doctor places on humans and our tendency to view animals as mere resources.

Human Beings and Other Livestock

SHOCKEYE: Such a soft white skin, whispering of a tender succulence . . . Let me buy it from you.

PATRICK TROUGHTON DOCTOR: My companion is not for sale!

—"THE TWO DOCTORS," 1985

Can you imagine the Tom Baker Doctor sitting down to eat sausages made of Sarah Jane Smith? How about the David Tennant Doctor chowing down on a roast Rose, or the Peter Capaldi Doctor dining on Clara cutlets and claret? That's only the tip of the iceberg of what we do to other species that the Doctor wouldn't do to us.

Farm animals are often exposed to extreme weather conditions of heat and cold, especially while being transported. Can you imagine the Tom Baker Doctor, having landed in Antarctica in "The Seeds of Doom" (1976), allowing Sarah Jane to be injured by frostbite just because it's too much trouble to raid the TARDIS costume room for some woolies? Young animals are routinely separated from their mothers at an age at which both have powerful emotional bonds. Can you imagine the Smith Doctor confiscating Amy and Rory's baby on the grounds that it's more convenient for him to store her separately? Young pigs are routinely castrated and de-tailed without anesthesia. Can you imagine the Smith Doctor deciding that he doesn't want Amy and Rory breeding anymore, and so aiming his sonic screwdriver at Rory's trousers and warning him, "Now, this is going to be extremely painful." Chickens are routinely kept together in close confinement, in cages too small to even stretch their wings, and with their beaks seared off so that they don't peck each other to death out of sheer stress. Can you imagine the Smith Doctor confining Amy, Rory, and River to a tiny, roundel-walled room, packed too tightly to stretch out their arms, with their teeth and fingernails pulled so that they can't tear each other to bits in their madness?

Yes, the images are gruesome, but that's the point. We regard the thought of doing such things to humans as horrific, yet we do them to other animal species. Rather than treating us as we treat animals, the Doctor would do almost anything to defend us. Flying over Victorian London in a balloon made of human skin in "Deep Breath," the Capaldi Doctor warns a Clockwork Robot, "Those people down there. They're never small to me. Don't make assumptions about how far I will go to protect them, because I've already come a very long way." Even when the Pertwee Doctor is exiled to Earth by the Time Lords (1970–1973), he works with UNIT to defend us rather than taking over our world and remaking it in a form more amusing to him, perhaps as a global showroom for classic cars.

Why should the Doctor value human wellbeing so much? Is it just favoritism, of the sort we show to our pets but not to farm animals? He's certainly fond of Earthlings. In "The Ark in Space" (1975), the Tom Baker Doctor confides to Sarah, "It may be irrational of me, but human beings are quite my favorite species." But if the only reason for the Doctor to treat us well is that he's fond of us, then it wouldn't be wrong of him to lose his fondness and to start treating us the way we treat animals. Yet we want to say (or I do, at any rate!) that there *is* something wrong with eating humans, locking them in small spaces, and otherwise treating them as livestock.

Asking whether the Doctor would be justified in treating humans the way that we treat animals isn't just a game. Philosophers test moral theories for consistency by asking what results they'd give in imaginary situations, called "thought experiments." For example, we might have a theory that it's always wrong to lie, but we should abandon the theory if it doesn't stand up in every hypothetical case, like that faced by the Smith Doctor in "Victory of the Daleks" (2010), in which the only thing preventing him from being exterminated is pretending that a Jammie Dodger is the TARDIS self-destruct button. Likewise, if the moral rules we use to justify our treatment of animals have unacceptable consequences when we apply them to the treatment of humans by aliens like the Doctor, then we need to change our moral rules. The Colin Baker Doctor has just such a moral revelation in "The Two Doctors" (1985). He's so repulsed by meeting the human-eating gourmets, the Androgums, he not only swears off eating meat, but takes it off the TARDIS menu, telling his companion Peri, "From now on, it's a healthy vegetarian diet for both of us."

Between Species, Might Makes Right

Daleks are supreme! Humans are weak!

—Dalek Jast, "Daleks in Manhattan," 2007

One common justification offered for the way that humans treat animals is simply that we have the power. People who believe that we're justified by power alone often maintain that rights are won by humans through political struggle, and so animals have no rights just because they've never been powerful enough to take any. But if might makes right between species, then there's no reason for the Doctor not to eat us, or otherwise do with humans as he pleases. Nor has there been any need for the Doctor to keep protecting humanity from enslavement or extermination by more powerful alien invaders. He's been saving us from mightier neighbors since "The Dalek Invasion of Earth" (1964), in which the William Hartnell Doctor interferes when the Daleks take over our planet to turn it into a jury-rigged spaceship.

Having gotten into the habit, he saves us again and again in each new incarnation, from the Troughton Doctor stopping the reptilian Ice Warriors from conquering Earth in "The Ice Warriors" (1967), to the Smith Doctor overthrowing the Silence who secretly rule us in "Day of the Moon," to the Capaldi Doctor preventing the invading two-dimensional "Boneless" from mashing us all flat in "Flatline" (2014).

Eat the Stupid

You humans have got such limited little minds. I don't know why I like you so much.

—Tom Baker Doctor, "The Masque of Mandragora," 1976

Another common justification offered for our right to treat animals as we like is that our intelligence is so superior to theirs. But again, if one species gains the right to treat another how it likes because it has superior intelligence, there's no reason for the Doctor not to use us as mere resources. Nor is there any reason for him to continually protect humanity from superior intelligences from space.

While some invaders have more advanced technology without being noticeably brighter than we are, others are clearly our intellectual superiors. The Great Intelligence is a great intelligence, yet the Doctor has been thwarting it from the time the Troughton Doctor first ruined its plan to conquer the Earth with Yeti robots in "The Abominable Snowmen" (1967) to the time the Smith Doctor stopped it from eating human minds through the Wi-Fi in "The Bells of St. John" (2013). The poor old Master, a brilliant Time Lord like the Doctor, has been trying to take over the Earth ever since the Pertwee Doctor prevented him from building an army of plastic killers in "Terror of the

Autons" (1971), but the Doctor always insists on getting in his way, about once a week in 1971 alone. Likewise, the Eccleston Doctor revealed in "Dalek" (2005) that the Daleks are all "geniuses," but that doesn't stop him from trying to wipe out the lone surviving Dalek before it can kill any more humans.

We could insist that what makes it morally alright for us to treat animals as we do isn't their relative intelligence compared to ours, but that their intelligence doesn't reach some minimum level required for moral concern. People who offer this justification usually claim that humans have rights because our species reaches this minimal level of intellect, while cows, sheep, and other non-human animals don't have rights because they don't reach this level. But this answer is arbitrary. Why draw the line at which rights appear at the point we humans just happen to be on, rather than drawing it above us at the level of the Time Lords, or below us at the level of cows? What could we say in principle to someone like the Master if they wanted to draw it at their own level instead? Besides, not all human beings reach a level of intelligence greater than that of non-human animals. If someone is badly mentally disabled, do they lose their rights?

Doctor Who avoids a lot of the difficult issues involving intellect and rights by rarely including species with intelligence between that of humans and that of other animals. As a rule of thumb, especially in the New Series, alien life is either animalistic—your leechlike "crimson horrors," your microscopic, shadow-loving Vashta Nerada, and your huge, reptilian Drashigs—or is as clever as, or cleverer than, humans. When the Smith Doctor learns in "The Rebel Flesh" / "The Almost People" (2011) that genetically engineered "gangers" are being exploited for the production of acid, the gangers turn out to be just like humans in intellect and psychology, making his decision that they must be freed as much of a moral no-brainer as the Hartnell Doctor's decision to free the enslaved and brutalized human miners in "The Dalek Invasion of Earth." Just as morally obvious have been the Doctor's decisions to liberate so many other oppressed alien species of human-level intelligence, like the tentacle-faced Ood rescued by the Tennant Doctor from the Ood Operations company in "Planet of the Ood" (2008), the feline Tharils rescued by the Tom Baker Doctor from slavery as temporal navigators in "Warrior's Gate" (1981), and the moth-like Menoptera rescued by the Hartnell Doctor from their ant-like Zarbi masters in "The Web Planet" (1965).

Realistically, intelligence for both natural and artificial life would exist on a spectrum rather than being a simple bifurcation which neatly divides creatures into those to be treated like animals and those to be treated like people. If gangers were halfway in intelligence between humans and chimps, would they still need to be freed, or would it be alright to leave them to burn in the industrial acid pools? There seems to be no non-arbitrary way to draw a line dividing species intelligent enough to have rights from species that aren't. So believing that a creature has rights depends on whether it reaches a certain level of intelligence seems less like a genuine moral solution than an excuse to do what we want.

It's Only Natural

On most planets, the animals eat the vegetation. . . . On planets where the Krinoid gets established, the vegetation eats the animals.

—TOM BAKER DOCTOR, "The Seeds of Doom," 1976

Another common justification offered for our treatment of animals, and especially for eating them, is that we're simply doing what's natural. People who hold this view will often point out that throughout nature, we find animals preying on other animals, and that our ancestors have been consuming other animals for at least two hundred million years or so, since we were shrew-like creatures munching on crunchy insects. Yet again though, if it's morally okay for a species to do anything that's in its nature, then the Doctor has been wasting a lot of time defending humanity from our natural predators.

The face-hugging Dream Crabs that the Capaldi Doctor saves us from in "Last Christmas" (2014) are only trying to eat our brains, as we humans might eat other animals on Earth. The Minotaur in whose nightmare hotel the Smith Doctor stays in "The God Complex," feeds on faith, a process that requires driving its victims insane with terrifying hallucinations. Yet, the fact that consuming the faithful is how its species eats doesn't stop the Doctor from killing it through emotional starvation to save the people it preys on. Likewise, the Tennant Doctor explains in "Blink" (2007) that the Weeping

Angels "live off potential energy" by consuming the energy produced when they send someone back in time. Yet, despite the
fact that sending people into the past is just part of the
Weeping Angels' lifecycle, the Tennant and Smith Doctors
intervene to stop them whenever they encounter them. The
Tennant Doctor shows the same lack of sympathy to the
energy-bodied, energy-eating Wire from "The Idiot's Lantern"
(2006), the spidery, flesh-eating Racnoss from "The Runaway
Bride" (2006), and the liquid, body-stealing Flood from "Waters
of Mars" (2009), all of who are just doing what comes naturally.

The Classic Doctors were no more prone to letting nature
take its course. When the Troughton Doctor learns in "Fury
from the Deep" (1968) that an ancient monster composed of living seaweed is poised to spread across the world, he drives it
back to the depths by playing it the amplified screams of his
companion Victoria. When the golden, energy-eating monster
Axos shows up from space to consume Earth in "The Claws of
Axos" (1971), the Pertwee Doctor uses the TARDIS to imprison
it in a time loop. When the Tom Baker Doctor finds in "The Ark
in Space" that a starship full of humans suspended in stasis
has been invaded by the insectoid Wirrn, who plan to lay their
eggs in the sleeping colonists, he electrifies the ark to stop
them. He likewise interferes with the perfectly natural invading behavior of the infectious plant Krinoid in "The Seeds of
Doom" (1976), the virus Swarm in "The Invisible Enemy"
(1977), the wormlike, life-eating Fendahl in "Image of the
Fendahl" (1977), and the eye-shadow loving, blood-drinking
Vampires in "State of Decay" (1980).

The Swarm even argues the point with him, insisting, "I
have every right! It is the right of every creature across the universe to survive, multiply and perpetuate its species." If the
Swarm is correct that it has a right to do anything that perpet-
uates its species, then this justifies not only the actions of creatures who must consume humans to survive, but also the
actions of those invaders whose survival depends on enslaving
or destroying us, like the Cybermen first encountered by the
Hartnell Doctor in "The Tenth Planet" (1966), the Zygons met by
the Tom Baker Doctor in "Terror of the Zygons" (1975), and the
Nestene Consciousness defeated by the Eccleston Doctor in
"Rose" (2005). Note, though, that even if the need for survival
gives the Swarm and other species the right to prey on humans,

it won't justify our treatment of animals. After all, humans in the modern West no longer need to prey on animals to survive.

The Suffering Standard

CYBERMAN: Why should we mind?

POLLY: Because millions and millions of people are going to suffer and die horribly!

— "THE TENTH PLANET," 1966

In my opinion, the best fundamental approach to our moral obligations to animals is that suggested by the English philosopher Jeremy Bentham (1748–1832). Bentham was an advocate of a philosophical view known as "utilitarianism." Utilitarianism is the theory that actions are right or wrong in proportion to the degree that they cause happiness or suffering. The more happiness they produce, the morally better they are, while the more suffering they produce, the morally worse they are. The social changes Bentham advocated on utilitarian grounds include welfare for the poor, political equality for women, the decriminalization of homosexuality, and the abolition of slavery, the death penalty, and corporal punishment (there will be no slapping the Doctor while Bentham is on the TARDIS. Companions who try that will go to "time out" immediately).

As for animals, Bentham concluded in *An Introduction to the Principles of Morals and Legislation* (1789) that "The question is not, 'Can they reason?' nor, 'Can they talk?' but, 'Can they suffer?'" Bentham was a founding member of the Royal Society for the Prevention of Cruelty to Animals and an early advocate of passing laws to protect animals from inhumane treatment. Unlike the Colin Baker Doctor, he wasn't a vegetarian, and didn't think that we have a moral duty not to eat meat. But he thought that the animals of his day were treated with an unacceptable lack of compassion. Given a TARDIS ride to a modern factory farm, he'd be horrified to see the new techniques we've developed for making the most profit from animals with the minimum fuss. He might even ask the Doctor why he doesn't *do* something to put a stop to it. He rescues the humans of Earth often enough. What about the pigs?

Bentham's demand for humane treatment for all species capable of suffering might require us to pay more for bacon and eggs, but it also requires Daleks not to turn us into slaves, and Clockwork Robots not to harvest us for spare parts. Utilitarianism explains why it's a *good* thing for the Doctor to continually intervene to rescue us from alien attack. It explains why the Doctor is being heroic, rather than simply eccentric, in caring about human well-being enough to stand in the way of alien species who would do to us the sort of things *we* do to the species we have in our power. After all, it would cause suffering for humans to be, say, exposed to terrible weather, separated from our young, operated on without anesthesia, or kept in confinement in small spaces, so it shouldn't be done—at least, not if it doesn't somehow bring about a benefit that outweighs the suffering it would bring.

But if Bentham is right that there's nothing wrong with eating animals per se, does this mean that there's nothing wrong with eating humans per se either? Would it be alright for the Doctor to eat Clara after all? Given that every regeneration of his will meet a version of her, thanks to the events of "The Name of the Doctor" (2013), he could even eat her once a regeneration, trying out a different recipe each time ("mmm . . . with celery" thinks the Peter Davison Doctor, while the Smith Doctor just wants to dip Clara fingers in custard).

However, I don't think that eating humans passes the utilitarian test. No matter how delicious a human might be when cooked to perfection according to the ancient Gallifreyan Recipe of Rassilon, the pleasure of eating one is presumably not so intense that it outweighs the loss of all of the happiness the human would've had in their life if they'd lived, along with all the good they could've done in the world and the all the grief their deaths will bring to those who love them. Some vegetarians insist that by this same standard, eating meat is always wrong. They claim that the pleasure gained from eating animal flesh never outweighs the cost to the animal, even if we try our best to be humane in rearing and killing it. That's an issue too big to tackle here, but if they're right, it had better be healthy vegetarian diets for all of us. Otherwise, we've no grounds for complaint if the Time Lords decide that turnabout is fair play.

The Tom Baker Doctor pushed himself contentedly back from the table and dabbed his lips with his enormous scarf. "It may be irrational of me," he grinned, "but human beings are quite my favorite species." The Troughton Doctor stifled a belch, steepled his fingers over his full stomach, and agreed: "There are some corners of the universe that have bred the most delicious things." The Colin Baker Doctor sat scowling, his plate empty. The Davison Doctor nudged him. "Come on. A well prepared meal is the sort of small, beautiful event that life is all about."

"You really must eat a little human flesh now and then, old chap," added the Pertwee Doctor, a glass of red wine in his hand. "Fungus is scrumptious, but it's low in protein. No wonder Jo got so stringy."

"And eating humans is easier than getting divorced," noted the Smith Doctor, picking his teeth. The Eccleston Doctor chimed in, "Humans have more uses than just eating, too. See this fantastic jacket? That's genuine Jackie Tyler leather." The McCoy Doctor's mouth was full, but he mimed that the food was getting cold.

The Hartnell Doctor leaned in to the Capaldi Doctor, smiling. "Ha-hm! It all started out as a mild curiosity in a junkyard, and now it's turned into quite a great nosh-up, don't you think?" The Capaldi Doctor was grim and thoughtful, his fingers knitted together on his knees.

"Maybe Six is right. I wonder, am I really a good man? Isn't it wrong to eat humans like this?" The Tennant Doctor raised his eyebrows and sighed. "Well . . . you know. Morality is complicated. Very complicated. It's a tangled web of morally-worally, ethicy-wethicy . . . stuff." The old man hooked his thumbs behind his lapels and grandly advised, "I don't know if you are a good man or not. But I do know this much. These men and women are excellent. Do have some more!" And at that, the Pertwee Doctor banged on his glass and called a toast—"To absent friends!"

14

The Doctor's Desire for Human Suffering

ANGEL M. COOPER

ROSE: Why no emotions?

THE DOCTOR: Because it hurts.

—"RISE OF THE CYBERMEN," 2006

We all suffer. Living is painful. And most, if not all of us, have wished we could eradicate suffering from our lives. We wish for peace. If only we could have peace, we think, then life would be better.

Many philosophers have focused on the elimination of suffering. John Stuart Mill, for one, grounds his entire moral theory on the eradication of suffering. He explains in *Utilitarianism*, "Pleasure and freedom from pain are the only things desirable as ends." We all desire to have pleasure and to avoid pain, according to Mill. Part of being human is to shun pain and try to escape it—often even to despise it. However, Friedrich Nietzsche defies traditional philosophy. Rather than shunning suffering, he champions it. Nietzsche holds that the best way to live is to affirm life. Yet, an essential part of our lives, which we usually reject, is suffering. All human beings suffer, and according to Nietzsche, suffering is what makes us who we are. Suffering allows us to grow, create, and overcome in life. In order to affirm life, we must value our suffering by recognizing the ways in which it improves us. Disregarding our suffering is weak and degenerative for Nietzsche.

In "Rise of the Cybermen" and "The Age of Steel" (2006), *Doctor Who* takes on a Nietzschean attitude towards suffering.

We can see this attitude through the contrast of two characters: the Doctor and John Lumic. The Doctor embraces his own suffering and the suffering of humanity, arguing that without suffering there's no humanity. For the Doctor, suffering and pain cultivate brilliance in us. Lumic, on the other hand, despises suffering and attempts to eradicate his own suffering as well as that of humanity. We can see the Nietzschean attitude reflected in the outcomes of these two characters presented in both episodes. The Doctor, in fighting against the elimination of pain, and in trusting his *all too human* companions, is victorious. Lumic, however, fails. Even though he's able to rid himself of his suffering, he loses everything that makes him who he is and eventually is destroyed.

The Peaceful Weakness of Lumic

Lumic creates the Cybermen in order to prolong his life and end his sickness. What Lumic values most is his rational capacity, his brilliance—what he values least is his suffering. He designs the Cybermen to preserve his brilliance but at the same time rid himself of pain. Lumic exclaims in "Rise of the Cybermen," "We're all flesh and blood but the brain is what makes us human. And my mind is more creative than ever." According to Lumic, the brain produces his creativity and brilliance. Lumic identifies who he is with his creative mind. So he maintains that the brain contains our humanity. Lumic believes that his sickness holds him back. If only he can rid himself of his suffering, then his creativity will thrive.

Nietzsche would disagree with Lumic because, for Nietzsche, our creativity stems from our suffering. In *Thus Spoke Zarathustra*, Nietzsche writes, "that the creator may be, suffering is needed and much change. Indeed, there must be much bitter dying in your life, you creators... To be the child who is newly born, the creator must also want to be the mother who gives birth and the pangs of the birth-giver." For Nietzsche, suffering and pain breeds creativity. We can't create something new without the influence of pain. To remove all suffering would lead to the end of creativity for humanity.

Lumic fails to recognize that he needs his pain in order to be the brilliant man he takes himself to be. When Lumic becomes the Cyber Controller, he succeeds in eliminating his sickness. But, with his pain goes his creativity—and losing his creativity means losing himself. When Lumic first meets his Cybermen, they explain that their thought is uniform.

> LUMIC: But in your mind, what do you think?
>
> CYBERMAN: We think the same. We are uniform.
>
> LUMIC: But you think of what?
>
> CYBERMAN: We think of the humans. We think of their difference and their pain. They suffer in the skin. They must be upgraded.

The Cybermen are all equal. They have no creative thoughts. They only think of one thing and that's creating more Cybermen. Although they've eradicated suffering in themselves, their entire existence is now only concerned with ending all suffering. When Lumic becomes the Cyber Controller, his thoughts also conform to that of the Cybermen. Lumic doesn't realize that in escaping his suffering, he loses the person he was. In order to end his suffering, Lumic essentially must die.

After becoming the Cyber Controller in the "Age of Steel," Lumic explains, "I will bring peace to the world. Everlasting peace. And unity and uniformity." Unlike Lumic, Nietzsche rejects the struggle to forgo suffering in order to procure a life of happiness, pleasure, comfort, and peace. In *Beyond Good and Evil*, he argues:

> You want, if possible—and there is no more insane "if possible"—*to abolish suffering*. And we? It really seems that *we* would rather have it higher and worse than ever. Well-being as you understand it—that is no goal, that seems to us an *end*, a state that soon makes man ridiculous and contemptible—that makes his destruction *desirable*. (p. 153)

For Nietzsche, to strive for "well-being"—a kind of peace and contentment—in life at the expense of suffering is to *end* humanity. To be human is to suffer. Lumic has rid himself of sickness and now strives for the peace that Nietzsche criticizes. He's no longer human because he's abolished his own suffering and in order to gain everlasting peace for the world, he'll destroy all humanity. Moreover, we, the audience, desire his destruction.

Lumic becomes part of what Nietzsche calls "the herd," because he's lost his individuality and uniqueness. Lumic explains that he now seeks unity and uniformity, whereas before his *upgrade*, he sought excellence and novelty. In *The Gay Science*, Nietzsche calls those who try to mediate between thinkers "mediocre" and writes, "They lack eyes for seeing what is unique. Seeing things as similar and making things the same is the sign of weak eyes." Lumic can no longer see uniqueness in the world. He craves uniformity. Those who want to reduce humanity to one equal level are weak and despicable to Nietzsche. They make everything similar, dull, and un-exceptional. Nietzsche calls these people "the herd" because they all think the same. Although the Cybermen view Lumic as a leader who may be more intelligent than themselves, with Lumic's loss of creativity and his quest for uniformity, he becomes just another member of the herd.

Furthermore, we can see a Nietzschean value of suffering when it comes to other characters' attitudes towards Lumic and the Cybermen. First, Lumic is clearly the villain of the episode. He's so villainous that he's greeted with less sympathy than most other antagonists in the series. (Spoiler: I will later discuss the sympathy the Doctor gives to the Family of Blood, the Slitheen, the Master, and even the Daleks.) The Doctor never offers Lumic the chance to redeem himself or retreat as he does with other antagonists. In fact, none of the protagonists—the Doctor, Pete, Rose, Mr. Crane, or even the Cybermen—in these two episodes offer Lumic any sympathy. When Rose encounters the Jackie-Cyberman she exclaims, "They killed her. They just took her and killed her." She doesn't see this thing as her mother. There's nothing left of her mother in the Cyberman. Likewise, when the Doctor opens up one of the Cybermen and explains to Mrs. Moore that Lumic implanted an emotional inhibitor inside them, Mrs. Moore says, "So they cut out the one thing that makes them human." The Cybermen are clearly no longer human.

Finally, at the end of the episode, the Doctor gives Pete his sonic screwdriver, telling him to use it on the rope they're climbing in order to destroy Lumic. This action is rare for the Doctor. He occasionally allows his enemies to be destroyed because of their own negligence. For instance, he doesn't save Cassandra from drying out in "The End of the World" (2005).

However, he rarely, if ever, actively seeks out the destruction of his enemies without first offering them a deal to save their lives. No, the Cybermen aren't human. The Doctor and his companions can only offer the Cybermen pity at their loss of life. However, Lumic is viewed as especially despicable and weak. Lumic, is, after all, the only character who "wants" to become a Cyberman—but only when he's about to die, of course—in order to end his suffering. Lumic's choice is despicable. Without emotions and the ability to suffer, Lumic gives up not only his creativity, but his humanity as well.

The Agonizing Strength of the Doctor

The Doctor, unlike Lumic, values suffering and so is not part of the Nietzschean "herd." Lumic, on the other hand, is a member of the herd. He's weak, and although he doesn't realize it himself, he is life-denying. Nietzsche depicts the denial of life in those who reject their suffering and seek the equality of the herd. In *On the Genealogy of Morals,* he claims that the notion "that every will must consider every other will its equal— would be a principle *hostile to life*." Embracing suffering and the uniqueness of the individual, leads to growth, which is life affirming for Nietzsche. By denying suffering and pursuing uniformity, the Cybermen destroy life, rather than preserve it. The Doctor, on the other hand, is unique, strong, and life affirming. When Lumic says that he'll bring unity and uniformity to life, the Doctor replies, "And imagination? What about that? The one thing that led you here, imagination, you're killing it dead!" ("The Age of Steel"). The Doctor's response is similar to Nietzsche's argument that suffering is needed for creativity. He further rejects Lumic's goal of peace and uniformity because uniformity breeds herd mentality by killing imagination. It's killed Lumic's creativity, which is what made him brilliant. The Doctor tells Lumic:

> But everything you've invented, you did to fight your sickness. And that's brilliant. That is so human. But once you get rid of sickness and mortality, then what's there to strive for, eh? The Cybermen won't advance. You'll just stop. You'll stay like this forever. A metal Earth with metal men and metal thoughts, lacking the one thing that makes this planet so alive. People. Ordinary, stupid, brilliant people.

The Doctor points out that Lumic was able to create because of his pain, and as a result of his sickness. Like Nietzsche, he praises the influence of pain and explains that it's fundamental to being human—for striving, for being creative. Without pain to force the Cybermen to strive and grow, they'll just stop. The Doctor has shown Lumic to be life-denying because the elimination of his suffering was an *end*. People, with their suffering, stupidity, and brilliance are what make the world alive—and the Cybermen aren't people.

Lumic, now the Cyber Controller, has lost all humanity and he can no longer understand the Doctor's values. The Cybermen only think of eliminating pain. They can't understand the desire to strive and grow to be more than what they are. Lumic, confused by the Doctor's diatribe, questions him about his emotions.

> LUMIC: You are proud of your emotions?
>
> THE DOCTOR: Oh, yes.
>
> LUMIC: Then tell me, Doctor. Have you known grief, and rage, and pain?
>
> THE DOCTOR: Yes. Yes I have.
>
> LUMIC: And they hurt?
>
> THE DOCTOR: Oh, yes!

The Doctor again follows the Nietzschean perspective, claiming that he's proud of his emotions, even the painful ones. Lumic then specifically focuses in on pain, asking the Doctor if he'd want a life without pain. The Doctor responds, "You might as well kill me." The Doctor understands that without his pain, he wouldn't be the same person. He wouldn't be a person at all. In *The Gay Science*, Nietzsche exclaims, "The poison of which weaker natures perish strengthens the strong—nor do they call it poison." Lumic's sickness and pain destroyed him because he's weak, but the Doctor is strong. His pain strengthens him and he praises it.

Not only does the Doctor praise suffering in opposition to Lumic in "The Age of Steel," but we can observe *Doctor Who*'s depiction of the value of suffering even more so by looking at the Doctor's character. The Doctor is a being who has suffered greatly. He destroyed two species, including his own people, and his past weighs on him. However, he uses that suffering to improve his character. He typically gives his enemies a chance to back down. When in conflict, he strives to allow everyone to live. In short, the Doctor's suffering has allowed him to become a more merciful being. In *On the Genealogy of Morals*, Nietzsche describes mercy as "the privilege of the most powerful man." We can see the Doctor grow more merciful through the two experiences that pain him the most: the act of destroying two species and the loneliness that comes from that act.

In the Time War, the Doctor destroyed both his own people and the Daleks in order to save the universe. The memory of this act causes him a tremendous amount of pain. He doesn't often talk about his people, but when he does, it's with a great sadness. In the few instances that he's accused of killing the two species—by a Dalek ("Dalek," 2005), the Slitheen women Margaret Blaine ("Boom Town," 2005), and the Beast ("The Satan Pit," 2006)—his pain is evident. However, the Doctor uses this pain to improve his character and grow stronger.

We can see the Doctor's strength in the mercy he shows his enemies. He often gives his enemies a chance to make a deal and escape destruction (which they, of course, decline). He even sometimes gives them more than one chance. He offers help to the Nestene Consciousness ("Rose," 2005), the Slitheen ("Aliens of London," 2005), the Empress of the Racnoss ("The Runaway Bride," 2006), and Martha's kidnappers ("Gridlock," 2007). He hides from the Family of Blood so that they may die in peace, only later punishing them for killing and terrorizing the people of the small town where he hides out ("The Family of Blood," 2007). But his mercy is most notable towards the Daleks. He doesn't destroy the Dalek in "Dalek" and offers to help the Daleks multiple times in "Evolution of the Daleks" (2007). In this two-part episode, the Daleks kill many people, but the Doctor offers to help them create a new race of Dalek-humans on another planet. When they betray him and Dalek Sec, destroying all the human Daleks, he still offers to help Dalek Caan. The Doctor states:

> Dalek Caan, your entire species has been wiped out. And now the Cult of Skaro has been eradicated, leaving only you. Right now you're

facing the only man in the universe who might show you some compassion. Because I've just seen one genocide. I won't cause another. Caan, let me help you. What do you say?

The Doctor offers compassion and mercy because of his pain from his acts in the Time War. Before the Time War, he was willing to sacrifice his people and the Daleks. However, his pain and suffering from destroying two species push him to grow and become a stronger, more merciful being. He shows compassion to his worst enemies, even when he's already given them a number of chances.

The Doctor's pain from loneliness also allows him to become more merciful. The Doctor's people are destroyed and his human companions always seem to leave him for some reason or another. The Doctor and other characters in the show often mention his loneliness. In "School Reunion" (2006) he tells Rose that eventually he'll have to live on without her. Alone. He calls this the *curse* of the Time Lords. In "The Lazarus Project" (2008) he states, "If you live long enough, Lazarus, the only certainty left is that you'll end up alone." After looking into his mind, Reinette comments, "Such a lonely little boy. Lonely then and lonelier now. How can you bear it?" ("The Girl in the Fireplace," 2006). One of the Doctor's greatest pains is his loneliness and it's part of what makes him who he is. But it also makes him better. He's strong enough to bear the pain of his loneliness; and later, it too, drives him to act mercifully even toward the Master.

In "Last of the Time Lords" (2007) the Master enslaves the human race, killing many people. Eventually, Martha and the Doctor overcome the Master and reverse time. Almost everyone who remembers what the Master did to humanity wants him dead, but the Doctor refuses. He explains to Captain Jack, "I'm not here to kill him. I'm here to save him." He tells the Master that he forgives him and plans on keeping the Master with him rather than killing him. However, the Master's human wife, Lucy, shoots him. The Doctor pleads with the Master to regenerate, yelling, "We're the only two left. There's no one else. Regenerate!" But the Master refuses. It's the Doctor's loneliness that gives him this compassionate and forgiving nature. He recognizes the value of life because of the pain he has from being alone. He's a better, stronger, more life affirming person because of his pain.

Being Human—It Hurts

Nietzsche describes mercy as a quality of only the most powerful individuals. The Doctor is merciful, compassionate, and forgiving. His mercy comes from his pain. The Doctor reflects a Nietzschean attitude, embracing his suffering and gaining strength of character from it. Lumic, on the other hand, opposes the Nietzschean attitude, shunning suffering and losing his humanity in the process. It's difficult for us to accept this Nietzschean perspective on pain and suffering. We spend so much of our time running from pain, embracing it seems ludicrous. But *Doctor Who* shows us that suffering is part of being human. Without it, a person is just "a living brain . . . with a heart of steel" ("Rise of the Cybermen"). But with it, we're "people. Ordinary, stupid, brilliant people" ("The Age of Steel").

15

The Way of the Doctor Is Deception

MICHAEL DODGE

Time and again, one galactic crisis after another, we've come to know and love the good Doctor. This is probably because he's always struggling against the darker natures of man and machine, showcasing his heroism, and reaching out to his human companions with compassion and understanding.

Yet, of all the things the Doctor says and does to save the day, sometimes he employs tactics we'd expect more from a villain than a hero. The Doctor isn't averse to deceiving or even lying to those around him—even to his friends. Ultimately, to better understand the Doctor, we need to explore the relationship between the concepts of lying and deception, as well as their philosophical "mirrors," honesty and truth. Beyond this, we also need to discuss the pragmatic essence of deception in *Doctor Who*, moving beyond the simple lies of necessity so often employed by the Doctor, companions, and antagonists, in order to question the rule underpinning so many of the Doctor's actions—Rule #1: the Doctor lies ("The Big Bang," 2010 and "Let's Kill Hitler," 2011).

Generally, but not always, lying and deception are employed by the Doctor to ensure positive outcomes for those for whom the Doctor feels responsible. When the Doctor "deceives" he's essentially leading others to believe that which isn't true—it's less direct than uttering a falsehood, and it allows others to come to their own, albeit false, conclusions. Sometimes airy and humorous, these deceptions may be the result when the Doctor simply fails to correct the false impression, like when he lets the store clerks think he and Craig are "partners" in "Closing Time" (2011).

At other times, the deception is deep, confusing, and painful, as when he plans his own "death" and invites everyone to it in "Impossible Astronaut" and "Day of the Moon" (2011). Still, deceptions can simply be critical sub-points in the overarching structure of the Doctor's work, as when the Vinvocci altered their appearance in order to repair the Immortality Gate ("The End of Time," 2009). However, in almost every instance, deceptions or lies employed by the Doctor are done to help or save those most vulnerable from the machinations of greedy pirates, dastardly Daleks, monotonous Cybermen, or any other form of Whovian villainy.

That Was a Clever Lie, You Idiot! Anyone Could Tell That Was a Clever Lie!

Lying is more complex than simply telling someone an untruth. It's possible, after all, for you tell someone something that is false, when you happened to believe it yourself. In that instance, you had no intention to deceive, you simply lacked correct information. No one is likely to accuse you of lying in that situation. They'd say you've made a mistake. For our purposes here, we'll take lying to be the same as that defined by philosopher Bernard Williams (1929–2003), which is ". . . an assertion, the content of which the speaker believes to be false, which is made with the intention to deceive the hearer with respect to that content." Williams's definition shows us that a lie occurs only when you believe what you're saying is false, *and* intend for the person to believe what you're saying is true.

Lies Are Words, Words, and Words

A common feature of lies is how they're communicated to people. While a lie needn't always be spoken to deceive, words are their most frequent medium. We've often seen a salesman or politician use hundreds of words, where a few dozen would suffice. The more someone tries to convince you to accept their view, the more likely it seems they're trying to deceive you. The truth should be simple, and easy to convey. It'd be simplistic to think that this was always the case, but perhaps the Doctor would do well to remember this principle, though, for whatever reasons, the Doctor often fails to abide by this notion, choosing instead to operate with guile and gumption, rather than just telling us outright what's happening all around us.

Chatty or not, most of us see the Doctor as a good human— ehhh, Gallifrey-man—and a hero. Such heroic men are supposed to be the epitome of virtue, showing the world their moral fortitude by resisting the temptation to do a wrong, and proving that the good guy needn't stoop to the depths of the villain to achieve his goal. Heroes like the Doctor dig around in their kits for the tools we should all be using to make our way through life—bravery, thoughtfulness, compassion . . . lying? If something seems off about this, it should. Most people, including most philosophers, condemn lying as a bad thing—an unethical, immoral act. If that's true, when we see the Doctor lie, is he doing the right thing? We need to know, after all, because he lies so frequently that it's become his Rule #1.

But if the Doctor tells a lie, it must be for a good reason, right? Yet for most of us, when someone lies to us, even if it's the Doctor, we feel they've done something wrong. When someone lies to us, we rely on that statement in our subsequent actions. Everything we do based on what we were told is tainted, resulting in ill feelings (at the least). Several philosophers have attempted to articulate this feeling, clarifying what exactly it is that makes deceit and lying such bad things. In particular, Aristotle is noted for the proposition that *all* lies are base, whereas truth is good and noble. When the Doctor lies, he takes this base, wrong thing and uses it against others. Even if he means well, for example, in trying to thwart Daleks, defeat the Master, or confuse Cybermen, the end result he seeks is always shadowed by the guilt of the lie—it's never truly noble, because it's always wrong to use lies, even when trying to do good for others. In essence, creating a "good" result by using "bad" tactics is immoral, and therefore ignoble.

Immanuel Kant (1724–1804) also objected to lies and deceptions. Kant was known for his categorical imperative, a duty which people ought to follow in order to live moral lives. In essence, you should act only in ways that you could expect to become universal rules of behavior—that is, your actions should echo a moral law that you should expect everyone to uphold. One such maxim is that lying to someone is wrong, and so you should never lie, just as you would expect no one should lie to you. The duty that this creates is a perfect one, admitting of no exceptions. Thus, we should always be honest, and never lie or deceive.

Kant's philosophy is also known for the "respect for persons" principle, where people should treat one another as an ends in themselves. According to Kant, you should always treat others as if they're valuable, special, and rational persons, and never treat them only as if they're mere tools to be used in order to accomplish your goal. The people around you *are* the goal, and treating them as anything other than free, thinking beings, including always being truthful with them, would be like taking away something precious—their ability to make rational choices.

If someone lies to you, not only do they disrespect your dignity as a person, but also when you act based upon the lie, you're harmed because you can't make a rational choice with false or irrelevant information. While the categorical imperative may seem too idealistic, there's something seemingly plain about the wrongfulness of lying to and deceiving others, especially when done to one's friends. Even lying to an enemy feels tainted, somehow.

The stringent nature of Kant's categorical imperative is felt even more acutely when judging minor deceptions that would rarely garner the condemnation of most philosophers. When the Vinvocci disguised themselves with "shimmers" in order to effect repairs on the Immortality Gate, their only wrong was in deceiving others into thinking they were human ("The End of Time"). Kant would hold the Vinvocci were wrong in deploying shimmers, because their disguises were a way of abusing the trust of those around them. Yet, their deceit seems understandable, and even preferable, considering the panic and mayhem the knowledge that green, intelligent, walking cacti ("that's racist!") exist would cause to society.

The moral status of lies and deceptions has also been addressed by Jeremy Bentham (1748–1832), a philosopher known for his development of a theory of ethics called Utilitarianism. Utilitarianism claims that there are two primary "masters" in life—pleasure and pain. Whenever someone contemplates an action, she should ask herself whether that action will cause more pleasure than pain, and therefore greater happiness than unhappiness. The rightness or wrongness of an action depends, for the most part, on whether its expression would produce more happiness than unhappiness.

Bentham would examine the Doctor's deceptions with less dogmatic zeal towards treating people as "means" or "ends," caring more for whether he was causing pain, or pleasure. In a way, this means that some of the lies and deceptions in *Doctor Who* are morally justifiable, since they pave the way for the Doctor to rectify some current or looming evil. However, whether they solve a problem or not, a lie would only be acceptable if it generates the greatest good for the greatest number of people. Unfortunately, sometimes lies cause a great deal of pain—too much to be morally acceptable for Bentham or any utilitarian.

One such instance occurred when the Impossible Astronaut emerged from Lake Silencio, shooting the Doctor, and apparently killing him for good by preventing his regeneration ("The Impossible Astronaut"). From the perspective of his friends, who witnessed the shooting, preventing his regeneration would've meant a permanent death for their Time Lord friend. The aftermath of the event was predictable—the Doctor's companions were absolutely devastated by his loss, thinking their friend and fellow adventurer would never return. At the Doctor's Viking funeral, you could feel the deep and abiding pain shared by Rory and Amy. That kind of loss haunts people, lingering, and evoking pain each time the memory of the event surfaces.

The ethical problem arises when you realize, later in the series, that the Doctor hadn't died, but only deceived everyone into believing he'd been killed ("The Wedding of River Song," 2011). While the Doctor had exceptional reasons for appropriating the Teselecta and faking his death (getting the vile Madame Kovarian off of his track, for one), doing so not only achieved the goal of fooling his enemies, but it made his friends suffer. One could argue that this "great lie" caused much more pain and unhappiness than pleasure, which, for a utilitarian, would be unacceptable.

The moral error is compounded when the Doctor, lionized, respected, and loved by so many, lies and deceives those around him in order to accomplish his task *du jour*. How can our beloved hero *be* a hero, when he routinely deceives those around him? Perhaps this concern can be alleviated if there's a way for deception and lies to be used for the greater good of the people, entities, and planets he encounters. For some philosophers, the unwavering wrongfulness of lying isn't so clear cut as is commonly believed.

Gallifreyan Guile—the Good Lie

So when is a lie a good lie? No—I don't mean when a lie is *convincing*, but rather, can a lie be a good thing in itself? If we do accept that lies can be good, as do some utilitarians, we should examine whether the so-called "good lie" is immune from the condemnation of the philosophers we've discussed. We've all heard that some lies are rather innocent, the kind commonly known as "white lies." For instance, lies are often used to alleviate fear and calm a person, as when a doctor about to give a child a shot, or River administering to Amy, tells the patient that it "won't hurt a bit" ("The Time of Angels," 2012). Certainly, it feels "off" to tell a parent that they've wronged their child by trying to lessen their fear.

Sometimes, lies are used to help the Doctor's friends, companions, and acquaintances keep on task. When exploring a supposedly haunted mansion, the Doctor arrives and insinuates himself into the pseudo-scientific investigation of the Witch of the Well ("Hide," 2013). Pretending to be from military intelligence, the Doctor found a wedge that allowed both him and Clara to not only gain entry into Caliburn House, but to co-opt the lead role in the investigation. Had the Doctor not effectuated this stance, the people studying the phenomenon would've rejected his presence, and the Doctor's efforts at saving the "witch" (who turned out to be a trapped time-traveling scientist) might have failed. Though he had to lie to do it, the Doctor saved a life.

In his famous dialogue the *Republic*, Plato claimed that there are times when telling a lie isn't only acceptable, but even righteous. This Noble Lie is told by an elite force, such as a government, to a common populace. In his example, members of an ancient society are told why their civilization is socially stratified, and the various classes of people are explained as being the will of the gods. The higher powers needed only a handful of people to rule, and so these people are seen as more precious, as if gold had been melded with their being. For workers, the gods had mingled their essence with silver, and iron or other lesser metals were wedded to the farmers and laborers. The occurrence of each of these metals in nature is mirrored by the quantity of each tier of society, so as gold is precious, rulers are few, whereas iron is common, as are laborers.

The idea behind this lie is that it helps people to accept their position in life, and keep society functioning properly. Its nobility arises in turn because, for Plato, society couldn't function without the existence of these classes, and civilization provides shelter, food, meaning, and leadership for all—something most would recognize as desirable and good. While not a precise parallel, the Doctor emulated this noble lie when he deceived most of the universe into believing he'd been killed, all to enable himself to overcome the problem of, in his words, becoming "too big" ("Day of the Moon"). Only an elite, god-like being such as the Doctor could convince both the powers-that-be and the common alike that he had expired, thereby enabling him to surreptitiously continue his mission of helping people. Depending on whether you think like Kant or a utilitarian, lying may or may not be morally preferable, but it's certainly noble to help the masses of beings who routinely benefit from the Doctor's actions.

Utilitarian ethics also allows for noble, or at least good, lies. While we've seen Bentham condemn lies for causing displeasure and unhappiness, it's equally true that his moral calculus allows for lies to be acceptable when they actually increase happiness and pleasure. The "death" of the Doctor at the hands of the Impossible Astronaut that we condemned above for causing so much pain also created great happiness. That deception not only fooled the companions, but also the Doctor's antagonists. In turn, this allowed the Doctor to produce an immeasurable happiness for the universe, since he could continue on traveling through time, helping those in need, but with less resistance from his enemies. Indeed, the Doctor's lies generally produce greater happiness and pleasure than unhappiness and displeasure. Seen through this lens, a utilitarian would rarely judge the Doctor harshly.

Finally, some philosophers would contend that lying is ethically neutral. In his work *Human, All Too Human*, Friedrich Nietzsche (1844–1900) famously asserted that lying isn't intrinsically unethical. He noted that while it's true that most people attempt to avoid lying in their daily interactions, they don't do so because of some heightened sense of ethical duty toward one another, or because truth-telling is a noble endeavor. No, they avoid lying because of the difficulty of maintaining the pretense. When people lie, they very often have to cover up the act with additional and more complex lies; and ensuring that the charade doesn't fall apart is exhausting work. If they could do so with ease, people would always lie when it gained them some immediate advantage.

While the Doctor probably wouldn't subscribe to this theory wholesale, he has lied and deceived others on many occasions when he felt it necessary. Consider that at a certain point during his travels, the Doctor realized that the real Amy had been duplicated by his enemies (Madame Kovarian, it turns out) and replaced with a "ganger" made from the Flesh, and yet he failed to share this knowledge with Rory ("The Almost People," 2011). Knowing that the Amy traveling on the TARDIS wasn't real while failing to inform Rory was surely a deception. For Nietzsche, the Doctor's decision was ethically neutral, because he didn't restrict Rory's knowledge out of insensitivity to Rory's interests. Rather, the Doctor needed to know more about the Silence before taking action, which he subsequently did with gusto at Demon's Run ("A Good Man Goes to War," 2011).

Experience Makes Liars of Us All

Perhaps lying and deception are inevitable in the Whoniverse. Often, both sides in a conflict employ these tactics, and we're never surprised when the Master or a Dalek lies to those around them. The Doctor, in turn, does what he needs to do to survive, and to defeat various galactic threats. No one doubts the Doctor loves to save the underdog, and particularly humanity. And given the challenges of his existence, the Doctor has learned that in order to save people and right wrongs, lying is sometimes necessary. Perhaps Professor Palmer was right to say that experience makes liars of us all ("Hide"). No matter which ethical theory we choose to apply to the Doctor, he always tries to do what, in his mind, is the right thing. Hence, Rule #1: the Doctor lies.

Does this excuse doing bad things for good reasons? Are the Doctor's lies morally excusable? Perhaps, and perhaps not. It's certainly the case that lying, in and of itself, isn't an admirable act. But we've also seen that some lies are morally acceptable, or at least justifiable, because of the good that they do. Ultimately, when the Doctor lies, he does so to help others.

Indeed, in understanding *why* beings (human or otherwise) lie or deceive in *Doctor Who*, we can understand the essence of what it means to be the Doctor—sometimes the hero lies, and for this, we ought to be grateful.

16
Divine Hatred—Dalek Beauty

COLE BOWMAN

The Doctor has no greater enemy than the Daleks. Malicious biological machines, the Daleks have spent nearly all of eternity at odds with the Doctor, exterminating anything that stands in their way to achieve total domination of the universe.

First appearing during the original Doctor's reign, they've been encountered by each and every one of his regenerations. While the Doctor has always been challenged by their appearances throughout the history of time, perhaps his most surprising encounter with them happened during his Eleventh iteration. In the seventh season of the series reboot, the Doctor was confronted not by Dalek armies or their psychological warfare. Rather, he was faced with the idea of what Daleks find beautiful.

In "Asylum of the Daleks" (2012), the Doctor is confronted with the concept of Dalek beauty in the form of the broken, battle-scarred, and insane Daleks who have been housed on their asylum planet. The Daleks have refused to exterminate these specimens because to do so would be to destroy "divine hatred," effectively offending their concept of beauty. While the Doctor is taken aback by the idea that the Daleks could find hatred beautiful, it isn't an unreasonable perspective for the Daleks to have given their conceptual scheme.

How is it that the Daleks might find something like hatred beautiful? Even further, how can they consider that very thing divine? Are divinity and hatred even capable of being in the same discussion?

A Concept of Beauty

To truly understand the Dalek asylum, we must first understand beauty itself. Perhaps one of the greatest quandaries in respect to beauty is whether or not it really *exists*. Is anything inherently real about beauty? Is beauty objective or subjective? Is beauty derived from some physical trait or quality, or is it simply in the mind of the person perceiving it? Or, is beauty a quality in and of itself? Are things beautiful if there's no observer to evaluate them? How can there be a consensus of what's beautiful if there's no objective value to agree upon? While these questions might seem easy to at first, the more you consider them, the more philosophical weight they carry. These are *just a few* of the questions that have plagued philosophers who have sought to reconcile the nature of beauty and there are many, many more.

Philosophers have debated for generations whether or not it's some inherent trait within a thing that makes it beautiful. Starting with Plato, a strong tradition of this *objective* beauty was established in classical philosophy, wherein things were believed to be beautiful because of immutable principles contained within them. This classical model of beauty states that these principles give us a pleasurable experience and we understand that pleasure as beauty. Music, art, food, and all manner of other thing were considered the same way. Jammie Dodgers are delicious and we perceive them as such. This objective perspective on beauty led to a great deal of effort on the part of philosophers looking for the underlying principles of beauty, with some brilliant results. Mathematical and artistic relations are the perfect example of this way of thinking, as we see in Da Vinci's *Vitruvian Man*.

Later, thinkers began to consider the *subjective* concept of beauty more and more seriously. According to subjective aesthetics, there's no such thing as a specific quality from which beauty is derived, but rather it's all a construct of the mind. We perceive Jammie Dodgers to be delicious, so they are.

But neither of these explanations of beauty are quite satisfactory, especially for later philosophers. Some of the most comprehensive contemplation of this topic came from Enlightenment philosophers David Hume (1711–1776) and Immanuel Kant (1724–1804). Though they differed on many things, Hume and Kant were in near agreement on the nature of beauty. The phrase "Antinomy of Beauty" came from this era's thinkers, and its usage has had a profound impact upon the perspectives of aesthetics that have since followed.

So, what's the "Antinomy of Beauty" and why is it so important? An "antinomy" is an irresolvable contradiction inherent in a single concept. To Kant and Hume, the very idea of beauty is an antinomy. It's both subjective and objective at once, though to varying degrees in different situations. While both would ultimately argue for the apparent subjectivity of beauty, neither could completely exterminate the idea that there was some objective quality to beauty itself.

Divine Hatred

While the Daleks use the terms "divine" and "beauty" as though they're inextricably interrelated, there's no such necessary correlation. What is it that connects these two concepts within the Dalek Prime Minister's mind? Philosophers have considered the possible link between divinity and beauty since Plato, and have used both as a tool to explore the other more fully. Beauty has been a way to understand that which a philosopher considers divine, and vice versa.

Is something divine because it's beautiful or is something beautiful because it's divine? It's an aesthetic version of the old chicken-and-egg problem. One of the founding fathers of philosophical thought, Plato of Athens offers a very clear-cut vision of how we might find divinity in a concept even as malignant as hatred. The cornerstone of Plato's teachings was what's called the Theory of the Forms, which asserts that all of existence as we know it is a mere reflection of a rarified, perfect version of existence that abides in abstraction. Everything that exists from bowties to solar systems is a derivative of a more perfect version of itself that's all but unattainable.

The Form of a thing is the immutable essence of that thing. It's the very idea that makes that thing's existence possible. According to Plato, the more closely a thing represents its Form, the more we should consider it worthy or beautiful. Beauty is a natural byproduct of a thing's relation to its abstract Form. The thing in question is in harmony with the Form that it's attempting to represent. So for him, anything that's beautiful is objectively so because of its apparent connection to the divine.

So, the most beautiful (and coolest) of bowties would be the bowtie that most accurately represents the very idea of bowties. Beauty is derived from a bowtie's closeness to the Form of Bowtie. So, first, the Form of Bowtie is divine, then bowties are beautiful. Similarly, acts of hatred are considered beautiful by the Daleks as they represent the Form of Hatred itself. Anything that exhibits hatred, therefore, can be considered beautiful by the Daleks—even the Doctor.

The contrary belief was held quite firmly by much later philosophers, such as Friedrich Nietzsche (1844–1900) and Arthur Schopenhauer (1788–1824). Both thinkers, while the intellectual descendants of Plato, differed quite distinctly from the early Greeks. For them and many other philosophers of the same generation, something was first beautiful *then* became divine to its observer. An object, say a painting, became an important piece of divinity if and only if it was first beautiful and imbued with value by its observer. The important difference between these two perspectives is at the very heart of objective-subjective struggle.

A useful example of this can be seen actively throughout the world's religions. Holy relics are considered sacred representations of divine principles and they're often associated with great beauty. Take specifically the *Pietà* by Michelangelo. Probably one of the most recognizable pieces of sculpture, it depicts Mary and Jesus of Nazareth after Jesus's execution. It's considered by some to be one of the most important scenes in all of the Christian story, and the sculpture that depicts it was crafted by one of the greatest sculptors ever to have lived. Therefore, it's both divine and beautiful. So, is it beautiful because it depicts the divinity expressed by its association with an extremely popular religious view or is it divine because its beauty is the result of a master craftsman unparalleled in his time? Well, it's kind of both. It all really comes down to your perspective, according to Nietzsche, which he expounds upon in his work *Human, All Too Human*. In this work, he relates the metaphysical joy that we derive from beautiful art to a religious experience. From this, he explains that the apparent paradox comes from the kinship between the two feelings of metaphysical and religious joy. So how does such a linkage work?

Say, for instance, you are a Christian and you hold to the opinion that all representations of Christ are sacred. The *Pietà* in its representation of Christ after the crucifixion is, therefore, divine in your eyes. Then again, so is the depiction of Jesus on a bumper sticker; and also the supposed manifestation of his visage in a piece of toast. Regardless of the level of craftsmanship behind the appearance of the Son of God, you see it as divine. In this way of looking at it, the beauty that you find within a work is a *direct result* of its association with your religion. Beauty is thus derived from divinity. If we apply the same mechanism as Plato did, it's obvious that the less accurate depiction of the divine, the toast, is significantly less beautiful than the masterwork *Pietà*.

On the other side of the coin, let's say that you aren't religious. Rather, you simply appreciate art and you've found that beauty has an inspiring effect upon your mood. For you, the beauty of a thing can lead to something akin to a transcendent experience, be it a movie or a painting or any other representative piece of artwork. The *Pietà*, therefore, acquires something akin to divinity from the excellence of its own beauty. That it's the masterwork of an artist with very few peers imbues it with a value that can't be measured. Because of this, you find inherently more beauty than you might if the same scene were made by a less skilled craftsman, and yet a work of equal skill depicting any other scene would have the same effect.

What's important in both of these concepts is the relation that they imply between an object and the observer of that object. The observer is the most integral part in the connection between the beauty of a thing and the divine according to Nietzsche. An association between them can't be made if there's not an agent to make the association. Because hatred has such an important role in the way that the Daleks relate to their reality, they associate it with a transcendent experience. Were the Daleks to have some sort of religion, it would involve a great deal of hatred, especially when we consider how shallow their range of emotions actually is. A "Dalek god" would harness hatred as a weapon and use it to exterminate any non-Dalek in the universe. And that which most beautifully resembles absolute hatred could become almost godlike to them. So it doesn't really matter whether the Daleks have ascribed divinity to hatred for its function in their lives or if they've made it a function of their lives because of its divinity. Kant would argue that it's the mere fact that they *do* value it that's important.

But Hello Again

One argument against the Dalek vision of beauty comes from the concept of *disinterested* appreciation of beauty. Both Hume and Kant touch upon this in their discussions of beauty as an integral quality of the "Judgment of Taste." This Judgment is Kant's criterion for effectively evaluating beauty *outside* of the subjective experience. In his *Critique of Judgment*, Kant writes:

> Now, when the question is whether something is beautiful, we do not want to know whether anything depends or can depend on the existence of the thing . . . We easily see that, in saying it is *beautiful*, and in showing that I have taste, I am concerned, not with that in which I depend on the existence of the object, but with that which I make out of this representation in myself. (p. 28)

Kant is saying here that the recognition of beauty must be independent of that thing's function in our lives. A thing can't be truly appreciated for beauty if we only look at what it can do for us, or how we depend on it. Beauty, therefore, must be independent of our own motives.

How do these motives work, exactly? Let's look at an example: Rory believes that Amy is the most beautiful woman in the world. More specifically, he's madly in love with her *and* he thinks that she's beautiful. While their romance is a wonderful thing, does Rory's love really show us an accurate perception of Amy's beauty? Not really, if you're to believe Kant. According to Kant, Rory is unable to see Amy for her beauty alone. Because he loves her, because he's invested in her well-being, his appreciation of her beauty is effectively skewed. That is, he "depends" on her (as Kant would put it), so he can't accurately assess her beauty. He's too wrapped up in her.

This sort of thing happens in reverse as well. In "The Girl Who Waited" (2011) Amy memorably says, "Rory is the most beautiful man I have ever met." She emphasizes this sort of appreciation several times throughout the series. But, she falls to the very same problem that Rory does in his appraisals of her: she's too invested in him to make an impartial judgment of taste. She has a vested interest in him as a romantic partner and, therefore, can't accurately evaluate his beauty. She's unable to remove her subjective motives from her evaluations of him.

However, this doesn't mean that Amy and Rory aren't beautiful. Just because Amy is too close to Rory to *objectively* estimate his attractiveness, doesn't mean that there's nothing there for her to be appreciative of in the first place. But, Amy isn't the only one who considers Rory beautiful. Perhaps most notably, the TARDIS "herself" thinks that he's pretty. In "The Doctor's Wife" (2011), the TARDIS is planted into the body of a woman and is able to express herself as a result of this implantation. While she shows very little interest in the companions, she refers to Rory as "pretty," even going so far as to make that his unofficial title when they're speaking together. The fact that the TARDIS refers to Rory as "pretty" implies that maybe not all of what Amy sees in him is entirely subjective. This is where the aforementioned antinomy comes from. If both Amy and the TARDIS agree that Rory is beautiful, maybe there's something there other than just what Amy's dependence on him suggests. Maybe there *is* an objective quality that both of them are responding to.

Here Kant offers us the idea of an "agreement of taste." Kant argued that there is a necessary universalization in the judgment of taste that would lead to an agreement in different people's preferences. Kant asserts that since the people who experience a beautiful thing must necessarily experience much of the same situations leading up to the recognition of this beauty there's a necessary agreement of their taste. Two individuals from a similar background with similar experiences will come to much the same aesthetic evaluation. The fact that both Amy and the TARDIS are familiar with human standards of beauty informs them of the quotient of beauty that Rory holds. Despite their unequal investment in the young nurse, they're both familiar with the human aesthetic traits that make up Rory's beauty.

Humans, Daleks, Time Lords and all manner of other alien races each have their own conceptual framework which has been derived from their mutual experiences and biology. For example, Sontarans have a significantly different conceptual framework from humans. Where Strax, the Doctor's reluctant Sontaran ally, is ashamed of his work as a nurse, Rory the human is quite proud of doing the same work. Where one culture considers it a miserable fate, another values it highly. Both of these opinions have been determined predominantly by their cultures, but are ingrained in their conceptual schemes. While each species' framework is unique, with individuals having varied schemes within them, they have a number of shared points with the other species that populate the universe by which they are able to identify. Both Sontarans and humans *have* nurses, but their perspectives on them differ greatly.

The conceptual framework goes well beyond just simple perspective, though. Think of it more like the deep structures of your brain at work, subtly informing everything that you're able to know. So when you consider something beautiful, you're referring to various points on your conceptual framework that help to identify the qualities that imbue it with beauty. Your judgment of taste is part of your conceptual framework for beauty, and it informs every potential aesthetic decision that you make. Because the TARDIS and Amy have a few shared, overlapping points on their own conceptual frameworks—like ideas about human form—they come to a similar conclusion about Rory's prettiness.

Given the Daleks' hive mind, the Dalek conceptual framework doesn't just have a few shared points. Rather, they share an entire conceptual framework. Because of this shared conceptual framework, beauty isn't in the eyestalk of a particular Dalek beholder—see Clive Cazeaux in *Doctor Who and Philosophy: Bigger on the Inside*. In other words, it's not individually subjective. Instead, their idea of beauty is shared throughout their entire species. So when one Dalek thinks that something is beautiful, they all do.

Subtract Love, Add Anger

To really get to the heart of the question about Dalek beauty, we must turn back to Kant. While his works are a cornerstone in the foundation of modern aesthetic theories, what's most important about his concept of beauty for our discussion is his well-known claim that "Beauty is a symbol of morality." Applying this to the Dalek way of interpreting the world, understanding what they take to be beautiful shows us their moral values, because beauty signifies value. Therefore, by understanding their concept of beauty, we'll be able understand their moral underpinnings.

If Kant is correct that beauty is, in fact, an indicator of morality within a system, then it follows that the Daleks value hatred in such a profound way that they've created an entire planet-sized asylum to preserve it. The Asylum itself represents a massive undertaking for the Dalek species, the likes of which are almost unparalleled. Except, of course, for the Library that the Tenth Doctor encounters. It's a tad eerie to think about it in this way, but the Library and the Asylum are more similar than they may seem at first. Both the Library and the Asylum exist for the sole sake of preservation. For the Library, its books and life records offer pieces of knowledge. For the Asylum, it's the broken down Daleks, all of whom represent the beauty found in hatred. The Asylum is a museum.

What, exactly, is so threatening to the Daleks, then, that they're willing to destroy their own museum of hatred? So threatening, that they're willing to ask their greatest nemesis for assistance in order to achieve that destruction? So threatening, that they fear the destruction of their entire way of life? Why, a girl from London, of course. Her presence threatens their entire conceptual framework.

Clara Oswald is something of an enigma in this outfit. While the events at Trenzalore ("The Name of the Doctor," 2013) have elucidated the circumstances that ultimately led to Clara's imprisonment within the Asylum, the problem isn't how she got there, but why she's been allowed to stay. In fact, her place within the Asylum is one of utmost security, where she can be held captive and contained, perpetually under watch by the system that runs the little planet. As far as the Asylum hierarchy is organized, Clara is located in something of a place of honor. While other Daleks, damaged by wars and driven insane are left to wander through the hallways of the broken down Asylum, Clara is under maximum security. So what's so different about her? Well, she's human on the inside.

In the very same episode, there's another human-Dalek hybrid that provides an interesting counterpoint to Clara's role. The woman at the beginning of the episode who was used as a lure to catch the Doctor, Darla, is human on the outside and Dalek within. While both of them are inverse versions of the same part-human, part-Dalek setup, they're treated entirely differently by the Dalek majority. Darla, while still physically human shaped, is accepted as a Dalek, even though she's seen as an insignificant member of their masses. While ostracized, Dalek Clara is held above the rest of the "beautiful" Daleks in the Asylum in a way that suggests she's a more significant part of the Asylum itself.

But wait, there's more. During their conversation, the Dalek Prime Minister openly insults the Doctor when the Time Lord expresses his disgust about the Dalek appreciation for hatred. The Doctor says: "I thought you'd run out of ways to make me sick. But hello again. You think hatred is beautiful?" To which, the Dalek PM responds: "Perhaps that is why we have not been able to kill you." *Ouch*. This dialogue goes deeper into the psyche of the old Gallifreyan than it might seem at first. For the Doctor, there's no more despicable way of life than that of the Daleks, so to be associated with that which they revere, it's more than just hurtful. It's insulting at the deepest of levels.

What comes from both of these situations is an eerie understanding of what the Daleks hold important. Hatred is so beautiful to them that it has become sacred in the Dalek conceptual scheme. The Dalek scheme shares hatred as a point of reference with both humanity and the Time Lords. While their exact perspective on hatred is quite different than the latter two life forms, they're able to recognize beauty in both the Doctor and Clara as they share this mutual point within their conceptual framework. And perhaps this is why it's so very disgusting to the Doctor that the Daleks have a concept of beauty. The shared experiences that they have on their own schemes allow for him to glimpse into their minds in a way that twists his very perspective into something Dalek. And perhaps this is why the Daleks have detained Clara in the way that they have: Because she allows them to glimpse into the human perspective of hatred, which is both beautiful and terrifying to them.

In the great arch of philosophy, it turns out that beauty is rather subjective. Depending on which way your philosophical bent leans, you may view it as an integral part of the universe—as did Plato—or you might view it entirely derived from the nuances of your own experience—as did Kant. Beauty is, therefore, something of a reflection of our conceptual framework. It's the ghost in the machine of our minds. Perhaps it's appropriate then that this faculty also exists within the Daleks. Though their conceptual framework for that which is beautiful is entirely different than a human's, they're still able to express some kind of beauty—as hatred.

The Doctor and the Daleks both have a concept of beauty. Like in all things about the old enemies, their perspectives will likely never be reconciled. What matters is that hatred has become important enough to the Daleks that their very identity is based on it. Hatred drives them, challenges them to persist in their mission and even terrifies them. Whether or not it's a quality that's inherently a part of the Dalek being or is cultivated through their culture, its importance to them is unquestionable. Hatred has transcended the boundaries of other Dalek experiences and remains singularly important to them in a way that nothing else has. To the Daleks, it's an aesthetic, something that moves them. It's no wonder, then, that the Daleks consider it divine.

17
The Friends of a Time Lord

GREG LITTMANN

Have you met Miss Smith? She's my best friend.

—TOM BAKER DOCTOR, "The Seeds of Doom," 1976

How would you like to be the Doctor's friend and companion? You'd have the entire universe at your feet, from the Big Bang that starts it all to the Big Freeze when all the stars go out; from the verdant forests of the planet Vortis where the spectacular Menoptera moth-people fly, to the caverns far beneath our Earth where the reptilian Silurians build their colossal cities of stone.

As River Song puts it in "Silence in the Library" (2008): "The Doctor in the TARDIS. Next stop everywhere." Who wouldn't want a friend who could offer so much? How many kids—and perhaps adults!—have looked to the sky and thought, "Come get me, Doctor!" But what would the Doctor want with the likes of you?

One of the few constants in the Doctor's personality throughout his regenerations is his need for friends. In more than fifty years of adventuring, the Doctor has only had nine televised adventures without a regular companion. It's true, the Doctor doesn't always recognize his need for friends. In fact, in the Classic Series, companions rarely start traveling with the Doctor out of feelings of friendship. More typically, companions are:

Kidnapped: Barbara, Ian, Dodo, and Harry

Refugees: Vicki, Steven, Katarina, Jamie, Nyssa, Turlough, Kameleon, and Ace

Accidental stowaways: Polly, Ben, Sarah, and Tegan

Deliberate stowaways: Zoe, Leela, and Adric

Simply entrusted to the Doctor: Victoria, Jo, K-9, and Romana

All the same, the Doctor makes friends out of most of his companions in the end. Sarah, for example, becomes an accidental traveler after she goes snooping in the TARDIS in "The Time Warrior" (1973), but the Jon Pertwee and Tom Baker Doctors keep her on afterwards, despite innumerable opportunities to leave her back on Earth.

The Doctor repairs the TARDIS navigational system in time for the New Series, allowing him to travel more or less where he likes. Gone are those staples of the Classic Series, unwilling or uninvited companions. If a traveler just wants to go home, like Barbara and Ian, or wasn't invited onto the TARDIS in the first place, like Leela and Tegan, the Doctor can easily drop them off. In the New Series, companions are almost always willing travelers who were invited by the Doctor. Rose, Jack, Martha, Donna, Amy, River, and Clara were all people whom the Doctor chose to travel with because he thought they'd make good friends.

Why does the Doctor need friends and what sort of friends should he have? This isn't just idle speculation. What we say in the case of the Doctor will have implications for how we answer these questions in our own case. Do we need friends and what sort of friends should we have? *Doctor Who* is a particularly useful resource from which to draw examples of friendship, since the Doctor has had so many friends over the centuries.

The most influential account of friendship ever is that offered by the Greek philosopher Aristotle (384–322 B.C.E.) in his *Nicomachean Ethics*. A brilliant generalist like the Doctor, Aristotle wrote seminal works on morality, politics, art, and science, and is the single most influential figure in Western philosophy. Aristotle tried to work out how life can be lived well. He saw having friends as essential for a good life and for happiness, claiming that nobody would bother staying alive without friends, even if they had everything else that's good. Aristotle believed that there are three types of friendship: friendship founded on pleasure, friendship founded on usefulness, and friendship founded on mutual goodness. He thought that we should strive for friendship founded on mutual goodness, regarding the other sorts of friendship as inferior.

Fun in Time and Space

Oh, come on! They're boarding now! It's no fun if I see it on my own.

—DAVID TENNANT DOCTOR, "Midnight," 2008

A friendship founded on pleasure is based on the enjoyment each friend gets from the other's company. Is this the sort of friendship the Doctor engages in? There's no doubt that, at least some of the time, the Doctor gets pleasure from the company of his companions. The original William Hartnell Doctor explores alien worlds with a sense of glee, and the presence of his friends only makes him enjoy himself more. The way he laughs and smiles as he explains the wonders of Vortis to Ian ("The Web Planet," 1965) makes clear how much having Ian there contributes to the fun. The pleasure of joint adventure is exhibited, at least sometimes, by all of the Doctors who were to follow.

The warm Patrick Troughton Doctor even introduced the idea that the Doctor and companions might engage in recreation together. In "The Enemy of the World" (1967), he plunges into the ocean for a swim and calls Jamie and Victoria to join him. The Pertwee Doctor upped the ante by conducting TARDIS flights specifically to show his companions something wonderful, inviting Jo and Sarah on tourist trips to see beautiful worlds like the blue Metebelis 3 and the fragrant Florana. Likewise, the Tom Baker Doctor takes Romana to the beach at Brighton in "The Leisure Hive" (1980), the Peter Davison Doctor drops by the Eye of Orion for a break with Tegan and Turlough in "The Five Doctors" (1983), the Colin Baker Doctor goes fishing for gumblejacks with Peri in "The Two Doctors" (1985), and the Sylvester McCoy Doctor goes to the psychic circus with Ace in "The Greatest Show in the Galaxy" (1988).

Understandably, given the Doctor's new tendency to choose his associates in the New Series, the pleasure he gains from his companions has been even more explicit. Having acquired Rose in "Rose" (2005), the Christopher Eccleston Doctor immediately becomes her enthusiastic tour guide, taking her to see the far future in "The End of the World" (2005) and the nineteenth century in "The Unquiet Dead" (2005). The David Tennant Doctor retains his role as tour guide and even takes Donna to the leisure planet "Midnight," to share with her the sapphire waterfalls and diamond deserts, begging her to join him on a tour. The Matt Smith Doctor takes the same delight in his crew. In "The Rings of Akhaten" (2013), the Doctor is enjoying introducing Clara to an alien world so much that he jubilantly shouts out to her the names of the various species they pass in the street. He explains to Amy in the minisode "Meanwhile in the TARDIS 2" (2010) that he took her onboard in the first place because seeing familiar sights through the eyes of his human friends allows him to enjoy them afresh: "You make all of space and time your backyard and what do you have? A backyard. But you, you can see it. And when you see it, I see it." The Peter Capaldi Doctor enjoys sightseeing with Clara so much that he becomes a positive pest, badgering her at home in "Time Heist" (2014), insisting "The Satanic Nebula. Or the Lagoon of Lost Stars. Or we could go to Brighton. I've got a whole day worked out!"

Someone to Hold Test Tubes, Make the Tea, and Save the World

Doctor, you take ordinary people and you fashion them into weapons.

—Davros, "Journey's End," 2008

Or perhaps the Doctor founds his friendships not on pleasure but on usefulness. Aristotle explains that such friendships are based on what the friends can do for each other. The Doctor can offer all of space and time, but companions can be very useful too. For the elderly Hartnell Doctor, Ian fills the role of action hero, taking on the jobs that require more brawn than brain, such as when he defeats the Aztec champion Ixta in single combat in "The Aztecs" (1964). The Doctor would continue to use companions as convenient heavies with Jamie, Leela, K-9, Ace, and the gun-wielding River Song. The skills the companions bring to the table go far beyond being able to outwrestle an occasional Aztec or take out the odd Sontaran with a thrown knife to the probic vent, as Leela does in "The Invasion of Time" (1978). Jo is an escapologist, Harry, Martha, and Rory bring medical skills, Adric has achieved "mathematical excellence," and River Song is able to fly the TARDIS. Zoe, Liz, K-9 and Romana are even brilliant scientific generalists, like the Doctor.

Yet the companions bring more than a skill set. They are, at least some of the time, clever, resourceful, and independent, and they frequently get to save the day on their own initiative. If Barbara hadn't decided to start a revolt against the Daleks by impersonating a Dalek official over the radio in "The Dalek Invasion of Earth" (1964), then humanity would've had it. We'd have had it again if Polly hadn't weaponized nail varnish remover for use against Cybermen in "The Moonbase" (1967), or if journalist Sarah hadn't gone investigating the nefarious National Institute for Advanced Scientific Research in "Robot" (1974), or if the companion hadn't come through to save us all on countless other occasions. In "Ghost Light" (1989), the McCoy Doctor even lets Ace tackle the mystery of a haunted house by herself as an "initiative test," recognizing that he needs his friends to be able to solve problems for him.

The companions of the New Series are even more likely to save the day. The Eccleston Doctor takes Rose aboard in "Rose" after she saves his life and the Earth by swinging through the air on a chain and kicking some anti-plastic into a Nestene Consciousness. Likewise, Martha is invited for her first trip on the TARDIS after saving the Tennant Doctor's life by improvising a medical treatment for aliens in "Smith and Jones" (2007), and proves so handy on subsequent adventures that he makes her a fulltime companion in "The Lazarus Experiment" (2007). Donna is invited onto the TARDIS in "The Runaway Bride" (2006) after helping the Doctor fight the spidery Racnoss, and saving his life by reminding him to run from the angry queen. Amy is on the point of being thrown off the TARDIS by the Smith Doctor in "The Beast Below" (2010), before she redeems herself by coming up with a plan that would save both the *Starship UK* and the oppressed Star Whale who serves as the ship's engines. As for Clara, she's not content with saving her Doctors alone: she saves the lot of them, again and again, in a variety of different incarnations, as revealed in "The Name of the Doctor" (2013). Even the Daleks know that the Doctor needs his friends in order to triumph.

When they send the Smith Doctor on a mission in "Asylum of the Daleks" (2012), they send Amy and Rory with him, explaining, "It is known that the Doctor requires companions."

Aristotle claims in his *Nicomachean Ethics* that friendships based on pleasure or usefulness tend not to last long. He writes: "these friendships are only incidental; for it is not as being the man he is that the loved person is loved, but as providing some good or pleasure. Such friendships, then, are easily dissolved, if the parties do not remain like themselves; for if the one party is no longer pleasant or useful the other ceases to love him" (Book VIII, lines 1156a17–21).

Perhaps this describes the Doctor's friendships, which tend to be very short-lived. The need to accommodate an ever-changing cast means that the Doctor's relationships usually last one to three years. Sometimes, companions leave because they want to go home and back to their old life and friends (Barbara, Ian, Dodo, Polly, Ben, Harry, Tegan, Turlough, Martha, Amy, Rory). Sometimes, they form new romantic relationships on their adventures that they care about more than their relationship with the Doctor (Vicki, Jo, Leela), or are driven by compassion to stay behind on an alien world to help out (Steven, Romana, Nyssa).

It's hard to imagine someone wanting to leave the TARDIS, a problem that the Classic Series sometimes solved just by having the Doctor dump or abandon his companions (Susan, Jamie, Zoe, Sarah, Peri), or even lose them to violent deaths (Katarina—*whoosh!* and Adric—*boom!*). The New Series tends to solve the problem by having the companions barred from rejoining the Doctor for weird sci-fi reasons that he can't do anything about (Rose, Jack, Donna, Amy, Rory). Once he's parted from a companion, the Doctor doesn't even stay in touch. When Sarah meets the Tennant Doctor in "School Reunion" (2006) it's the first contact she's had with the Doctor since the Tom Baker Doctor dumped her in "The Hand of Fear" (1976). ("School Reunion" ignores the events of "The Five Doctors," so we will too.) Even the Doctor's own granddaughter, Susan, who he unceremoniously ditched against her will on a ruined twenty-second century Earth in "The Dalek Invasion of Earth," is barely mentioned again, and never visited. If Amy is right in "Amy's Choice" (2010) when she claims that "Friends are people you keep in touch with," the Doctor's friendships end at the TARDIS doors.

The Company of Heroes

Amy: But why didn't it feed on us, too?

Matt Smith Doctor: On the darkness in you pair? It would have starved to death in an instant. I choose my friends with great care.

—"Amy's Choice," 2010

The best kind of friendship, in Aristotle's view, is one based on mutual goodness. In this kind of friendship, people are friends because they each love whatever's good and their friend is good. Not only are good people the most pleasant to be around for someone who loves goodness, but only within a friendship based on goodness can there be the trust required for friends to be able to help one another well. More important than our friends' ability to help us, though, is our ability to help our friends. For Aristotle, the most important thing in life is being good. Having friends that we can help gives us special opportunities to be good. He wrote:

> To confer benefits is characteristic of the good man and of virtue, and it is nobler to do well by friends than by strangers. (*Nicomachean Ethics*, Book IX, lines 1169b10–13)

Are the relationships between the Doctor and his companions founded on the mutual love of goodness? The Doctor is certainly a very good chap. Even though his New Series regenerations sometimes suffer from guilt, he remains a quintessential hero. He can't stumble across an evil on his travels without intervening to put things right, even if he has to overthrow a government to do it. As Clara reminds the Capaldi Doctor in "Robot of Sherwood" (2014), "You stop bad things happening every minute of the day." From 1979 to 1983, the Doctor even occasionally received the backing of the White Guardian, the personification of the force of good—as symbolized by the stuffed dove he sometimes wears on his head, a fashion choice that makes a stick of celery in the lapel look restrained. The companions, like the Doctor, are also generally heroic individuals who'll risk their lives to save strangers. They help the Doctor in every righteous battle he fights.

However, Aristotle insists that relationships based on mutual goodness will be long-lasting, since someone who's good is liable to remain good, and so what their friend loves about them won't change. That doesn't sound much like the Doctor's brief relationships. Aristotle also thinks that relationships based on goodness take a long time to form, since to appreciate someone's character requires getting to know them well. This also doesn't sound much like the Doctor's relationships, not just because they're brief, but because he doesn't let his companions get to know him well. In fact, his companions know almost nothing about him—not his history, not his family relationships, not even his *name!* Aristotle would probably rule that the Doctor and his companions can't have the right kind of friendship because the companions have no idea who he is. In Aristotle's eyes, the need to know your friends well also rules out the possibility of having many good friends. You just can't know a lot of people well enough, though this is less of an issue for millennia-old Time Lords.

Aristotle believes that a "perfect friendship" of this moral sort is a friendship between equals. The friends should, ideally, be equals in station, intellect, education, and morality. Once again, this doesn't sound like the Doctor's relationships. It isn't clear exactly how to rate the Doctor's social station. He's been everything from Lord President of Gallifrey to an intergalactic hobo. Still, given the way that he relates to powerful rulers like Davros, Rassilon, and Richard Nixon, he should rank as a king at least, if not a god—and Aristotle specifically notes that a human could never be friends with a god. The Doctor's companions, on the other hand, are more often than not from the working and middle classes. Aristotle wouldn't be able to understand why a Time Lord would hang out with a mere shop attendant like Rose or kiss-o-gram like Amy.

Even greater than the difference in station between the Doctor and his companions are their usual differences in intellect and education. To call the Doctor "brilliant" is like calling the Master "a bit naughty." He easily outclasses any human being who has ever lived. Likewise, to call the Doctor "well-educated" is like calling the Daleks "unfriendly." The writers can and do have him know pretty much anything. Not only has he mastered every field of science, but you can land him on a random planet among the three hundred billion or so in our galaxy alone, and the chances are that he can recognize the world on sight and recount its history.

Even Romana, a fellow Time Lord, can barely compete with his cleverness.

Aristotle does allow that an inferior sort of friendship based on moral goodness could hold between non-equals. Such a friendship could even be morally beneficial for the friend who's inferior in understanding, since they'll have the opportunity to learn from the friend who is wiser. Aristotle could certainly appreciate the way that the genius Doctor has so often served as a moral authority for his companions. Most obviously, the Doctor helps them to understand the moral duties of time travelers. Barbara criticizes the Hartnell Doctor for failing to interfere in Aztec sacrifice in "The Aztecs," Steven criticizes him for not saving the French Huguenot protestants from slaughter in "The Massacre of St. Bartholemew's Eve" (1966), and Donna criticizes the Tennant Doctor for not saving the citizens of Pompeii in "The Fires of Pompeii" (2008). However, they do so out of ignorance.

The Hartnell Doctor clarifies matters in "The Aztecs" when he explains that "you can't rewrite history. Not one line!"—a restriction that's later replaced with the limitation that the Doctor can't interfere in certain "fixed points" in time. The Doctor's moral advice goes far beyond the field of time-travel ethics. For example, the Pertwee Doctor scolds the Brigadier for his genocide against the Silurians in "Doctor Who and the Silurians" (1970), while the Tom Baker Doctor tries to wean Leela from unnecessary murder, the Colin Baker Doctor tries to wean Peri from eating meat, and the McCoy Doctor tries to wean Ace from the casual use of explosives.

In the New Series, the Doctor has been even more eager to improve his companions morally. "It's a different morality. Get used to it or go home" the Eccleston Doctor instructs Rose in "The Unquiet Dead," when she places the sanctity of human corpses over saving the lives of the vaporous Gelth who need them. In "The Parting of the Ways" (2005), Rose states: "The Doctor showed me a better way of living your life . . . You have the guts to do what's right when everyone else just runs away . . ." Donna undergoes a transformation with the Tennant Doctor, going from a selfish jerk when we first see her in "The Runaway Bride" to someone who genuinely cares about strangers. The Smith Doctor teaches Amy not to be prejudiced against artificial life in "The Almost People" (2011), and by showing a good example, manages to transform River Song from an amoral assassin into a heroine who'll give up her remaining regenerations to save his life in "Let's Kill Hitler" (2011). Given time, the Capaldi Doctor might even teach Clara not to hit her friends when they say something she doesn't like (a moral duty mastered by most precocious five-year-olds).

Giving the Doctor a Taste of His Own Medicine

My friends have always been the best of me.

—Matt Smith Doctor, "The Wedding of River Song," 2011

While Aristotle would understand why the Doctor would try to morally improve his companions, he wouldn't understand why the Doctor would allow his companions to attempt to improve *his* moral behavior in return. In the first *Doctor Who* adventure, "An Unearthly Child" (1963), a horrified Ian prevents the Hartnell Doctor from killing a helpless caveman with a rock. Not long after, in "The Edge of Destruction" (1964), Barbara gives the Doctor a dressing down for his ingratitude towards his companions after the help they'd given him, snapping, "You ought to go down on your hands and knees and thank us. But gratitude's the last thing you'll ever have, or any sort of common sense either." This is a Doctor who sometimes needs to be reminded of his moral duties by his friends.

The idea of the companions being moral advisors of the Doctor mostly disappears from the Classic Series after the early Hartnell episodes. The Doctor is simply too *good* to require moral advice. However, the theme of companion as moral critic returns with a vengeance in the New Series, as the show seeks to give the companion a more proactive role. For instance, in "Dalek" (2005), the Eccleston Doctor is on the verge of murdering a Dalek before Rose brings him to his senses by demanding, "What the hell are you changing into?" Donna decides in "The Runaway Bride" that the Doctor needs companions to help him resist his more callous instincts. "I think you need someone to stop you," she warns him. Donna's interpretation is backed up in "A Town Called Mercy" (2012), in which the Smith Doctor is about to force a war criminal out of town and into the hands of the cyborg who'll kill him. Amy intervenes, pointing her gun at the Doctor and telling him that "this is what happens when you travel alone for too long. Well listen to me, Doctor. We can't be like him. We have to be better than him." Moved by the swelling violins behind Amy's speech, the Doctor is convinced. Likewise, in the multi-Doctor special "The Day of the Doctor" (2013), it's Clara who reminds the three Doctors to "never give up. Never give in," and inspires them to find a solution that doesn't involve sacrificing Gallifrey.

To Aristotle's mind, the way that the Doctor has often been moved by his companions' moral advice just demonstrates how messed up their friendship really is. If the Doctor already knows so much more than they do, and especially if he knows enough about morality to be in a position to offer moral instruction to his companions, then it makes no sense for them to be offering moral instruction to *him*. The teacher should teach the student and not vice versa.

For all of these reasons, if Aristotle were given a chance to hear the story of the Doctor's friendships, perhaps as he and the Doctor share a cell in the bowels of a Dalek starship on a long flight to Skaro, he'd judge that the Doctor doesn't make the best sort of friendships. This is an important problem, he'd insist, wiping the gruel from his beard. What the Doctor needs, in his view, is someone he can spend many years with, someone in which he can confide his secrets and mysteries. Only then can the Doctor truly be loved as he should be loved—for his goodness. Aristotle would insist that the Doctor must choose as a close friend someone of excellent background, great intelligence, and upstanding moral character—and he'd be pointing both of his thumbs at himself when he said it. Then he'd add, as the Doctor climbed onto his back to examine the ceiling again, "When I think of this TARDIS of which you speak, I cannot help but be reminded of something I wrote in my *Nicomachean Ethics*: 'there is nothing so characteristic of friends as living together'" (Book VIII, lines 1157b18–19).

Should the Doctor Listen to Aristotle?

Just as long as you understand that I won't follow your orders blindly.

—WILLIAM HARTNELL DOCTOR to his companion Ian, "An Unearthly Child," 1963

That's what I think Aristotle would say to the Doctor, but would he be right? You'll have to make up your own mind, but I think Aristotle partly has it right and partly has it wrong. Aristotle is right to praise friendship based on a mutual recognition of moral goodness. He's right that good people are trustworthy and that it's useful to have friends we can trust. For example, when the Smith Doctor sends out a general call for help to his old friends in "A Good Man Goes to War" (2011), he knows that they'll come running from across time and space to help him face the headless monks.

Less convincing is Aristotle's claim that people who love goodness will find other good people pleasant. Plenty of morally upstanding people are utterly unpleasant to be around, and much less fun than many people of a shadier moral character. The Star Whale from "The Beast Below" is so kind that it volunteers to spend centuries giving the people of the UK a ride through space to a new world, but that doesn't mean that it wouldn't be a boring conversationalist, eternally mulling over stellar tides and the subtle flavors of space plankton. Fans of the Classic Series might try imagining eternally taking tea with the virtuous but staid White Guardian or Keeper of Traken.

Aristotle's suggestion that friendship based on mutual goodness is best when it's between equals is partly right. He's wrong that friends should be equal in social station. If anything, having friends of different social stations can give us important new perspectives. What might the Doctor learn from someone who has to work for a living? To be fair to Aristotle, though, such friendships can be practically difficult, even today. You can phone President Obama just to shoot the breeze as often as you like, but you'll never get him on the line. As to the importance of our friends being our equals in intelligence, Aristotle is right insofar as the cleverer and better educated we and our friends are, the more tools we'll have to determine the right way to act.

Aristotle is also right that our friends provide us with important opportunities to be good to them, and he appreciates also that kindness to friends isn't an excuse for injustice to strangers. However, Aristotle misses that there's nothing noble about treating your friends better than people you have no connection with, and he misses that the instinct to look after the in-group is more poisonous to society than mere selfishness.

Ironically, while Aristotle thinks that it's a fine thing to give preference to your friends, it's the way in which the Doctor gives such preference that's his most frequent moral failing. As noble as the Doctor is in general, in this regard, he has often been flawed. Most of us today recognize the wrongness of giving preferential treatment to people based on the fact that they're of the same ethnicity, or sex, or religion as us, but fail to notice the moral problem of discrimination in favor of our friends. Yet a consideration of the Doctor's friendships should make the problems clear.

The Doctor is always loyal to his companions when they're in danger, which is to say that he's often risked the lives of vast numbers of strangers in order to save his friends. For example, in "Genesis of the Daleks" (1975) the Tom Baker Doctor tells Davros the reasons for all future Dalek defeats, just to stop him from torturing Sarah and Harry any more. More typically, the Doctor risks lives by spending time saving his friends while the fate of a world hangs in the balance. In "Bad Wolf" (2005), the Eccleston Doctor puts off dealing with the Dalek fleet poised to exterminate humanity because Rose is aboard, and must be rescued first. The Smith Doctor even encourages Rory in "The Big Bang" (2010), when Rory weighs Amy's life against the existence of the entire universe and judges Amy more important to save. To call Rory a monster here would be an insult to the monsters of *Doctor Who*, who are generally only looking to sacrifice a planet or two to their ambitions. Danny (or at least Clara's dream-version of him) takes a similar attitude, assuring the Capaldi Doctor in "Last Christmas" (2014), "I didn't die saving the world. I died saving Clara. The rest of you just got lucky."

Even the Doctor's self-sacrifice in giving up a regeneration to save a companion, as the Davison Doctor does for Peri in "The Caves of Androzani" (1984), the Eccleston Doctor does for Rose in "The Parting of the Ways," and the Tennant Doctor does for Wilf in "The End of Time" (2009), aren't heroic acts, but selfish ones. He gets to save the people he cares about but the greatest price is paid by strangers. How many worlds will burn or be enslaved because the Doctor won't be there, having cut his life short by centuries to save Peri, Rose, and Wilf? This isn't to criticize the writers of *Doctor Who*, whose job it is to entertain us, not to present us with examples of moral perfection. Rather, the point is to note that even when we're acting out of nothing but love for our friends, we do wrong if we treat them as being more important than strangers.

Finally, Aristotle misses what's most useful about having morally good friends. It's that good friends can serve as moral advisors even if they aren't morally superior to us in general. To Aristotle's mind, in order for someone to give us useful moral criticism, they'd have to know more about morality than we do. However, this isn't how moral behavior really works. We all make moral mistakes even when we should've known better. We all allow ourselves, now and then, to be pushed by our emotions to adopt an unfair double standard or to overlook our own moral principles. Someone doesn't need to be an expert in morality to help us to see these errors. They don't even need to be morally superior to us. They just have to point out what we're overlooking because our feelings have run away with us. Consider the case in "Dalek" in which the Eccleston Doctor is about to murder the Dalek and Rose snaps him out of it by asking "What the hell are you changing into?" In real life, a conversation may have to last longer to change someone's mind, but the idea of the Doctor lowering his gun once he's reminded of his own moral principles is entirely plausible. Rose doesn't have to know more about morality than the Doctor to point out where he's being inconsistent. She just has to help him see past his own rage. *That's* what friends are for.

The Doctor sat back in his chair with an enormous sigh, feeling the weight of more than two thousand years slipping from his shoulders. He exclaimed "You were right, Aristotle. It took us a long time, but now that I've told you everything, and let a friend really get to know me, I feel so much better." Aristotle's eyes were wide with amazement.

"What an astounding life you've led!" he cried, "The story of your origins on Gallifrey! The secrets hidden in the depths of your TARDIS! The thing with the Zygons and the Infinity Bomb and President Obama's pants! And your name! No wonder you won't tell it to anyone!"

Suddenly, a shower of sparks erupted from the time rotor and the TARDIS corridors began to echo with the deep and sepulchral tolling of the cloister bell. The Doctor sprang to his feet and studied the console, his face growing grim. He murmured "Of course, friendships based on usefulness are handy too. Do you remember the story of River Song and the Silents? How are you with a laser pistol?"

18
Sex for Dummies, Humans, and Time Lords

COURTLAND LEWIS

> Man loves woman. Man loves man. Woman loves woman. Who cares? People *hating* each other, that's what bothers me.
>
> —TWELFTH DOCTOR, *New Adventures with the Twelfth Doctor*, Number 4

In Classic *Doctor Who*, love and sex were the last things we expected to see. Of course, there were many beautiful companions—I always had crushes on Sarah Jane, Romana II, and Peri, but the thought of them and the Doctor flirting, schnogging, knoodling, or engaging in any other sort of hanky panky was beyond the pale of imagination. Even with Leela in her loin cloth and Peri and Turlough in their bathing suits, the thought of sex just didn't arise—though I'm sure some of the cheeky older fans had their fingers crossed!

Fast-forward to the roaring 1990s and love just seemed to be in the air. Not only was the president of the United States enjoying an unexpected period of love, but the Doctor, too, decided to take the plunge and smooch his companion Grace Holloway (*Doctor Who: TV Movie*, 1996). By the time *Doctor Who* achieved its reboot in 2005, the smooch blossomed into a full-blown sexual revolution. Not only do characters now talk of having sexual trysts, but many of them openly flaunt their sexual libidos and exploits. There's the sexual tension exhibited between Mickey, Rose, and the Doctor. There's Captain Jack who knows no bounds, illustrated nicely by his full frontal nudity in 2005's "Bad Wolf"—"Ladies, your viewing figures just went up!" Other examples include Madame de Pompadour,

Jenny Flint and Madame Vastra, Tasha Lem, the thin-fat gay married Anglican Marines, and of course, the vivacious Amy Pond and her irrepressible daughter River Song. And let's not forget the Doctor's polygamy. If "until death do us part" is true, then he's married to at least two women, River Song and Queen Elizabeth I, and for all we know, the half-human Tennant Doctor—technically, Number Twelve, according to the Smith Doctor—is married to Rose. That means he has at least three wives—Yowzah, indeed!

Doctor Who's menagerie of man-on-man, man-on-woman, woman-on-woman, human-on-alien, polygamy, and everything else that doesn't make it to the small screen probably has Doctor Ruth itching to become the Doctor's next companion. Why include such material in what used to be—and for many, still is—a family show? What's the Doctor trying to teach us about the nature of sex and relationships? It must be something important, or it wouldn't continually appear throughout the New Series. From what I can glean, the Doctor is trying to teach viewers a fundamental ethical principle: as long as two rational autonomous persons willingly enter into a relationship, then there's nothing in the whole wide universe that's wrong with it. Some people might not like some of the relationships seen in both the Whoniverse and our own, but there are no good *ethical* arguments to show that they're immoral. To see why this is so, let's put on our serious fezzes and talk about love and sex.

Master of My Domain, Doctor of My Manor

The deeply held beliefs you have about right and wrong are your morals. If you share outrage with Donna when she discovers the plight of the Ood in "Planet of the Ood" (2008), then you have a certain moral belief that it's wrong to enslave and torture the Ood. How do you know your indignation is justified, and not merely the result of sentimental emotions? You need ethics. Ethics attempts to justify our moral beliefs, and though there are many different ethical justifications for our moral beliefs, most ethical theories share certain principles. One such principle is that of autonomy.

The concept of autonomy is traced back to Ancient Greece, where capable city-states were allowed to govern their own affairs. Analogous to these city-states, when humans reach a point in their lives when they can adequately govern themselves, when they're competent to make important decisions that affect their lives and the lives of others, we say they're autonomous.

Autonomy has two requirements. It requires individuals be capable of making competent, free, and well-reasoned decisions, while at the same time requiring that they be responsible for their decisions. It's this duality that makes autonomy the fundamental building block of morality, because it grounds the notion that people with certain rational capacities are free and responsible *moral* agents, as opposed to mere *causal* agents. For example, in "Aliens of London" (2005), you shouldn't be upset at the pig for crashing the spaceship into Big Ben. The pig was genetically enhanced, and lacked the ability to make any autonomous decisions, let alone fly a spaceship. The pig and the ship were mere causal agents; they were like a big rock being thrown at London. However, it's perfectly justified to be upset at the Slitheen, since they're the ones who devised the plan and purposely caused the ensuing destruction and death. They're moral agents because they're autonomous.

Autonomy isn't an all or nothing affair. It comes in degrees. When you were born, you had little to no autonomy. You were completely dependent upon some caretaker. As you grew and gained more knowledge and the rational ability to process this knowledge, you gained more autonomy. For instance, the Doctor is more autonomous than young Amelia Pond. She's a child with very little knowledge of the world, whereas the Doctor is a nine-hundred-something-year-old Time Lord. Amelia's decision to travel with the Doctor shouldn't be considered a fully autonomous decision, due to her age and lack of knowledge about the world. Sure, the Doctor has a time machine, a sonic screwdriver, and impeccable fashion sense, but it's really no different than a stranger walking up to a young child and enticing them into their van with chocolate, video games, and things that go "ding." The child is enticed and says, "Yes, I want to go with you." This isn't a rational autonomous decision, which is why we have laws to protect children from nefarious adults. Of course, as viewers, we all know the Doctor wouldn't purposely wrong or allow Amelia to be wronged by others, but she simply lacks the ability to make such a life-altering decision.

On the other hand, adults can freely choose to go with strangers because they're autonomous, even if they're completely ignorant of some things. For instance, the Doctor is more autonomous than the adult Amy in regards to flying the TARDIS. She might randomly hit several buttons and accidently get it right, but the Doctor knows what the buttons do—at least most of the time. Amy, however, is more autonomous in regards to her own life, because, at least theoretically, she knows more about herself than anyone else. Still, Amy and the Doctor are both autonomous, and even though we might question their motives from time to time, they're knowledgeable and rational enough to have their decisions respected. Unless we have knowledge about what the Doctor and Amy need in order to make better choices, we should respect their autonomously chosen life-decisions. To not do so is to treat them like children, and unless properly justified, being parentalistic wrongs autonomous agents.

Let's Get It On

Why all this talk of autonomy, when we're supposed to be talking about sex? The answer is easy. Morally permissible adult relationships require both parties to be autonomous decision-makers. Just imagine if the Doctor went around forcing people to travel with him, we'd call him an alien abductor. He usually asks his new-found friends if they want to travel. This allows them to autonomously *choose* whether they want to join the adventure or not. There are times when the Doctor doesn't ask, like with Ian and Barbara, but this is usually the result of some extreme circumstance. In other rare cases, for example, if the only way to save you from a batch of Cybermen is to take you away on the TARDIS, the Doctor would be morally justified in abducting you for a short period of time.

Intimate relationships begin in a similar way. One party asks: will you go out with me? The other party must choose: yes or no—please circle one. The question gives the courted party an opportunity to consider all of the relevant facts in order to arrive at a desired answer. It appears, then, if both parties are autonomous, there's nothing immoral about the relationship. Others might not like the relationship, but it's really none of their business.

However, simply being autonomous doesn't ensure the relationship is moral. Other moral considerations must be taken into account. For instance, if one or both of the parties is already engaged in an exclusive relationship, then it'd be wrong to enter into another relationship. Another example is that if one of the parties manipulates the other to such a degree that she can't make a well-informed decision, then the manipulator is immoral. Manipulation occurs in every relationship, to some degree or another. Consider, for example, Rory's asking Amy's friends what kind of flowers she likes in order to win her heart with a beautiful bouquet. We might think this is, to an extent, manipulative, but it doesn't seem immoral, since Amy is still capable of making a well-informed decision about whether or not to date Rory.

On the other hand, imagine if the Doctor has the "hots" for you. Now, imagine he's the creepy stalker-type of Time Lord who uses his TARDIS to go back into your history and find out everything there is to know about you: your likes, dislikes, favorite color, favorite Doctor, and so forth. As he's visiting your past, he begins doing things that will make you love him in the future. For instance, he prevents you from watching Tenth Doctor episodes, and replaces them with his episodes. As a result, you grow up loving his Doctor, not the Tenth Doctor.

These actions would be manipulative to such an extent that you wouldn't be able make a well-informed decision. Your memories have been changed. So, the creepy stalker Doctor doesn't respect your autonomy, and therefore, is immoral. This is exactly what happens when someone "trolls" your information from different social media websites, in order to get you to like them. They're simply manipulating you to get what they want, and this doesn't respect your autonomy.

The best way to avoid this problem is to start off each relationship with as much honesty and respect for autonomy as possible. The Ninth Doctor illustrates this nicely in his promos for Series One:

NINTH DOCTOR: Do you wanna come with me? 'Cause if you do, then I should warn you. You're gonna see all sorts of things: ghosts from the past, aliens from the future, the day the Earth died in a ball of flame. It won't be quiet, it won't be safe, and it won't be calm. But I'll tell you what it will be: a trip of a lifetime!

Being upfront and telling the truth is the best way to respect the autonomy of other people, because it respects their ability to make a rational decision based on the available information.

Two Hearts Just Ain't Natural

A more prominent criticism of the types of relationships seen in *Doctor Who* is to claim that they're unnatural, and therefore, immoral. Such critics claim that even if both parties are rational autonomous agents, their relationship runs counter to the natural order of the world, which, for some, makes it immoral. In order to make sense of this criticism, we need to examine a case to which we have access. Since we've yet to have credible accounts of alien and human relationships, homosexual sex is our best test case, and John Corvino provides one of the most lucid and effective examinations of the morality of homosexual sex in his essay, "Why Shouldn't Tommy and Jim Have Sex?" So, let's see what 'unnatural' really means.

As Corvino notes, we should recognize that much of contemporary life is "unnatural." Clothes, homes, and most of our food and medicines are manufactured, processed, and synthetic. Yet, disease, suffering, volcanoes, and death are perfectly natural. So, if we aren't careful with how we define 'unnatural', and if 'unnatural' means 'immoral', then many things we all want are immoral—including our attempts to fight off disease and death. Since those who speak out against homosexual sex aren't usually against clothes, advanced medicine, and modern homes, 'unnatural' must mean something different.

One way we might understand 'unnatural' is to equate it with 'unusual' or 'abnormal'. The problem with this definition is that being unusual doesn't equate with being immoral. There are all sorts of behaviors that are unusual. In fact, until very recently, watching *Doctor Who* in America was unusual because no one had heard of it, but there seems to be nothing intrinsically immoral about watching *Doctor Who*. The fact that the Doctor is an alien with two hearts makes him abnormal, but that doesn't make him immoral. If we assume that the unusual is immoral, then we would have to conclude that giving to charity, reading a book, and a whole host of other activities would be immoral. Such examples show that there's nothing inherently immoral about being unusual.

Corvino notes that some people use the word 'unnatural' to mean 'something not practiced by other animals'. This definition leads to equally absurd results as the previous one. Not only do several other species of animals engage in homosexual behavior, like Teiidae lizards, Laysan albatrosses, and some penguins and giraffes, but the majority of human activities aren't practiced by other animals. For instance, other animals don't create dramas and about time traveling and mass-EX-TER-MIN-ATE-ing aliens, nor do they write books, cook their food, hold elections, or wear clothes. So, unless nearly all human behavior is immoral, this definition won't work.

A third way of defining 'unnatural' is to say it means 'that which doesn't proceed from innate desires'. This definition is used by opponents and proponents of homosexual sex. Opponents claim homosexual sex is a lifestyle choice, while proponents claim that it's a natural act based on innate desires. According to Corvino, both sides are wrong because innate desires don't determine whether behaviors are moral or immoral. The Doctor appears to have an innate desire to destroy that which is evil. Rusty recognizes such a desire in "Into the Dalek" (2014), and we see it manifest itself in "Dinosaurs on a Spaceship" (2013), when the Doctor executes Solomon. The same almost happens with Kahler-Jex in "A Town Called Mercy" (2013), but we're shown—thanks to Amy—that the true test of moral character is how we, as rational autonomous persons, react to our innate desires, not the innate desires themselves.

The fourth definition equates 'unnatural' with 'unintended', by nature or the divine. There are three ways we might determine what's unintended. First, we might use efficiency to determine what's intended. However, being efficient doesn't make something moral, nor does being inefficient make something immoral. The most efficient way to solve world hunger would be to convert the hungry into Cybermen or hire the Daleks to exterminate them. Both of these options are clearly immoral, so efficiency doesn't show us what's moral.

Second, we might use 'natural purpose' to determine 'unintended', meaning that what prevents or doesn't contribute to a thing's natural purpose is unintended. To make sense of this definition we need to know our natural purpose. What is it? Make love. Make war. Watch *Doctor Who*. Is it all three, or some combination? If it's simply, keep the species going, then having sex for fun is immoral, along with masturbation, sex enjoyed by infertile couples, and possibly people who choose to not have sex at all. Are all of these immoral? If only one isn't, then this definition should be rejected.

Finally, a critic might claim 'unintended' means 'God doesn't approve'. Leaving aside questions about God's existence, there's still the issue of knowing how to properly interpret holy texts. You can spend your entire life researching texts, interpretations, and archeological evidence, and still not arrive at a concrete, consistent, and full-proof set of answers for what God (or the gods) approves or disapproves. Whether you're Jewish, Christian, Muslim, Hindu, Sikh, or a member of one of Earth's other wonderfully meaningful religions, it's up to you to conduct your own honest research into the issue, seeking out both positions that favor and oppose your current interpretation. If you're unwilling to perform such a task, yet you oppress and condemn those who don't meet your standards, then your belief system is no better than any number of *Doctor Who*'s monsters who ignorantly and dogmatically despise all that's different from what they consider "natural." In other words, don't be a Dalek when it comes to your understanding of religious truth and how you treat others.

Slippery Slopes—Geronimo!

Not all arguments against the types of relationships seen in *Doctor Who* are so straightforward. Some people suggest the relationships are immoral due to the consequences that allowing them would produce. For instance, imagine after watching an episode with Madame Vastra and Jenny schnogging, some talking head gets on TV and says, "This has been my point for years: once homosexuality becomes socially acceptable, bestiality, pedophilia, and all sorts of other morally abhorrent sexual acts will become socially acceptable." This is a type of argument that good critical thinkers will recognize and avoid. It's called an "empirical slippery slope," and is a fallacy—a common error in reasoning.

Empirical slippery slopes make predictions about the future, and should be avoided, since no one can accurately predict the future. Sure, there are times when certain events can be predicted based on previous events, but empirical slippery slopes often turn the mundane into the extraordinary, in order to create fear and to destroy reason. The TV talking head's prediction of the moral decay of society because of homosexual "relationships" is an empirical slippery slope. People used the same argument against interracial relationships. Since no one on Earth has a TARDIS or other future-seeing device, we should avoid stepping on empirical slippery slopes at all costs.

The truth of the matter is that the slippery slope suggesting homosexual relationships will lead to the acceptance of bestiality and pedophilia in our society is simply *false*—not to mention objectifying and insulting. As noted above, the type of sexual relationships exhibited in *Doctor Who* involve two (or more) rationally autonomous consenting adults. Even if someone objects to Vastra's and Jenny's homosexual relationship as promoting the decay of society, the criticism is hollow. Both parties are rational autonomous beings, which means they can choose to engage in whatever relationship they like. To show they ought not to requires a different sort of argument for why members of the same sex shouldn't engage in certain relationships. Such arguments will probably be as speciesist as the anti-interracial relationship arguments were racist.

The Beauty of Diversity

With the above arguments in mind, there seems to be no moral grounding for denying two autonomous people the right to enter into a consensual relationship that isn't the result of coercion, manipulation, or some other feature that prevents one or multiple parties from being reasonably autonomous. In fact, the examples of intimate, cross-gender/species/technology relationships seen in *Doctor Who* are those seen in all consensual autonomous relationships. So, why do people get so upset over two autonomous people of the same gender or of different species being in a relationship? The truth is, and they don't know this, but they're not really upset about the *relationship*. Most friends are same-sex. Many of these same-sex friends live together, pay bills together, and attend movies, festivals, and dinners together, and a lucky few get to travel in the TARDIS together. The Doctor isn't human, yet no one gets up in arms about him traveling with humans. No one seems to care about these relationships, which implies it isn't the actual relationship that people are so upset about. What they're upset about is they find the sex-act between people of the same gender ugly, and the problem with this sort of position is that "ugliness" is an *aesthetic* category, not an *ethical* category.

Corvino suggests that there's a fifth understanding of 'unnatural' that equates it with terms like 'disgusting' and 'offensive'. To understand this claim, we must look at aesthetics. Aesthetics is the philosophical attempt to describe what's beautiful and why it's beautiful. For instance, I find the Slitheen beautiful—and no, it's not the gas conversion process that causes them to poot! My wife, on the other hand, finds them disgusting. I also seem to be in the minority when it comes to loving the Sixth Doctor's costume. Who's right? I would say we're both right, because the cuteness of the Slitheen and the Doctor's outfit are matters of personal taste. Because it's a matter of personal taste, then it'd be morally wrong to go around forcing—or trying to force—others to agree with me.

Too often, aesthetics gets confused with ethics, usually because they share a similar vocabulary. Aesthetics sometimes uses terms like 'good' and 'bad', but when it does it's referring to attractive/beautiful and unattractive/ugly. When ethics uses 'good' and 'bad', it refers to actions and thoughts that violate some sort of moral principle. For instance, when a fan says that last week's episode was "bad," they don't mean it violated a moral principle. Instead, they mean it was an unattractive or unpleasing episode. Unlike ethics, aesthetics is, for the most part a matter of personal subjective taste. "Beauty is in the eye of the beholder."

Aesthetics seems to be the only solid grounding for people's aversion to some autonomous sexual relationships. As a result, they have a right to their aesthetic opinion, but they don't have a right to force their preferences onto others. That's the beauty of autonomy. Morally, we're free to do what we want, as long as we don't wrong others; and as long as *all* parties are rationally autonomous, we should let them enjoy their relationship. Aesthetically, if you don't like it, you don't have to watch—isn't freedom great? Personally, I like watching aliens and humans, regardless of their gender, enter into loving and monogamous relationships of mutual respect. I don't like watching men and women have casual intercourse with multiple random people, which seems to be the norm for the majority of TV, because it's often disrespectful and deceptive. So, I autonomously choose to watch *Doctor Who*—isn't autonomy great?

Sometimes the actions and words of humans make us wish we had a TARDIS, so we could escape the ignorance and bigotry that sometimes dominates Earth. Thankfully, as rational autonomous persons we can think, learn, and grow. We can challenge and examine our moral positions and change them accordingly. We can recognize when we're doing something wrong, and we can commit to never doing it again. We've seen progress in terms of women's rights, the rights of people of African and Asian descent, children's rights, and even animal rights. We have a long way to go, and we continue to have setbacks, but if we persevere we can make a difference. Being a mindful moral person starts with working hard to become a more rational autonomous person, and ends with respecting the moral worth and rights of others. That's the lesson *Doctor Who* is trying to teach viewers about sex, love, and relationships. It's one our universe desperately needs.

19

The Doctor Is a (Wo)Man!

NATHAN KELLEN

When Matt Smith's exit from *Doctor Who* was announced, signaling the end of his run as the Eleventh Doctor, the Internet lit up with rumors about who'd join the Whoniverse as the Twelfth Doctor. Countless actors were suggested, with the role of the Twelfth Doctor eventually being handed to Peter Capaldi.

The public spectacle and debate over the casting of the next Doctor is of course nothing new, but this time something special occurred. Amongst the regular debate over whether this or that actor should get the role, whether the Doctor should be old or young, white or black, the emphasis was on "Should the next Doctor be a woman?"

This question wasn't unprecedented—there were a few suggestions here and there of a female Doctor after David Tennant's run as the Tenth Doctor. What spurred and fueled the discussion of the possibility of a female Doctor were several hints throughout the New Series, from "The End of Time" (2009), "The Doctor's Wife" (2011), and "The Night of the Doctor" (2013).

Even with 2014's "Dark Water," which wrote into *Doctor Who* canon that Time Lords can change gender when they regenerate, there's a question of whether fans would accept a change in the Doctor's gender identity. Is the Doctor's character fundamentally masculine, or is it just some sort of bias that prevents some of us from accepting a female Doctor? It's here that the philosophy of sex and gender can help us understand the limitless possibilities of *Doctor Who*.

The Mystery of Regeneration

Over the course of fifty years of *Doctor Who*, we've grown accustomed to the nature of Time Lord regeneration. When Time Lords get old, injured, or just plain bored of their current bodies, they can regenerate into new bodies. The ability to regenerate is the key to *Doctor Who*'s longevity, by allowing the show to continue on after actors have had their fill as the title character, or executives desire a change.

When William Hartnell's Doctor regenerated for the first time in "The Tenth Planet" (1966) into Patrick Troughton's Second Doctor, we learned that the Doctor's appearance and age could change. Throughout the series we've seen many other examples of regeneration, both from the Doctor as well as other Time Lords. When Time Lords regenerate, their age, appearance, and personality changes, but until recently, the big question was: can their *gender* change as well?

During the Eleventh Doctor's tenure, three hints were dropped which can settle this question. In "The End of Time," as the Doctor examines his brand new body to see how it turned out, he exclaims, "I'm a girl! No, no! I'm not a girl." Next, in the fan-favorite Neil Gaiman penned episode "The Doctor's Wife," the Doctor mentions his interactions with a long-lost friend, the Corsair. In his excitement about the possibility of another living Time Lord, the Doctor mentions that the Corsair didn't feel like himself, or *herself* without their distinctive snake tattoo, keeping it in each regeneration. Further, this line was a deliberate addition by Gaiman as a tease to suggest the possibility of a future female Doctor.

Finally, in the mini-episode "The Night of the Doctor," which documents the Eighth Doctor's final moments, we get one last hint. The Sisterhood of Karn offer the Eighth Doctor several different elixirs which utilize perfected Time-Lord science. Each offers him a different choice, including "fat or thin, young or old, man or woman." With the help of the Sisterhood of Karn, the Doctor could've transformed into a woman by his own volition.

All hints and speculations were put to rest during the Twelfth Doctor episode "Dark Water," when it's revealed that Missy is the Master regenerated as a woman. With this revelation, all questions about the Doctor's ability to regenerate as a woman should be put to rest, right? Not so fast! There are some deeper issues that we must address.

Time Lords, Clownfish, and Sex Changes

Not all people are excited at the possibility of a female Doctor. Peter Davison, who brought the Fifth Doctor to the screen, claimed in 2013 that:

> I'll probably get into trouble for saying this but I think it sort of has to be a man. To have a female would be like having a female James Bond. It would be a rather odd thing. If you suddenly make the Doctor a woman, you effectively say, "Well let's give him a sex change," and I don't think that works.

But what's 'odd' about this, and why wouldn't this work? One way to answer this question is to look at biology. Time Lords certainly wouldn't be the first species to change sexes. Even without moving to the Whoniverse, there are several fish on Earth that exhibit sex changes, including clownfish, moray eels, and gobies.

Clownfish are interesting because they're sequential hermaphrodites, that is, all clownfish are born as males and only develop later, if at all, into females. In a typical clownfish school, there's only one female who gives birth and keeps the school's reproductive cycle going. When something happens to the female clownfish, like getting killed, a male clownfish can biologically change its sex from being physically a male into physically a female. This former-male clownfish can now reproduce as if it were always a female. In becoming a female, the clownfish adopts a whole new biological function, now laying scores of eggs and giving birth to future generations, moving from a fish who likely never bred, into a breeding position.

Even humans can, rarely, exhibit natural sex changes. Some females with certain enzyme deficiencies can develop into males slowly over time, producing more androgens and displaying typical male characteristics. However, some humans actually choose to change their sex. Since the late 1960s, transsexuals, people who don't identify with their birth sex, have engaged in sex reassignment therapy to change their bodies to better match how they identify as male or female. Sex reassignment therapy often involves hormone replacement therapy which prompts physical changes in the body, including altering body structure. For some (but not all) transsexuals, sex reassignment therapy concludes in a "sex change." Sex changes involve genital surgery, changing the genitals of the person undergoing the surgery to match which sex they identify with.

Thus, sex changes aren't as unusual as one might think. All sorts of Earth creatures change their sex, without even having to resort to wibbly-wobbly, timey-wimey *Doctor Who* sci-fi explanations.

Time Lords and Gender Trouble

With the Master regenerated as a woman ("Dark Water" and "Death in Heaven," 2014), and several biological explanations to ground this change, it's perfectly intelligible to think that the Doctor's body could change into a female body. But can *the Doctor* truly be a woman? This question seems to be at the heart of Davison's comments. The Doctor's personality has changed drastically from one incarnation to the next, but is changing gender too much of a stretch for Whovians? Is Davison correct that the Doctor must be a man?

Philosophers and gender theorists often make a distinction between *sex* and *gender*. Sex is a biological feature, based in physical characteristics like genitalia, hormones, and chromosomes. Most humans fall into one of two sexes: the typical male and female biological categories we all know. A small percentage of individuals fall into a third category, *intersex*, which is a bit of a disingenuous term, since there's a lot of debate about which syndromes and conditions should count as intersex. According to the most common definition, intersex applies to those who are born with a set of chromosomes that is neither XX nor XY; this condition is present in roughly 1 in 1,666 births.

Gender, on the other hand, is socially constructed—being built out of something like social *identities* and *roles*. Sexual identity is the result of the type of gender a person identifies with. Most people identify as one of two genders: man or woman. However some people don't identify as either man or woman; they identify as both, or perhaps as some other gender identity altogether. These individuals, together with transsexuals, make up the category of *transgender*—people who don't identify with or conform to their perceived or assigned gender or expectations about that gender.

On the other hand, gender roles are the result of social expectations of what people of each gender do. Most theorists maintain that gender is constructed out of the social roles in which we all participate. Simone de Beauvoir famously claimed in her foundational work on gender, *The Second Sex*, that "One is not born, but rather becomes, a woman." Being a woman is more than simply having female sex organs or XX chromosomes—it's occupying a particular role in the social realm and viewed by society in certain ways.

Can the Doctor's gender role be female? The Doctor is no stranger to being viewed in new and different ways, having had many faces, lived thousands of years, interacted with countless cultures and even been viewed as both a hero and a villain, by different people. While the role of the Doctor is that of a warrior for the peoples of the Gamma Forests, the Doctor's fundamental role for many other societies (including ours) is to heal and help. To heal and help are typically associated with feminine roles, which the Doctor not only plays but has defined. His adopted ethical system is that of the feminist ethics of care, at least according to J.J. Sylvia in *Doctor Who and Philosophy: Bigger on the Inside*. So, maybe the Doctor is already more feminine than we think.

Simone de Beauvoir is of course not the only person to posit a theory of gender, Judith Butler developed a theory about the *performativity of gender*, which is meant to inspire a comparison to performances in arenas like theater. According to Butler in *Gender Trouble*:

> Gender ought not to be construed as a stable identity or locus of agency from which various acts follow; rather, gender is an identity tenuously constituted in time, instituted in an exterior space through a stylized repetition of acts.

Butler maintains we shouldn't conceive of gender as something that we're born into, something that's locked in by our biology, or given to us by one action. Rather, she argues that we exhibit our genders by continuously performing certain actions, like those that we might recognize as stereotypically female or male—wearing dresses, liking sports, and so on. This process happens over time, likely from the time we're born when the doctor delivering the baby (sadly not *the* Doctor!) declares it "male" or "female." Further, the actions we perform are always influenced by society and its expectations.

Could the Doctor be a woman under Butler's and de Beauvoir's accounts? Yes. As each Doctor appears and each new actor attempts to make his mark, the Doctor engages in different behaviors, different mannerisms, and other different performative acts. Sometimes these performative acts add up to a different personality altogether. Following Butler, we could interpret the Doctor's performing stereotypical "male" acts, like being flirty, or fatherly (at very different times) as his gender. But nothing stops the Doctor from acting differently, performing different acts and taking a new identity—in fact, this happens every couple years with respect to everything apart from gender (and race, so far). The Doctor has lived a long life, with many adventures. Some of these performed actions are bound to be more feminine than masculine. So, on both de Beauvoir's and Butler's accounts of gender, the Doctor can be a woman just as easily as a man.

Because of its performative nature, Butler claims that gender isn't something that we *are*, but something we *do*. You, I, and the Doctor aren't simply individuals with gender labels attached to them, and to which we must conform, but people who constantly perform acts throughout life around which we can develop a sort of theme, or identity. So, even though viewers might see the role of the Doctor as being "male," nothing requires the Doctor to identify and act according to viewers' expected roles. Our actions form our gender, and as Butler suggests, our gender identity is "tenuously constituted in time." So, there's nothing preventing the Doctor from breaking free from the role and identifying with being female.

The Doctor's Identity Crisis

Biologically, there's nothing inconsistent in the Doctor's becoming a woman, and as we just saw, there's nothing preventing the Doctor from playing a female gender role. In fact, in many ways he's already playing such a role. So, what's left? The only possible way to interpret Davison's criticism is that the Doctor's identity is intrinsically male. In other words, despite how much the Doctor changes from one incarnation to the next, there's a core personality trait that's male, which must remain for him to be considered the Doctor.

Could the Doctor handle the change from a man to a woman? Psychologically, given the Doctor's mental constitution, the answer is "yes." He's undergone just as significant psychological changes before. Sometimes the regeneration process can be quite frightening, as in the transition from Four to Five ("Castrovalva," 1982), when the Doctor comes "unraveled"; Five to Six ("The Twin Dilemma," 1984), which has the Doctor almost killing Peri; Ten to Eleven ("The Eleventh Hour," 2010), where the Doctor must develop new tastes; and Eleven to Twelve ("Deep Breath," 2014), where he's "definitely" not flirting with a T-Rex. In fact, the Twelfth Doctor suffers a full mental breakdown. Again, the best evidence that the Doctor could survive this identity change is that the Master seems to be managing to cope with *hers* just fine.

The Doctor's characters that we Whovians know and love is tied to things like empathy, wit, intelligence, a certain amount of quirkiness and a passion for doing the right thing, no matter the difficulty, and none of these require a particular gender identity. The main outline of the show, involving a character who travels through time and space as a venerable Time Lord, saving the universe from various threats, could equally have started with a woman in the title role as a man (ignoring political realities about the time-period in which the show began). As noted above, some aspects of the Doctor's personality, like his empathy for others, are commonly thought to be more feminine in nature. If that's what fans admire about the Doctor, then it appears that the Doctor's character is already partially feminine. Why not let those features bloom to new heights, by changing the Doctor to a woman? We don't love and admire the Doctor because he's a man, but because the Doctor is a symbol of hope and goodness. Like de Beauvoir claimed, one isn't born a woman, but becomes one. The Doctor has certainly done enough to become a woman.

The Time of the (New) Doctor

The Twelfth Doctor has just begun his adventure in time and space, and we all hope that it's a long and happy journey for

Peter Capaldi and *Doctor Who*. But this is *Doctor Who*, and there's always room for another incarnation of our favorite Time Lord. Next time, when it's time for the Thirteenth, or Fourteenth, or so on, to step up and protect the universe from all manner of threats, Daleks, Cybermen, or otherwise, perhaps it won't be a male Doctor.

And that'll be just fine, because in the end, "Trust me, I'm the Doctor" are the words we want to hear, regardless of the gender of the person who utters them.

SERIAL 4

Gallifrey Falls
No More

Martin Stone Hennessee

TIME LORD PRESIDING

Terrifying, and Mad, and Bloody Brilliant

Martin Stone Hennessee, Time Lord Presiding

It's 1984, I'm twelve, and my channel-surfing has found an English girl in a yellow raincoat being captured and dragged away by a wobbly robot, while a man in a crazy scarf tries to clamber out of a pit. She's delivered to the clutches of a helmeted spaceman, but as the alien reveals his terrifying, potato-like visage . . . *that* music screams in, the credits roll, and I know I can't miss what happens tomorrow. What I don't know is that I've stepped into the TARDIS, and I won't be coming back.

It's 2014, I am forty-two and trying not to panic. For thirty years now, the Doctor and his rollicking adventures have inspired and intrigued me, found me new friends, shaped my musical, literary, and visual tastes, informed my morality, fired speculations on the nature of time, free will, and the illusion of the self, prompted me to consider vegetarianism, Marxism, Buddhism, and the semiotic thickness of a performed text. It's a dreamscape and a mythology that's kept me company through good times and bad, a thread of continuity in my life, ever-evolving but always constant, that good old Doctor, that mad man in his magic box.

It's 1994, and I don't have time for *Doctor Who* anymore. I'm going to college in New York, and "a fan" is the last thing I want to be. My Target novels and VHS tapes are in Mom's attic, and while *Love and War* was a masterpiece, I just can't be seen with that cover art in public. Like the family I love, and yet moved far away from, sometimes *Doctor Who* embarrasses by making it obvious just how much it formed every part of you.

It's 2014, and in my head live multiple Martins that may have been or may yet be, as day-by-day "I" become "me" at their expense. I remember being that boy in 1984, but do I really know him? Would he recognize me? If I could see myself circa 2044, would I recognize that guy? Martin Who?

It's 1984, and I'm not yet aware that my lack of interest in girls has any broader significance to my life. I am a chubby bookworm who thinks more about musical theater and the Loch Ness Monster than about romance. *Doctor Who* appeared in my life at exactly the right time, as did David, my first real friend, the only other *Doctor Who* fan I knew, cute but straight (story of my life), the person I thought the most about for a good twenty years of my life, and the first person to show me how little caring for someone means when they don't want or need your care.

It's 2014, and I had a friend once. We ran together when I was little, and I thought we were the same, but when we grew up, we weren't. I still wonder sometimes if he's watching.

It's 1994, and how many *Doctor Who* fans does it take to change a light bulb? None, but they wish it would come back on.

It's 2004, and I find a Xerox of a goggle-eyed Tom Baker on a bookstore corkboard. The secret handshake can't be ignored—I call the number, arrange to meet at a diner. Ashley is fun and easy to talk to, cute but straight (story of my life). We talk for seven hours that night, annoying two shifts of waitresses. We know the show is slated for a return, and that somewhere in Wales an army of meanwhiles and never-weres are coalescing into "the Doctor," whether we like it or not. We're excited, but feel it best not to get our hopes up—we remember last time.

It's 2014, and I am in a room in Atlanta with people who were watching *Doctor Who* from the very beginning, and kids younger than "Rose." It belongs to each of us uniquely, to none of us exclusively. Perhaps *Doctor Who* only finds its fullest expression in the individual imaginations of its fans. What was once a secret handshake for a small but dedicated tribe is now a global brand, a sprawling hall-of-mirrors of books, comics, Big Finish, webisodes, fanfic, so vast and sprawling that no mere mortal can take it all in. Perhaps *Doctor Who* keeps going because it's a genius idea that never has been, never *can* be, done justice.

It's 2004, and somewhere in Wales, a group of professional fans are hard at work changing a light bulb. But into what?

It's 1994, and my new boyfriend and I find "The Tomb of the Cybermen" (1967) in a video store. Maybe I am too sophisticated for *Doctor Who* now, but this is *the* lost classic! Later, we both sigh in pleasure as Patrick Troughton confides, "Nobody in the universe can do what we're doing." Maybe there was something to this old show, after all.

It's 1984, and if I'd known how many new friends the Doctor would introduce to me—and how many friends I'd introduce, in turn, to the Doctor and his world—I'd never have believed it.

It's 2014, and what does *Doctor Who* mean to me? May as well ask what life itself means. All I know is they're both terrifying, and mad, and bloody brilliant, and I wouldn't miss them for the world.

20
The Doctor Lies

KEVIN MCCAIN

The Doctor has many rules:

#408 Time is not the boss of you ("Let's Kill Hitler," 2011)

#27 Never knowingly be serious ("Let's Kill Hitler")

#7 Never run when you're scared ("Let's Kill Hitler")

#1 The Doctor lies ("The Big Bang," 2010; "Let's Kill Hitler"; "The Wedding of River Song," 2011)

Perhaps unsurprisingly given the nature of **Rule #1,** at times the Doctor says that **Rule #1** is something different—"Don't wander off" ("The Girl in the Fireplace," 2006). The rule that the Doctor lies seems like a pretty simple rule. However, it brings up interesting philosophical questions when we stop to think about the nature of the Doctor's lies. Can the Doctor lie to himself? Should the Doctor lie, if it's going to be for a noble cause?

The Doctor Lies to Others

The Doctor lies to his enemies at times, or at the very least he uses trickery and deceit to defeat them. How else could he always come out on top against Daleks while armed with only a screwdriver? A great example of the Doctor using deception to defeat his enemies comes in "The Two Doctors" (1985) from the original run of the series. In this episode, the Sixth Doctor gives his companion, Jamie, a bunch of false information because he knows that Stike, the Sontaran, is listening in on the conversation. Later, Jamie asks the Doctor, "You knew he was there?" The Doctor replies, "That's why I said what I did. None of it was strictly true, but he believed it because I was talking to you."

In this case the Doctor doesn't lie *to* Stike—lying is very special kind of deception which requires directly conveying false information to someone else with the intention of getting her to believe false things. The Doctor doesn't meet both conditions of lying with respect to Stike. He does intentionally get Stike to believe false things, but he doesn't directly tell Stike anything false—after all, the Doctor isn't speaking to Stike at all. The Doctor's talking to Jamie; he simply knows that Stike is listening. So, the Doctor doesn't lie to Stike in this case, since his conversation is with Jamie. However, the Doctor clearly knowingly tricks or deceives Stike. After all, the Doctor gets Stike to believe something that's false by saying the things that he does to Jamie. Part of what makes the Doctor so entertaining to watch is his ability to trick or outwit his numerous enemies in this way.

The Doctor doesn't just deceive or lie to his enemies though. At times the Doctor lies to his allies, and he definitely deceives them on numerous occasions! For example, the Eleventh Doctor (or the Thirteenth, depending on how you count your Doctors) tells the Mother Superious of the Church of the Papal Mainframe that the TARDIS can't be flown by remote. Although this is true, strictly speaking, the Doctor later reveals that he can get the TARDIS to home-in on one of the TARDIS keys and come to him remotely ("The Time of the Doctor," 2013). So, the Doctor wasn't technically lying to Tasha because what he told her was true, but he was surely deceiving her. More clearly, the Eleventh Doctor flat out lies to Mels about guns working in the TARDIS when she brings guns onto the ship and later openly admits to lying about it after she's foolishly fired a gun inside the TARDIS, "That was a clever lie, you idiot! Anyone could tell that was a clever lie" ("Let's Kill Hitler," 2011).

The Doctor also lies to his own companions. The Eleventh Doctor admits to Amy on multiple occasions that he lied to her—"The Big Bang" and "The Pandorica Opens," 2010. In fact he tells her "Amy, you need to start trusting me. . . . If I always told you the truth, I wouldn't need you to trust me." And then, of course, there's the time that the Eleventh Doctor tricks

Clara and sends her away *literally* right after he promises, "Clara Oswald, I will never send you away again" ("The Time of the Doctor").

So, obviously the Doctor can—and does—lie to other people. But, this isn't all that interesting because we can lie to other people too. After all, it's quite possible that you've said you didn't know how the cookie jar broke in order to get yourself or someone else out of trouble, when in fact you knew full well how it happened. Or you may have told a friend that a particular outfit looks great on him when you didn't really think that it did. No, the interesting question is not "can the Doctor lie?", but rather "can the Doctor lie to himself?" Not just attempt to lie or deceive, but actually intentionally—and successfully—deceive himself?

The Doctor Lies to the Doctor

The question of whether the Doctor can lie to himself is more complicated than the question of whether we can lie to ourselves. It's exceedingly plausible that we can deceive ourselves about various things. After all, people tend to be subject to a vast array of cognitive biases such as thinking that we're above average on most things, taking ourselves to be more responsible for positive outcomes of our actions than negative outcomes, and so on. What's more, we tend to still fall prey to these sorts of biases even after we're made aware of them. So, it seems that we're capable of deceiving ourselves about a number of things.

Although it's plausible that we deceive ourselves to some degree, it's unlikely that we can directly lie to ourselves. Lying plausibly requires knowing, or at least believing, that a particular claim is true and then intentionally trying to deceive someone else into believing that the claim is false by saying things that aren't true. For example, the child who knows that she broke the cookie jar is lying when she tells her mother that she has no idea how the jar was broken.

This is, of course, something that we can do to others, but it isn't clear that we can lie to ourselves in this way. In order to actually succeed in lying to yourself you would have to at the same time know—and believe—that a claim is true and get yourself to believe that that claim is false. So, you'd have to both believe and not believe the same thing at the same time;

and be aware of so believing. Unless you're the Red Queen from *Through the Looking-Glass*, you're going to have a tough time doing that! This isn't to say that you can't continually tell yourself that things are different than they actually are until the point that eventually, you begin to misremember what actually happened. This sort of thing happens. But, this kind of indirect self-deception, where you bring about a change in your memories as a way of deceiving yourself, is very different from directly lying to yourself, where you get yourself to believe something that you know to be false.

The Doctor, though, is different from us in many ways: two hearts, regeneration, thinking fezzes are cool, and so on. Another way that we might think that the Doctor is different from us is that, whereas it doesn't seem that we can lie to ourselves, there's a straightforward way in which the Doctor can lie to himself. One incarnation of the Doctor could lie to another. In "The Day of the Doctor" (2013), the Eleventh Doctor could easily lie to the Tenth Doctor or to the War Doctor, or to both when the three of them are together. Being a later incarnation, the Eleventh Doctor would have some information that the others lack. He could certainly provide them with false information. This isn't too surprising.

A bit more interesting is the question of whether an earlier incarnation of the Doctor could lie to a later Doctor. This would appear to be much more difficult because the later Doctor could remember when he was the earlier incarnation and tried lying to his later self. Hence, it looks as if the later Doctor would likely be aware that the earlier Doctor is trying to deceive him. This is similar to when we try to directly lie to ourselves. We fail because we know that we're lying.

Although an earlier Doctor trying to lie to a later Doctor might at first seem just like our lying to ourselves, it's not quite the same because it does seem possible that the Doctor could lie to himself in this way. In "The Day of the Doctor" there's a point where the Tenth and Eleventh Doctors are trying to figure out what to do about a fissure in time and space.

TENTH DOCTOR: Okay, you used to be me, you've done this all before. What happens next?

ELEVENTH DOCTOR: I don't remember.

TENTH DOCTOR: How can you forget this?

ELEVENTH DOCTOR: Hey, hang on. It's not my fault. You're obviously not paying enough attention.

Assuming that the Eleventh Doctor isn't lying to the Tenth in this situation, it appears that there's a way that an earlier Doctor *could* lie to a later one. The earlier Doctor would simply have to convince the later Doctor that the claim in question is one that the later Doctor has forgotten, which would involve lying about what the Doctor has forgotten. Such a scenario clearly seems possible. So, in at least some sense, the Doctor can lie to himself.

But, can a current incarnation of the Doctor knowingly deceive that very same incarnation? That is, can the Eleventh Doctor lie to the Eleventh Doctor? Or the Tenth to the Tenth? Again, it seems that he can if he's dealing with himself earlier in his time stream. In other words, it appears that the one-thousand-one-hundred-year-old Eleventh Doctor could lie to the one-thousand-year-old Eleventh Doctor in the same way that he could lie to the Tenth Doctor if the Eleventh Doctor were to cross his own time stream. And, perhaps the one-thousand-year-old Eleventh Doctor could lie to the one-thousand-one-hundred-year-old Eleventh Doctor in the same sort of way that the Tenth Doctor could lie to the Eleventh.

One last possibility is worth considering. Can a current incarnation of the Doctor lie to his current self? That is, could the Eleventh Doctor lie to himself at his current point in the time stream? It appears that the answer here is "No." When it comes to the Eleventh Doctor lying to himself in this fashion, he's simply like us. After all, if he knows that he's deceiving himself, then it would seem that he isn't deceived at all. So, the Doctor can lie to himself in many ways, but not in this way.

The Importance of the Doctor's Lies

We've seen that there are numerous ways that the Doctor can lie, not just to himself, but also to others. At this point you might be wondering, why does this matter? Or, who cares? Don't worry; you're not in violation of the Doctor's dictum "Don't ask stupid questions" ("The Eleventh Hour," 2010).

These are always fair questions when dealing with philosophy, and most other things for that matter. There are two good reasons for thinking that this discussion matters.

First, it's simply philosophically interesting to think about how and who the Doctor can deceive. His special nature opens up many different ways of lying to himself that aren't available to us. It's interesting to consider what might happen in those various circumstances. Perhaps our consideration of this topic up to this point has helped us to understand ourselves and our own deceptions a little better, which is a worthwhile accomplishment in itself. After all, we've seen that while there are ways that we can deceive ourselves, it looks as if lying, a very specific form of deception, is something we can't do to ourselves.

Second, many—including the Tenth Doctor—wonder if the Eleventh Doctor should forget the genocide that he committed. Perhaps more importantly, many wonder if the Doctor is blameworthy if he does forget. In "The Day of the Doctor" the following conversion occurs:

> **WAR DOCTOR:** Did you ever count . . . how many children there were on Gallifrey that day?
>
> **ELEVENTH DOCTOR:** I have absolutely no idea.
>
> **TENTH DOCTOR:** [*to the Eleventh Doctor*] Two point four seven billion. You forgot? Four hundred years, is that all it takes?

Clearly, the Tenth Doctor thinks that the Eleventh Doctor has done something wrong by failing to accurately remember his role in the Time War. But, has he?

First of all, it's far from clear that the Eleventh Doctor really has forgotten anything about his role in the Time War—even the number of children on Gallifrey that day. Let's not forget **Rule #1**! It's quite possible that when the Eleventh Doctor says, "I have absolutely no idea," we are witnessing an instance where he's lying to his earlier selves. When pressed by the Tenth Doctor, the Eleventh Doctor never says that he forgot. Instead, the Eleventh Doctor says, "I moved on."

Plus, there's evidence that the Eleventh Doctor does in fact remember what he did in the Time War. He tells Clara, "There's one life that I've tried to very hard to forget. He was the Doctor who fought in the Time War, and that was the day he did it. The day I did it. The day he killed them all." Clara tells the War Doctor: "The Doctor [the Eleventh], my, my Doctor, he's always talking about the day he did it. The day he wiped out the Time Lords to stop the war… He regrets it. I see it in his eyes every day." Finally, when the three Doctors (Tenth, Eleventh, and War) are about to press the button to activate the Moment box, the Eleventh Doctor says, "Gentlemen, I have had four hundred years to think about this. I've changed my mind," and then he uses his sonic screwdriver to put the big red button back in the Moment box ("The Day of the Doctor"). In light of all of this, it's plausible that the Eleventh Doctor hasn't forgotten his role in the Time War at all. In fact, it seems that he's spent a lot of time—four hundred years!—thinking about his actions and their consequences. If this is so, then it doesn't appear that he's done any wrong in forgetting the exact details of his involvement in the Time War, because he hasn't forgotten them at all!

Despite the fact that it seems reasonable to think that the Doctor hasn't forgotten his role in the Time War, we're left with an interesting question. What if he did forget? And, more to the point, what if the Doctor deceived himself or somehow made himself forget? Would the Doctor have done something wrong by employing self-deception in order to forget his role in the genocide of two races?

According to philosophers like Immanuel Kant (*Grounding of the Metaphysics of Morals*) and St. Augustine (*Retractationes*), the answer to this question is easy. The Doctor would've done wrong in this case because lying is always wrong. While Augustine seems to allow that you can hide the truth in the sense of refusing to tell someone the truth about some matter in special circumstances, he agrees with Kant that lying is always wrong—no exceptions. So, if we accept the position of these philosophers, it's clear that the Doctor would've been doing something wrong if he were to deceive himself into forgetting his role in the Time War.

But, should we accept the sort of position that Kant and Augustine offer? Perhaps not. There seem to be clear cases in which the right thing to do is to lie. Say you're trying to keep an innocent person safe by hiding her in your home and the killer comes to your door and says, "Tell me whether she's here, and if you refuse, I will simply assume that she's here." In this situation it's clear that you should lie to the killer and tell him flat out that the person isn't in your house. In fact, you should give the killer whatever assurances and promises you can that the person isn't in your house, if doing so might save her life. So, in some cases, it isn't at all wrong to lie.

Philosophers such as Plato (*Republic*) and Henry Sidgwick (*The Methods of Ethics*) have both defended the idea that there can be "noble" lies. That is, there can be lies that morality not only allows, but requires us to tell. These aren't lies that simply allow us to avoid punishment or to gather ill-gotten gains. No, these are lies that serve a higher purpose such as saving another's life or strengthening society in a crucial way. Telling the truth is important, but there are some instances where the obligation to be honest is overridden by the value of other moral goods.

Since there can be occasions in which it's morally right to lie and occasions in which it's wrong to lie, deciding whether the Doctor would've done wrong in making himself forget the genocide he committed isn't a cut and dried matter. The question comes down to what the Doctor's *motivations* for deceiving himself would be. Robert C. Solomon, in "Self, Deception, and Self-Deception in Philosophy," holds that when it comes to self-deception, the motivation almost always comes down to coping with an unbearable situation rather than simply enjoying believing false claims.

Although it isn't an example of self-deception, consider the Tenth Doctor and Wilf's agreement to keep Donna from learning about the Doctor or from even starting to remember anything about him in order to keep her mind from burning up with memories ("Journey's End," 2008). This appears to be a case where deception will, at least at times, be necessary to cope with an unbearable situation—a situation that would literally destroy Donna. Could something similar occur with respect to self-deception? It seems so. Plausibly, if the Doctor were to deceive himself about his role in the Time War, it would be so that he could cope with the guilt for what he'd done. He'd be motivated by the need to deal with an unbearable situation. Would that be enough to justify his making himself forget?

It might be. After all, the Doctor may have needed a way to cope with the genocide in order to function well enough to save countless other people, planets, and even the universe itself, as he did after the Time War. Should we think the Doctor morally blameworthy if he were to deceive himself into forgetting what he did as the War Doctor? Perhaps. But, we should bear in mind that he's the "good man" referred to in the old saying "demons run when a good man goes to war" ("A Good Man Goes to War," 2011).

Perhaps if the Doctor were to deceive himself about his role in the Time War, it would simply be a good man doing the best he can with a bad situation. Maybe Clara said it best: "You've been asking a question, and it's time that someone told you you've been getting it wrong. His name, his name is the Doctor. All the name he needs. Everything you need to know about him" ("The Time of the Doctor").

21
Forgetting Is the Human Superpower

Jessica Seymour

My entire planet died! My whole family! Do you think it never occurred to me to go back and save them?

—Ninth Doctor, "Father's Day," 2005

For Time Lords, the temptation to go back and fix the world must be unbearable. But that's their burden, as the Tenth Doctor loves to remind us. The Doctor has access to the most powerful ship in the universe, and yet he's helpless in the face of the fixed points in time—the death of Adelaide Brooke at Bowie Base One ("The Waters of Mars," 2009), Volcano Day in Pompeii ("The Fires of Pompeii," 2008), his own death at the hands of River Song ("The Wedding of River Song," 2011), and, of course, the Time War ("The Day of the Doctor," 2013).

When *Doctor Who* rebooted in 2005, with "Rose," we met Christopher Eccleston's dark, quirky-yet-guilty, Ninth Doctor. Nine was haunted by the Time War, where he destroyed the Daleks and the Time Lords in one lethal blow. The memory of what he did, of the lives he took that day, influences his decisions throughout the series—particularly when alien species play on his guilt. Over the next two regenerations, the Doctor relives his memory of the Time War again and again, reminding himself of the terrible threat he poses to the world should he lose control.

During the Fiftieth Anniversary Special, "The Day of the Doctor," we meet the War Doctor (played by the delightful John Hurt) who destroyed Gallifrey and the Daleks. The War Doctor, along with his Tenth and Eleventh regenerations, travel back to the Time War to retroactively save Gallifrey—and while his past selves forget that day, the Eleventh Doctor knows that Gallifrey is safe.

The emotional trauma he suffered during the War affects how he sees himself, and so his continued storyline revolves around the Doctor paying penance and protecting innocents from the various villains of the Whoniverse. What does that mean for the Doctor's character development over the last two regenerations? Should the Doctor forget the lessons he learned after the Time War, now that he knows that he isn't to blame? What happens if the Doctor forgets that he destroyed the Time Lords and the Daleks?

I'd Love to Forget It All

Stories allow readers to see how characters develop their sense of "Self"—who they believe they are and how they believe they fit into the world—through their experiences and the lessons they learn. As Kirsty Waugh suggests in "Mixing Memory and Desire: Recollecting the Self in *Harry Potter* and *His Dark Materials*," by creating this life "history," stories place emphasis on those moments in a character's life which are crucial to who the characters are.

The Doctor presents an interesting figure for a conversation about memory and the Self. As discussed by Patrick Stokes in *Doctor Who and Philosophy: Bigger on the Inside*, the Doctor changes his personality with every regeneration. This personality change occurs, despite each regeneration having access to the same memories as the previous "Doctor." During the Fiftieth Anniversary Special, the Tenth, Eleventh, and War Doctor all get along famously—after they're done sorting out their differences and making fun of each other's fashion choices. The fact is, the Doctor is always different when he regenerates; and yet, he remains the Doctor.

What changes during regeneration is how the Doctor *approaches* his memories, and how he constructs his "Self" through the memories he takes from one regeneration to the next. After the 2005 reboot, the Doctor's motivations seem to be fixated on atonement for the Time War. Despite the many differences between the Ninth, Tenth and Eleventh Doctors, they each want to make amends.

Memory, as described by Freud's *Studies on Hysteria* (1893–1895), is a constant forging and reforging of our sense of Self. He uses the term '*Nachträglichkeit*', or Afterwardness. Freud was mainly interested in memories of trauma, and the theory of Afterwardness is used to describe how we understand the importance of events after we see what they've done to us. Our memories define us because they make up the story of us—the story we tell ourselves and others to explain why we are the way that we are. Our Self is a continuous construction, and learning new information about our past can change the way we see and define ourselves. Essentially, Freud argued that memory is rearranged or reforged when we learn new information.

This is particularly interesting in storytelling, where we can see an earlier plot point contextualized or re-examined when fresh information comes to light. When the Doctor learns that the Time Lords were saved, he turns from penance to hope: "at last, I know where I'm going, where I've always been going: Home" ("The Day of the Doctor"). The Doctor has been regenerating before our eyes since the 1960s, but this is a new change. This time, it isn't the Doctor himself who has changed, but his *memories* of himself.

Coward or Killer?

When we meet the Ninth Doctor for the first time, he's haunted by the Time War. He takes Rose on their first "date" to the end of the world, the day the Sun swallows the Earth, and seems put off by her melancholy when she realizes that her world and her life aren't as permanent as she'd believed. At the end of the episode, the Doctor takes Rose back to the modern day and confides in her: "You think it'll last forever: people and cars and concrete. But it won't. One day it's all gone. Even the sky. My planet's gone. It's dead. It burned, like the Earth" ("The End of the World," 2005). For the Doctor, impermanence is a way of life. He exists everywhere, and everywhen, but he can never go home. By sharing that with Rose on their first trip in time and space, we get an inkling of what will be motivating the Doctor during this regeneration.

When the Gelth, a ghostly race of aliens infesting the gas pipes in a funeral home in Victorian Cardiff, mention the Time

War which nearly destroyed their race, the Doctor agrees to provide the Gelth with corpses of humans so they can be corporeal again ("The Unquiet Dead," 2005). Naturally, the Gelth double-cross the Doctor. They don't want to borrow corpses, they want to invade the planet and possess living people. The Doctor's response is disbelief: "I trusted you! I *pitied* you!" The Gelth took advantage of the Doctor's guilt and desire for atonement, and the Doctor learns to be more cautious with his generosity. His encounter with the Gelth only fuels his anger, because it leads to the death of Gwyneth, the clairvoyant servant girl.

The Ninth Doctor, despite proving himself to be an excellent dancer, is still a killer. This is brought home to the audience during "Boom Town" (2005) when the Doctor and his companions capture the Slitheen masquerading as Margaret Blaine, the mayor of Cardiff. The Doctor plans to return Margaret to her home planet, where she faces the death penalty for her crimes.

The Doctor ended the War by wiping out both sides; an action which he believes was necessary to prevent the destruction of the universe. To this Doctor, delivering Margaret to Raxacoricofallapatorius and her death sentence isn't as troubling as it is to his companions. Margaret tries to play on his sympathies, but by "Boom Town" he's learned from his experience with the Gelth and turns a deaf ear to her claims of having spared one of her victims:

> NINTH DOCTOR: You let one go, but that's nothing new. Every now and then, a little victim's spared. Because she smiled, because he's got freckles, because they begged. And that's how you live with yourself. That's how you slaughter millions. Because once in a while, on a whim, if the wind's in the right direction, you happen to be kind.
>
> MARGARET BLAINE: Only a killer would know that.

Margaret is right—the Doctor understands her because they're the same. While the Doctor would almost certainly have taken her home to be tried and executed, the TARDIS reaches a compromise by turning Margaret into an egg. This will allow her to repeat her life and, hopefully, not make the same mistakes. The Doctor is hopeful for her future because he believes that her predatory nature is the result of her upbringing, just like his murderous nature is born from what he's been forced to do for the good of the universe. But there's one race for which the Doctor has no pity: the Daleks.

During "Dalek" (2005), we see the almost paralytic rage which the Doctor carries for the Dalek race. He becomes so enraged after discovering the Dalek in Van Staten's basement, a Dalek that survived the destruction of both of their species, he tries to torture it to death. Later, he aims a gun at Rose because she won't give him a clear shot at the Dalek outside of its armor. His rage doesn't frighten the Dalek—on the contrary, it's impressed: "You would make a good Dalek." But it does frighten Rose, and her reaction forces the Doctor to reflect on what the Time War and the hatred for the Daleks has made him into.

The Ninth Doctor encounters the Daleks again during the two-part conclusion to the series "Bad Wolf/The Parting of the Ways" (2005). When he has the chance to destroy the Daleks, he hesitates because it would mean killing half of the population of Earth as well. Despite the Dalek Emperor's reminder that mankind "will be harvested for your weakness," the Doctor can't bring himself to commit another act of genocide—at least, not one which would cost the lives of innocents as well.

The Man Who Regrets

For someone who's always moving on because he dares not look back, the Doctor's memories remain a constant source of inspiration for the actions he takes in the present. His sense of Self depends on it. The memory of the Time War is so deeply important to the reboot Doctor's continued sense of Self that when the War Doctor meets his future selves, he can't recognize them. He only sees two angry men, forged by fear and regret, keeping the world safe from creatures like themselves.

The Tenth Doctor, called "The Man Who Regrets" by the Moment during "The Day of the Doctor," often dwells on his past. Unlike Nine, the Tenth Doctor tends to channel his anger at his own actions into helping others—even his most bitter enemies. When he runs from the Family of Blood ("Human Nature/Family of Blood," 2007), it isn't out of fear of them, it's out of fear of what he'll do to them when they catch him: "He never raised his voice. That was the worst thing—the fury of the Time Lord. And then we discovered why, why this Doctor, who had fought with gods and demons, why he had run away from us and hidden: he was being kind."

During "Evolution of the Daleks" (2007), the Tenth Doctor extends a hand of friendship to the Daleks—something his previous incarnation would've considered unthinkable. But this Doctor has learned to be merciful, if only to avoid repeating the mistakes of the past: "Right now you're facing the only man in the universe who might show you compassion. 'Cause I've just seen one genocide. I won't cause another."

Despite his desire to avoid mass-murder, the Tenth Doctor becomes more destructive as his story progresses. The Doctor tends to forget, after a while, just how much damage he's capable of. When he's separated from his companions or isolated in grief, his hubris takes over. The Tenth Doctor is often referred to as the most "human" of the Doctors; being both incredibly compassionate and incredibly flawed. It's when he forgets the Time War and how the power he wields can be so easily destructive, that he becomes frighteningly human.

Humans are dangerous in the Whoniverse. They destroy Sycorax ships with nuclear weapons ("The Christmas Invasion," 2005), they work alongside Daleks for profit ("Daleks in Manhattan," 2007), and they turn themselves into monsters in the quest for eternal youth ("The Lazarus Experiment," 2007). The Tenth Doctor becomes more "human" as the series progresses, and he constructs his Self as more and more powerful without the memory of the Time War to temper him. His pride is demonstrated in "Midnight" (2008), and particularly in "The Waters of Mars" (2009), when he changes a fixed point in time to save Adelaide Brooke: "For a long time now, I thought I was just a survivor, but I'm not. I'm the winner! That's who I am. The Time Lord Victorious!"

Adelaide's suicide appears to knock some sense into him because later, in "The End of Time" (2009), the Doctor has remembered some of his humility. He regrets his actions on Mars, although he still tries to delay his death for as long as possible by making the Ood wait for his assistance. He tells Wilfred Mott that the human race "look like giants," a sentiment repeated by the Twelfth Doctor in "Deep Breath" (2014), and that it's the Doctor's honor to die for him. When the Time Lords return to "complete the Ultimate Sanction" and end time itself, the Doctor fights to stop them, even though it means destroying his species for a second time. The memory of the Time War, of the destruction which the Time Lords are capable of when they choose, is driving the Doctor to prevent the end of time.

The Man Who Forgets

The Eleventh Doctor is all about memory. If the Tenth Doctor is the most "human" Doctor since the Time War, then Eleven is arguably the least human. He's mad, impulsive, and aggressively alien. He imprints himself on the memories and hearts of everyone he meets—human, alien, and enemy alike. At first, he draws strength from it. He constructs his Self as a weapon. He can "turn an army around at the mention of his name" ("A Good Man Goes to War," 2011). Eleven can be quite fierce because he knows *exactly* what he's capable of. He has the memories to prove it. When he, Amy, and Rory are captured by the Daleks in "Asylum of the Daleks" (2012), he tells Amy to "Be brave . . . Make them remember you."

Later, Oswin reminds the Doctor that the Daleks have grown stronger because they fear him. Because they *remember* him. The Time War, and everything which came after, has created a universe which loves and fears the Doctor. As a last gift, Oswin erases the Doctor from the Daleks' hive mind, and the Doctor, taking his cue from her, sets out to wipe himself from every data stream he can find. The fear he instilled in his enemies has only caused him trouble—ever since the Time War, when he wiped out two species in one stroke.

The Doctor's memory, notoriously foggy when it comes to his own shortcomings, needs constant refreshment. Amy, like other companions before her, serves the story by reminding the Doctor and the audience exactly how bad things can get when he forgets himself. In "A Town Called Mercy" (2012), the Doctor calls back to his Ninth incarnation when he tries to send Kahler-Jex to his death—but Amy is having none of it:

ELEVENTH DOCTOR: Today, I honor victims first. His, the Master's, the Daleks', all the people who died because of *my* mercy!

AMY: See, this is what happens when you travel alone for too long. Well listen to me, Doctor. We can't be like him. We have to be better than him.

The memory of the Time War, and the fear which his own name instills in his enemies, leads to a renewed desire for peace: "Don't you see? Violence doesn't end violence, it extends it" ("A Town Called Mercy"). With Amy's not-so-gentle reminder, the Doctor remains pacifist, but still dangerous.

What the Hell Are You Changing Into?

When the Doctor forgets the Time War, when he forgets that he's capable of murder and genocide, he becomes increasingly dangerous. During "The Day of the Doctor" (2013), Clara intervenes when the three Doctors plan to go through with the destruction of Gallifrey for a second time. After hearing the Tenth and Eleventh Doctors deliver a grand speech about their actions during the Time War, and how despicable they were in retrospect, the War Doctor still believes that the genocide of Time Lords and the Daleks must happen—if only to ensure that his future selves take the lessons of the Time War into their motivation for their new Selves.

It's Clara who demands they reconsider. She addresses the Eleventh Doctor, who has the most knowledge of all of his Selves about how the Time War affects his future.

> CLARA: Look at you. The three of you. The warrior, the hero, . . . and you.
>
> ELEVENTH DOCTOR: And what am I?
>
> CLARA: Have you really forgotten?
>
> ELEVENTH DOCTOR: Yes. Maybe, yes.
>
> CLARA: We've got enough warriors. Any old idiot can be a hero.
>
> ELEVENTH DOCTOR: Then what do I do?
>
> CLARA: What you've always done. Be a doctor.

The Doctor's name is a promise. A promise to care, nurture, and defend. The Doctor has always constructed his Self through his various regenerations as a man who heals—but his actions during the Time War prove that he can also be a murderer.

The War Doctor makes it clear to Clara that his future selves need that reminder of what atrocities they're capable of in order to ensure that they don't make those mistakes again: "How many worlds has his regret saved, do you think?" ("The Day of the Doctor"). This is how the War Doctor makes the decision to go through with the destruction of Gallifrey. But Clara shows that there's a third option.

The Doctor's memory of the Time War made him angry and vengeful, compassionate and prideful, pacifist, yet barely concealing his rage. When he succumbs to his fury, a reminder of the War—a reminder that he needs to be *better*, that he needs to atone for his sins—will draw him back from the brink and help him live up to his name. Although he has retroactively saved Gallifrey, the hope for reconciliation with the Time Lords needs to be tempered with the memory of his regret, because his regret is what drives him to be better.

He remembers the horrors and deaths, and acts accordingly. He heals the hurt. He is the Doctor.

22

The Mnemotechnics of Amy Pond

A.G. HOLDIER

Once upon a time there was a girl who believed in stars. Her name (like something out of a fairy tale, she'd been told) was Amelia Pond and she had a crack in her bedroom wall—a crack through which she would swear she could hear voices as she slept. This strange crack frightened her, but she could always remember her imaginary friend and feel a little better.

This Amelia didn't realize just how special she was—or how frightening that strange crack should be—but she was happy to grow up with her family and her Rory and the whispers of a most fantastic Story in her head.

You see, what Amelia didn't understand, and what she would later grow up to forget, was the importance of a tale she was told on a night in Leadworth when the shed in her yard should've been destroyed, but mysteriously wasn't. Not only was it a fairy tale worth telling, but it's a tale of Faerie that's worth pondering—the best kind of Story that enchants us, educates us, and opens us up to the wonderment of a new world.

It was a Story that saved the Universe.

Nothing Is Ever Forgotten, Not Completely

You'll recall the scene, I'm sure: after being caught by an alliance of his greatest enemies, the Doctor was forced to jerry-rig a time-traveling escape from the most secure prison in the universe—the Pandorica ("The Big Bang," 2010). By the end of the adventure, the Doctor was flying his prison into the heart of his exploding TARDIS in a desperate attempt to reboot the broken universe. Brilliantly successful (as usual), there was but a single price: because of his placement at the heart of the Big Bang Two, outside the reboot, the Doctor no longer belonged within the universe he had saved.

Enter Amy Pond. While watching his life rewind itself out of existence, the Eleventh Doctor made one last desperate bid for survival: he tucked the young Amelia into bed and told her one last story of their adventures in his magic box—a story that she wouldn't remember until her wedding day. The next time 2010 came around, after fighting the nagging feeling that there was "someone so, so important" missing, Amy's new husband reminded her of that "old wedding thing," finally allowing all of the shadowy pieces of her memory to fall into their proper place and causing her to start shouting:

AMY: *Sorry!* Sorry, everyone. But when I was a kid, I had an imaginary friend.

TABETHA: Oh no! Not this again . . .

AMY: The Raggedy Doctor. My Raggedy Doctor. But he wasn't imaginary, he was real.

TABETHA: The psychiatrists we sent her to—

AMY: *I remember you.* I remember! I brought the others back, I can bring you home, too. Raggedy Man, I remember you, and you are *late* for my wedding!

[*The glasses start rattling, very gently.*]

AMY: I found you. I found you in words, like you knew I would. That's why you told me the story of the brand new, ancient blue box.

[*A strong wind blows the balloons around.*]

AMY: Oh, clever. Very clever.

RORY: Amy, what is it?

AMY: Something old. Something new. Something borrowed. Something blue.

And as the TARDIS materialized back into the universe, the brand-new Mister Pond asked the question that was on everyone's minds: "It's the Doctor. How did we forget the Doctor?"

Perhaps an even more interesting question, particularly for those of us in the audience who know the frustration of feeling a memory slip away: "How did Amy simply remembering the Doctor actually bring him back into the world?"

I Will Always Remember *When* the Doctor Was Me

If you aren't the forgetful type, you'll recall that *memory* is something that has always followed the Doctor, a fact especially true since the series reboot: from the tragic fate of Donna Noble ("Journey's End," 2008) to the terrifying enemy of the Silence ("The Impossible Astronaut," 2011) to the antics of Strax and his memory worm ("The Snowmen," 2012), *forgetfulness* is a motif that has given *Doctor Who* every color in the emotional spectrum.

On occasion, memory loss has been seen as a well-intentioned comfort measure ("Forest of the Dead," 2008 and "Listen," 2014), but it has also been abused to quiet the guilt from a horrible choice ("The Beast Below," 2010) or corrupt a loved one by deleting part of their personality ("Death in Heaven," 2014). More than once, forgetfulness has come as a side-effect of untwisting a paradox (as in "Mawdryn Undead," 1983; "Last of the Time Lords," 2007; "The Wedding of River Song," 2011; and "Journey to the Center of the TARDIS," 2013), something the Eleventh Doctor sought to avoid when he was erasing himself from the memory banks of the universe ("The Angels Take Manhattan," 2012). Ultimately, it was thanks to an insane and dying (and impossible) Dalek that he was able to force the galaxy to truly forget about him ("Asylum of the Daleks," 2012). The Doctor has sacrificed his memories to fight planet-sized gods ("The Rings of Akhaten," 2013), sacrificed his enemies' memories to convince them to co-operate ("The Day of the Doctor," 2013), and seen the memories of his friends sacrificed to those nasty cracks in reality ("Flesh and Stone," 2010; "Cold Blood," 2010).

Our favorite Gallifreyan himself sometimes struggles with his memory, whether due to an unexpected transmat beam ("Bad Wolf," 2005), an unexpected prison sentence ("The War Games," 1969), or an unexpected regeneration (particularly in the 1996 *Doctor Who: The Television Movie* and "The Time of the Doctor/Deep Breath," 2013/2014). And let's not forget how many years he spent torturing himself with guilt because he forgot how heroic he actually was at the end of the Last Great Time War ("The Day of the Doctor"). Indeed, the list goes on: our Doctor has danced on the edge of where time and recollection part ways since many of us first met him.

But using memory itself as a creative tool seems like a horse of a different color (though he's still called Susan, thank you). Before we go too far, though, the Doctor should never travel alone and neither should we. We'll need a few helpful companions on our adventure to understand the trickiness of Amy Pond remembering the Doctor back into the universe.

I Brought the Others Back, I Can Bring You Home Too

Much like the mustachioed Brigadier, our first companion, Friedrich Nietzsche, is as well-known for his fiery confidence as he is for his facial hair. No stranger to controversy, Nietzsche spent a good portion of his philosophical career proposing wildly counter-cultural perspectives on everything from what a human being is to how the nature of time itself works (no wibbly-wobbly stuff here, though; he actually saw the universe as bound by a sort of fate). For example, Nietzsche spent much of the second essay in his 1887 work *On the Genealogy of Morals* discussing the historical origin of human society and concluding that the deciding factor in spurring humanity to develop into the dominant animal on the planet, an "animal with the right to make promises," was the collective choice to intentionally use pain in the institution of punishment.

See, to Nietzsche, it's only insofar as we can remember our pledges to each other that we're capable of functioning cohesively as a group, therefore, our power to remember our promises isn't only the foundation for our responsibility to others but also for the very institution of society itself. The tricky part, though, is to explain how calculating humans can overcome a defining feature of all animals: the natural faculty of forgetfulness. Nietzsche took the pain and difficulty that often comes in life quite seriously and argued that it's only by forgetting such things that "psychic order"—a Nietzschean term for something like "mental health"—can be maintained.

Consequently, sentient animals have developed a natural power (like breathing or digestion) to repress our past experiences so as to be able to genuinely feel happiness, hope, and all the fleeting good things of the present moment, to move on from the past and to focus on the "now." Friedrich Nietzsche would take one look at the Doctor's choice to forget (albeit, temporarily) the tragedy he experienced as the War Doctor and say, "Exactly."

So, in addition to our forgetfulness, Nietzsche suggests that it's the defining feature of the most powerful animals to also possess a competing faculty that, through an act of strong will, allows someone to avoid repressing a memory and, instead, retain it. This choice is grounded entirely in the force of an individual's will—only the best and strongest human beings are truly able to accomplish it. Consider what happened in the moments following Rory's death outside the Silurian city and his subsequent plunge into the time field emanating from the Cracks in the Universe: the Doctor frantically tries to coach Amy into focusing on Rory so that she, as a time-traveler, might be able to withstand the force of her time-stream being re-written in order to remember her fiancé. Unfortunately, the TARDIS shakes, distracting Amy Pond, thereby erasing Rory from her memory—her will to remember wasn't strong enough to counteract the equally strong natural force pressing on her to forget ("Cold Blood")—it may also be worth noting that the strong-willed Doctor suffered no such weakness.

But wait! As Vincent Van Gogh noticed, some part of Amy did, in fact, remember the loss of her Rory, even if she wasn't consciously aware of it ("Vincent and the Doctor," 2010). You see only the best humans (to Nietzsche, the most powerful ones) can remember things through an act of will. The rest of us, he explained, must have our memories burned into our minds through the painful process he dubbed *mnemotechnics*. As he said in his *Genealogy*, "only that which never ceases to *hurt* stays in the memory." Nietzsche saw the history of human society as the development of ever-more-clever ways of inflicting pain on each other (both physically and mentally) so as to maintain the foundation on which we all live together—the remembrance of our promises. The "social straitjacket," to use Nietzsche's term, is intentionally far from comfortable—anything else and society would simply be forgotten.

So, if Amy Pond was unable to consciously remember the most important man in her life by simply willing herself to do so, Nietzsche would point to the scars left on her *sub*conscious heart by the pain of her loss as the reason for her confusing tears in both nineteenth-century France and outside Stonehenge in front of a strangely familiar Roman centurion ("The Pandorica Opens," 2010). But although pain is a powerful element connected with human memory, Nietzsche's *mnemotechnics* alone aren't enough to explain how Amy could go on to simply remember the Doctor out of the Total Event Collapse—let's turn to our other companion for some advice.

That's Why You Told Me the Story

Whereas many are familiar with the novels of J.R.R. Tolkien, his academic work is somewhat more obscure—though no less imaginative. Like Nietzsche, Tolkien was also concerned with how societal-level memories operate and affect individual members of those groups, but he was more optimistic than our German friend. Instead of pain, Tolkien was interested in fairy tales—and not just "The Three Little Sontarans" or "The Emperor Dalek's New Clothes" ("Night Terrors," 2011).

Particularly in his 1947 essay "On Fairy Stories," Tolkien described fairy tales as something far more significant than a simple fable involving tiny, flying people; instead, he saw these narratives as one of the most complex and important genres of human storytelling. To Tolkien, a fairy story is much like a TARDIS: after entering either one, you will find yourself transported into a complicated and fantastic world filled with wonderment and adventure. This should come as no surprise from the creator of Middle-Earth, with all of its richness and depth, but Tolkienesque fairy tales contain far more than dragons and dwarves. They hold "the seas, the sun, the moon, the sky; and the earth, and all things that are in it: tree and bird, water and stone, wine and bread, and ourselves, mortal men, when we are enchanted." Fairy tales, to Tolkien, involve the fictional creation of an entire *realm* of existence—the realm of Faerie.

The crucial thing for Tolkien is for the world of the fairy story to make internal sense. For example, Tolkien highlights that Magic is, quite often, an element of fairy stories, but it only works if it's taken seriously as a natural part of the fictional world. Whatever rules an author wishes to create for her world are fine for Tolkien, provided that they're consistent and coherent—Magic must never be laughed at or belittled as unreal (no more so than something like gravity, the number twelve, or the color blue). Say, for example, that the entire run of *Doctor Who* were to finally conclude (Gallifrey forbid) with the final incarnation of the Doctor waking up from a dream to discover that he was a mere human having a nap like Dorothy visiting Oz. Not only would this undercut the "reality" of the decades-long show, but it would utterly destroy the Magic of the fictional world and turn the beauty of the story into a simple plot device.

No, the value of a fairy story is precisely the fact that it's at once comfortably familiar (so that we recognize it), but also strangely and magically alien (so that, much like our attraction to our alien Doctor, we are captivated by it). The enchantment that Tolkien discusses goes beyond a simple suspension of disbelief for the audience to something he calls "secondary belief," or a positive sense that the fictional world could actually be real. This is far from easy, and, in Tolkien's words, likely requires a certain type of "elvish craft," but the practice serves a vital role in maintaining the cultural memory of a society.

Much like how Gallifreyan stories about the Shakri can be traced back to an otherwise forgotten element of the universe, all fairy tales allow their story-tellers to come to grips with complicated, confusing, frightening, and entertaining elements of their culture's history ("The Power of Three," 2012). Consider how the Doctor describes the stories born from the reality of creatures like the Fendahl ("Image of the Fendahl," 1977), the Vashta Nerada ("Silence in the Library," 2008), or the Beast of the Impossible Planet ("The Satan Pit," 2006): the important thing wasn't that the myths of night demons or the Devil that were scattered across a thousand worlds were either true or false. The point was for all of those fairy tales to lead their hearers back into a world where the memory of the important creatures that inspired each story was preserved. And humanity is no different: the Doctor has fought against enemies that resemble our myths of vampires ("The Vampires of Venice," 2010), werewolves ("Tooth and Claw," 2006), zombies ("The Unquiet Dead"; "The Empty Child," 2005; and "Death in Heaven," 2014), and Frankenstein's monster ("The Brain of Morbius," 1976), indicating that we, too, draw our myths from the same sort of source.

Even more than that, fairy stories, Tolkien said, offer us an opportunity to compare our Real World with the fictional worlds of our characters, thereby allowing us to appreciate elements of our universe that would otherwise be taken for granted or forgotten. Screwdrivers can be rather mundane until you imagine a glowing green light at one end. Tolkien dubbed this "regaining of a clear view" of the everyday beauty of reality and the value of everything in it "Recovery."

Which is, as you will recall, precisely what the Doctor needed after tucking Amelia in one last time. What could possibly be done? Remember the Doctor's words:

> Well, you'll remember me a little. I'll be a story in your head. But that's okay. We're all stories in the end. Just make it a good one, eh? Because it was, you know. It was the best! ("The Big Bang," 2010)

I Found You in Words

The Eleventh Doctor was faced with an impossible problem: he'd saved the universe, but no longer belonged within it. He needed to find two things quickly: a spell to cast and the words to do so. Knowing that all memory of himself was about to be erased from existence, the Doctor remembered both Amy's connection to Rory after he fell into the cracks, and, perhaps, Nietzsche's observations of the power of pain to engrave memories deeply onto a person's soul. Without delay, the Doctor latched onto one last, desperate bid for survival by planting a tiny seed of himself inside Amy Pond's memories. If experiencing the loss of a friend as great as the Doctor isn't unbearably painful, then I suggest we don't understand the meaning of the word.

However, the Doctor knew that this wasn't as simple as merely sending Amy a postcard (that would come later)—he needed to burn the painful memory of himself into Amy's subconscious while also wrapping that memory in a protective cocoon that would serve to both safeguard and supercharge her mind with a creative, world-fashioning power. So, following Tolkien, the Doctor employed a tool that has always been about allowing a society to see the world clearly by considering a fictional one in comparison: the fairy tale. Unwittingly anticipating Tolkien's recognition of fairy tales as masterful examples of created worlds, Nietzsche writes in his 1872 book *The Birth of Tragedy* that art is "the highest task and the properly metaphysical activity of this life," or that genuine creation in the Real World is the business of all human artists—perhaps even one working with her painful memory as her medium.

And the Doctor is no stranger to seeing stories come to life, whether it was through the willful machinations of the Master and his Toclafane ("The Sound of Drums," 2007), the frightened ability of Chloe Webber while possessed by an Isolus ("Fear Her," 2006), or the strange happenings surrounding the little alien called George who just needed some parents ("Night Terrors"). The Second Doctor once found himself stranded in the Land of Fiction itself where he was able to rub elbows with Lemuel Gulliver, Rapunzel, and several famous monsters from Greek mythology ("The Mind Robber," 1968)—which makes the Twelfth Doctor's cynical reaction to meeting Robin Hood all the more quizzical ("Robot of Sherwood," 2014). And let's not forget where we started this discussion: inside the Pandorica, the most secure prison in the Doctor's universe, surrounded by Roman centurions, all of whom were created literally out of the remembered stories once loved by little Amelia Pond.

Little Amelia Pond who loved the Doctor, who watched him save all existence, and who spent her entire childhood with the universe pouring into her mind through the Crack in her wall, was uniquely positioned to combine Nietzschean *mnemotechnics* with Tolkien's idea that fairy tales have power to preserve and recover forgotten elements of our world. She, more than most, lost something crucial in the Big Bang Two, but it was only after the words of the Doctor's final Story sparked the gears of her adult mind to start turning again that those seeds planted by the Doctor sprouted and blossomed.

And the next thing we knew, the TARDIS was blocking the dance floor.

Once upon a Time Lord

So, was the Doctor actually as surprised as he claimed to be when he opened his door to his in-laws' wedding? Judging by our discussion here, his formal attire, and his parting "Gotcha" to Amy as the Pandorica flew away, we should clearly think not. As usual, the Doctor knew exactly what he was doing when he told that little girl one last story. Let's not forget the temporally un-synced River Song's parting comment to the Doctor at the Byzantium ("Flesh and Stone"):

> RIVER: You'll see me again quite soon when the Pandorica opens.
>
> THE DOCTOR: The Pandorica? Ha! That's a fairy tale.
>
> RIVER: Doctor, *aren't we all*? I'll see you there.

Tolkien knew that nothing is "just a fairy tale" and a Nietzschean eye might see how the significance of that fact could weigh upon everyone involved with these nasty Cracks— even the strong-willed and fearless Doctor ("The God Complex," 2011 and "The Time of the Doctor").

In the end though, as with all good fairy tales, there's a wedding, a party, and they all lived happily ever after—at least until the TARDIS whisked them away to the next adventure.

23
Failing and Forgiving in the *Name* of the Doctor

MATTHEW A. HOFFMAN

The Doctor has spent the first seven years of the series revival mourning Gallifrey's destruction, and condemning himself for having caused it. In fact, destroying his own people is so horrendous to him that he denies the name "the Doctor" to the incarnation who fought and ended the Time War. Though he admits his own guilt, he can never truly face what he's done, viewing his other self as a monster.

Despite the differences between human and Time-Lord lives, the Doctor's response to his moral failing is like the reaction a human might have in similar circumstances. Even after hundreds of years and several regenerations, the Doctor is unable to forgive himself for both his action and for falling short of his ideal of character.

Self-forgiveness has often been ignored by philosophers who write on forgiveness, many assuming it doesn't make sense or doesn't count as "true" forgiveness. However, self-forgiveness certainly applies in the case of a Time Lord with multiple selves. Not only is self-forgiveness necessary for the Doctor to heal fully from the war, it allows him to change his own past. In the Fiftieth Anniversary Special, we see the Tenth and Eleventh Doctors forced to come to terms with their past, working with the War Doctor and accepting their earlier actions. Forgiving the War Doctor allows the Doctor to move on from the war, but it also allows him to save Gallifrey, which wouldn't be possible without this reconciliation.

Last of the Time Lords

When we first meet the Ninth Doctor in "Rose" (2005), presumably set shortly after his regeneration, he introduces himself to his future companion by calling himself the Doctor, but it's clear from how he acts that much has happened to him since *Doctor Who: The TV Movie* (1996). He first tells Rose that he's the only one of his people left ("The End of the World," 2005), but in later episodes we learn the full story of how the Time War ended. Not only was Gallifrey destroyed along with the Dalek fleet, the Doctor's actions were the cause. Coming out of the war as the only survivor of his own genocide, the Doctor has something of a death wish, sending Rose away and expecting to die confronting the Daleks one final time ("The Parting of the Ways," 2005).

The Doctor prefers to die rather than commit genocide a second time, even if not acting means the Daleks succeed. He'd rather die himself than directly kill innocent people again. He survives thanks to Rose's intervention, but is forced to regenerate as a result of saving her from the energy of the Heart of the TARDIS. In regenerating, he's able to distance himself from the immediate survivor's guilt of his previous self. Yet beneath his cheerful façade, the new Tenth Doctor remains haunted by his actions during the war, hoping to never have to let his enemies die, going so far as even trying to save Davros ("Journey's End," 2008). The Eleventh Doctor is, however, finally able to put the Time War behind him in "The Beast Below" (2010), referring to it merely as a "bad day."

The Doctor shows a willingness to put the past behind him in his post-war lives. Despite this change wrought by successive regenerations, the Doctor remains the last of the Time Lords, well aware of his complicity in being such. The Time War has done more than make him aware of his losses, however, and we later learn he's been carrying another secret. He's able to remain the Doctor in the present only by shutting away the memory of the man he was when he destroyed Gallifrey. The Doctor can, and frequently does, admit his guilt, but only to blame himself. For him, the man who ended the Time War is not the Doctor at all.

A Man Is the Sum of His Memories. A Time Lord Even More So

Not only does regeneration change the Doctor's appearance more drastically—and more quickly—than happens in most people's lives, his personality undergoes a similar transformation. While we can look in the mirror and wonder at physical and mental changes over time, we're able to connect our present to our past by reflecting on how our past choices led to the present. Unlike humans, each physical incarnation of the Doctor exists as a separate man, rather than his present self being a result of his past. This leaves the Doctor with only memories of his past actions by which to tell a coherent story of his life. Lacking any name he's willing to (or can) go by, and since his past selves are quite different, the connecting thread for him throughout his lives is his title of "Doctor." He doesn't correct the Master, who defines the Doctor as "the man who makes people better" ("The Sound of Drums," 2007). Indeed, the Doctor appears to accept this as an accurate description of what it is to be "the Doctor." In labeling himself like this, though, he becomes defined by the sort of actions "the Doctor" would do.

As Jeffrey Blustein says in his aptly-named "Doctoring and Self-Forgiveness" (though about a different sort of doctor), one kind of self-respect involves "developing and living by commitments and attachments that ground a set of personal . . . standards by which the individual is prepared to judge his self-worth." This is precisely what the Doctor does in locating his life in relation to a set of principles summed up by his title. The Doctor views choosing his name as making a promise to only act a certain way. In taking on the name "Doctor," he's made a vow to help others wherever he finds himself, to not be "cruel or cowardly," to "never give up" and "never give in." Certain actions not only are contrary to this standard, they would in his mind make him no longer able to call himself the Doctor. Faced with lobotomizing the Star Whale in "The Beast Below," the Doctor tells Amy he won't be the Doctor afterwards. In his eyes, the lack of a better choice doesn't make the action right, and the Doctor sees his action as forcing him to renounce his identity. Acting contrary to how "the Doctor" should act necessitates this change in identity, even though he sees no other option open to him.

However, defining himself in this way makes the Doctor's self-understanding fragile. He takes himself to be a man who helps rather than harms, yet it appears that any future situation he faces might be one in which he must make a similar impossible choice. Lacking another name, it isn't only his self-respect but his identity at stake. He's quite lucky in this regard, very rarely having to decide between outcomes that run opposite his principles. However, without a name, the Doctor can't create a narrative about the man he once was—who was able to destroy Gallifrey—turning into the man he is now. The only thread he has to connect his lives is calling himself "the Doctor," and that he defines by characteristic actions.

Even though various incarnations argue with each other, they all recognize themselves as the same man, save for one. They might share memories, but as far as the post-war Doctor is concerned, the war was ended by another man. Since the Doctor accepts responsibility for the genocide, it isn't that action alone which he can't face. He hides his Time War-era self not only because he can't forgive himself for destroying Gallifrey, but because he finds it impossible to forgive himself for being the sort of man who could kill his own people. Moreover, the Doctor's choice to bury his past self allows him to continue calling himself "the Doctor" in the present. In distancing himself from his past, he can allow himself to feel shame and guilt, but he doesn't have to think of the War Doctor as anything more than an aberration. Rather than trying to remember the motivations and concerns they share, the Doctor refuses to see himself in the War Doctor at all, for fear it would reflect on his present.

The disassociation of the sort the Doctor has with his own past stems from not wanting to compare his post-war life to his past. This shame for his actual Ninth self, as Jeffrie Murphy puts it, involves "fear that the seeds of such a person might still remain" within him. Despite trying to live up to his ideal of what it means to be "the Doctor," he remains suspicious of his own motives. This fear, along with the shame of the action itself, gives rise to a deep self-loathing. Thus when facing the Dream Lord in "Amy's Choice" (2010), the Doctor quickly realizes who this mysterious antagonist is, recognizing the Dream Lord's hatred for the Doctor as his own subconscious given physical form. Ultimately the Doctor's fear lies, not in believing himself evil deep down, but in having been the same man all along, yet unable to save Gallifrey. His fear isn't that he gave up the mantle of the Doctor during the war, but that he failed *as* the Doctor.

This "moral hatred of self," in Murphy's phrase, is centered on the breaking of his promise to do good, as the Eleventh Doctor explains to Clara. The fault the Doctor sees is that he wasn't able to do better, to find another way. After all, that's what the Doctor's supposed to do. Since the Doctor thinks he should have been able to do otherwise, he won't accept that there was no better way in those circumstances. Not only does he hold the War Doctor responsible for the genocide itself, the Doctor also considers his old self blameworthy for being able to go through with his plan. The incarnation who ended the war becomes what Robin Dillon in "Self-Forgiveness and Self-Respect" calls "one's 'self-as-feared'." To the Doctor, his past incarnation is proof not only that his action was wrong, but that it revealed his promise to be hollow, and his life to be meaningless. Of course the Doctor has been running from this!

The Man Who Regrets and the Man Who Forgets

In "The Day of the Doctor," the Tenth and Eleventh Doctors have to work with the War Doctor to stop a Zygon invasion, forcing them to reconsider their past. Since they've omitted the War Doctor from the narrative of their lives, they haven't had to work through the guilt and shame of their choice to end the war. Without being confronted by an unwanted past, the post-war incarnations of the Doctor haven't come to terms with who they were, nor who they are as a result of the war. Having their past self alongside them gives the two Doctors no opportunity to hide from themselves any longer.

When first they meet, the War Doctor recognizes their look as one of dread. The Doctors' personal anxiety isn't quite the same as their response to a genocidal being like a Dalek, so it doesn't seem to reflect the view of the later Doctors that the old man before them is a monster. Rather, their fear involves having to face themselves and their past. If we think someone *able* to be forgiven—even if we find ourselves unable to forgive—we must also view this person as responsible for her actions.

Where a person can be held responsible for the genocide of Gallifrey, a monster can't. A being incapable of moral understanding can only be stopped, not reasoned with. Yet that's exactly why the Doctor prefers to think of his secret incarnation as monstrous. To face his past self as anything but an unreasoning evildoer, the Doctor would have to consider his past self's motives. Though holding himself responsible is in tension with thinking himself a monster, the pull between these exists because the Doctor prefers not to understand who he was. Viewing himself as a reformed monster makes Gallifrey's destruction the act of someone else, preferable to seeing that act coming from recognizable, "Doctorly" motives.

Following the Time War, the Doctor consciously works to prevent such a situation from occurring again, as well as refusing to commit genocide, even against the Daleks. The War Doctor clearly sees them as better men *because*, in the face of his actions, they value the universe and other people more keenly. The Doctor not only remains committed to the meaning he places in the name "Doctor," he tries to make up for his past wrongs, and this reaffirmation of his values is an important step in forgiving himself. If the Doctor had truly been as evil as he sees himself, yet repented, forgiveness would have been at least more difficult, and potentially impossible for him. Jeffrie Murphy argues that a "fully changed life" is necessary before we can forgive those who commit atrocities. However, even if the War Doctor had been a reformed villain, self-forgiveness would probably have been impossible for the Doctor. Being a certain kind of man, and acting accordingly, is so important to the Doctor's self-worth that even reform might not be enough for him to forgive. The Doctor's journey of forgiveness is therefore one of learning to judge correctly the actions of his other self, without focusing only on that man's moral integrity, or his own fears of imperfection.

The Doctor can forgive himself in the end partly because, while he was forced to make a terrible choice, his motivation wasn't that of the malicious figure he saw himself as in retrospect. Isolating his true Ninth incarnation to the corners of memory led the Doctor to self-recrimination beyond merely regretting his choice. When forced by circumstances (and the Moment itself) to interact with their past, the post-war Doctors are made to confront the reality of their decision instead of their preferred account. The dreaded figure hidden away in their memory, rather than being a terrible man, is much the same as they are, but forced into a hopeless situation with no good alternatives. In choosing to destroy Gallifrey, the War Doctor isn't killing billions for its own sake, but in order to save everyone else in the universe. This common motivation connects the three men as the Doctor. Given how regeneration works, this is both self-forgiveness and forgiving someone else, especially because the later Doctors haven't wanted to recognize their connection to the man who fought the Time War.

Once the Doctor recognizes that his guilt lies in the action of destroying Gallifrey, he's able to come to terms with the War Doctor's choice, without thinking that the lack of better options that day reflects on his character. Accepting the War Doctor doesn't mean the future Doctors see their action as good, nor does it even mean the Doctor stops blaming himself. They forgive him, not thinking that the destruction of Gallifrey is any less terrible, but no longer refusing to acknowledge the reality of the person behind that action.

Most all philosophers would agree that forgiveness, even self-forgiveness, doesn't extinguish holding someone responsible for wrong acts. However, some think that feelings of blame and reproach are incompatible with having completely forgiven someone. Charles Griswold, for example, sees forgiveness as a process, so while he thinks one can retain negative feelings and forgive someone, he thinks this antipathy shows there's more forgiveness to be done. Others, like Dillon and Andrea Westlund, see complete forgiveness as compatible with moderated antipathy for others, no longer being controlled by one's resentment or loathing. Similarly, self-forgiveness doesn't rule out self-reproach. Dillon holds that self-forgiveness involves ending the alienation one feels towards one's past self, no longer being bound by self-hatred. Forgiving isn't the same as excusing someone, so it isn't incompatible with continuing to blame someone when warranted. For the Doctor, forgiving himself means facing that the end of the Time War was a day when "it wasn't possible to get it right," in which even the Doctor couldn't save everyone. The future Doctors are able to understand the War Doctor as the same man they are, standing with him to end the war and finally move on with their lives.

Be a Doctor

The Doctor forgiving himself might've been impossible without Clara, for no matter his actions in the present, the specter of genocide makes him question the good he does. Clara, as an outsider to the Doctor's life, is able to answer his question of "who am I"; whereas, he can't. Having traveled with one version and seen all his past selves when she jumps into his time-stream in "The Name of the Doctor" (2013), she can give an outsider's perspective on her friend's character hundreds of years after the war. This third-party forgiveness, with her affirmation of his present integrity, lets the Doctor face his past truthfully for the first time without fear of his present. In doing so, he finds himself, not changed from a monster into a Doctor, but as an old man who needs to be told that he too is the Doctor.

Reconciliation leads the two Doctors to their past self, intending to help him through his darkest moment. Clara, however, despite being an integral part of the Doctor's path to self-forgiveness, wouldn't be able to forgive the Eleventh Doctor—her Doctor—for taking part in Gallifrey's destruction, even as part of his forgiving his past self. Despite the Doctor's acting in remembrance of all the people on Gallifrey he can't save, Clara can't imagine him participating in the genocide. Knowing who he is, seeing him having become a better man trying to prevent further catastrophe and atone for his actions, she can't accept that his present self could ever help to destroy Gallifrey. Not only would helping his past self re-open the Doctor's wounds instead of helping him to heal, Clara trusts the Doctor to do the impossible. Her stubborn faith in the Doctor forces the three men to realize they were wrong to think there was no better choice, and that because they're all the Doctor, together they can find a way to save Gallifrey.

Thus finally, only Clara can reaffirm all three men's continuity of identity, reminding them what it means to be the Doctor. That the Doctor, in being unable to forgive himself, thinks there should've been another way, gives him the opportunity to change his past, finding a path between the horns of his dilemma. He has spent centuries replaying that moment, trying to think of other options, and thinking it's his fault for not having any. Once he lets go of his shame for being in that situation, he's able to put those centuries of recrimination to use, able to devise a plan giving him another option. He's the Doctor, after all, and for him to call some decision impossible merely indicates he hasn't looked closely enough at the situation to see all the possibilities. Some circumstances may leave the Doctor only bad choices ("Mummy on the Orient Express," 2014), but they can never take the form of a dilemma forcing the Doctor to renounce his identity. Not only was the Doctor wrong in the particular instance of ending the Time War, but there are no such dilemmas at all for him. No matter how bleak and identity-destroying the circumstances appear, the Doctor can always find a way out.

In the minisode "The Night of the Doctor" (2013), the newly regenerated Time Lord declares himself, "Doctor no more," pre-emptively giving up his usual title with the realization of what he must do fighting the Time War. In the end, however, his future selves realize that they've always been the Doctor, and the Doctor isn't a man who could ever commit genocide. Ultimately not even this incarnation born to fight a war can stray very far from the Doctor's ideals. Clara makes this clear to the Doctor—and later the Time Lords—in "The Time of the Doctor." The name he's chosen is more than a promise of how he will act; it describes who he is, and never more so than when faced with a seemingly impossible choice. The Doctor may not always be kind or caring, or even very heroic. He may only be "an idiot, with a box and a screwdriver" ("Death in Heaven," 2014), but he's always able to live up to his name. Regardless of what the future brings or the personal idiosyncrasies of succeeding Doctors, that'll remain the fundamental truth uniting them all.[1]

---

[1] I would like to thank Jorge Oseguera Gamba for making me aware of this project, and Sara Kolmes for her valuable feedback.

24
Who's Duty to Whom?

PAUL DAWSON

A staple of TV viewing in the 1970s, aside from *Doctor Who*, was the wildlife documentary. These invariably showed animals of one sort hunting, killing, and eating animals of some other sort. Disquieting and indeed disgusting as the spectacle very often was, the average viewer seldom felt compelled to take sides, morally speaking. The lion disembowelling the gazelle might have put me off my fish fingers and custard, but I neither condemned lions, nor thought that, if ever I got the chance, I'd save and protect the gazelles. Lions hunting gazelles was, after all, the natural order of things, and I, being neither lion nor gazelle, thought only to observe disinterestedly.

Why, then, should a Time Lord make, and act on, moral judgments about relations between different species of non-Time Lord? More specifically, why should the Doctor side with humans—or humanoids, anyway—against highly intelligent non-humanoids? Granted, he doesn't *always* do this. Overwhelmingly, though, if it's a question of humans vs. Nestenes or Racnoss or Daleks, the Doctor is on our side. But *why*? And is such partisan behavior on his part *morally justifiable*?

A Rational Doctor?

Suppose that the Doctor asks himself such questions. Searching for answers, he travels first to Prussia in the late eighteenth century, there to converse with Immanuel Kant (1724–1804). Kant's moral theory clarifies and defends what he takes to be our ordinary view, that moral imperatives—moral requirements—are essentially *categorical*. They apply *universally*, to all who can understand them, regardless of differences of time, circumstance, species, culture, character, personality, personal history, need, desire, taste, and even planet of origin.

Categorical morality requires a categorical foundation, and that can only be logic. Why? Well, *all* thinking presupposes logic. Even a Dalek couldn't genuinely think that Davros *was* its sole creator and at the same time think that Davros *wasn't* its sole creator, or that someone else was its sole creator. This is an instance of the logical law of exclusive disjunction (either A or B, but not both), and that law is a necessary condition of all thinking.

Any being that thinks is subject to logic, then, and this includes beings devoid of benevolence, like the Daleks. Therefore, founding morality on logic rather than benevolence would permit Kant and his followers to extend moral imperatives even to the Daleks, and explain and justify the conviction of the Daleks' victims and opponents everywhere—that the Daleks *really are* morally wrong to exterminate and enslave. We could hardly say this of the Daleks if morality depended on benevolence, for then they, congenitally lacking in benevolence, would be literally *incapable* of choosing *not* to exterminate and enslave, and so couldn't have any moral *obligation* not to do such things. They'd be *amoral* creatures, rather than the *immoral* monsters we rightly regard them as being. So, if the Daleks are immoral rather than amoral—if they act morally wrongly, rather than outside of morality altogether—they must be subject to the moral law.

Logic prescribes answers for all thinkers, whatever their desires. The Ninth Doctor might wish that the War Doctor wasn't the same person as he, but if the Ninth is the same person as the Eighth Doctor, and the Eighth the same as the War Doctor, logic imposes this numerical identity upon him. In morality too, though the right thing to do might not be what an agent wishes to do, and the wrong thing to do might be what he'd love to do most of all, logic dictates the same answers for all thinkers. If logic so dictates, then likewise, regardless of contingencies of tradition and culture, the Aztecs oughtn't to have sacrificed people industrially, the Sontarans oughtn't to glory in war, the Cybermen oughtn't to impose conversion upon the unwilling, and the Daleks oughtn't to exterminate or enslave all non-Daleks. Again, logic might seem the ideal foundation for morality, as ordinarily construed.

Take the example of Daleks enslaving non-Daleks. Kant's moral theory implies that slavery is morally wrong, because it's logically incoherent to suppose it to be okay for everyone to enslave. If everyone enslaved everyone, no one could enslave anyone, nor even *will* to enslave anyone. The very idea of slavery is logically parasitic upon there being non-slaves, therefore slavery can't rationally be universalized. Therefore it's morally wrong.

The Doctor would see immediately that it would be hopeless to try to appeal to the Daleks with this argument. Even if they agreed with Kant about the logical incoherence of universalizing slavery, they'd simply retort: "EV-RY-ONE *WILL NOT* EN-SLAVE EV-RY-ONE!! ALL OTHER RACES ARE WEAK AND COM-PA-SSION-ATE. THE DA-LEKS WILL EN-SLAVE ALL!!" They'd insist, that is, upon viewing Kant's universalizability test *consequentially*—in terms of what would be *likely* to *happen* in the *actual* world—rather than in a way that permits the abstract, theoretical self-refutation that Kant intends. And indeed there's nothing *illogical* about thinking about such matters in consequentialist ways, rather than in a purely logical way.

More likely, the Daleks would fail even to *grasp* the universality that Kant holds to be essential to morality. *Why* must it be permissible for every rational agent to enslave everyone, if it's permissible for *the Daleks* to enslave everyone? Surely any normative system that could have any influence at all upon the Dalek psyche would have to enshrine the Daleks' conception of themselves as the *exception*, by dint of their inherent superiority.

Master Morality

Or take the Master. He might agree with Kant that rationality has special value, but view this value as *instrumental* rather than *intrinsic*. That is, he might fail to see why rational agents' rationality obliges him to treat them as ends in themselves, rather than merely as means to his ends. There are times, after all, when thinking human slaves suit his purposes better than mindless Ogron slaves ("Day of the Daleks," 1972 and "Frontier in Space," 1973). And even if he "oughtn't" merely to use and exploit rational agents, why *oughtn't* he do what he "oughtn't"?

Such reflections upon his arch enemies might lead the Doctor to conclude that Kant's theory fails. Conceiving of moral imperatives as categorical, Kant attempts to found morality upon pure reason. Pure reason, however, shorn of all interest and inclination, can't *motivate* anyone to act or refrain from acting. Kant's sought-after "categoricality" strips morality of its power to require behavior, so that *the very idea* of a categorical imperative implies a logical contradiction. Since it's *essential* to morality that it be able to influence will and behavior, Kant's view of morality must be false.

The apparent failure of Kant's moral theory might come as something of a relief to the Doctor. If Kant were right, then every time the Doctor helped others because he *wanted* to, in order to *make their lives better*, his actions lacked all moral worth. This is partly because those actions were motivated by desire rather than by reason alone. According to Kant, desires can't be proper moral motives since they vary from agent to agent, whereas moral requirements are universal. It's also because the objects of the Doctor's desires were certain *consequences*, and Kant regards consequences as morally irrelevant.

Even more seriously, the truth of Kant's theory would render certain aspects of the Doctor's assistance of humans/humanoids against rational non-humanoid aggressors morally unjustifiable. On Kant's view, all rational (and semi-rational) agents ought to be treated with equal respect just because of their rationality, and regardless of what they've done, or might do, to other rational agents. Consider the many occasions upon which the Doctor lied to murderous rational aliens in order to save human or humanoid lives. Kant says that it's always morally wrong to lie to rational agents, since this is to treat them merely as means—as tools or instruments—rather than also as ends in themselves, undermining their sacred rationality. Stealing is likewise always morally wrong, Kant maintains. Thus, regardless of his intentions and regardless of all that he's achieved subsequently, the Doctor's entire career has been based upon an initial act that was absolutely immoral: stealing the TARDIS from the Time Lords.

Suppose that Kant responded to this criticism by suggesting that the Doctor's "morality" was nothing more than pure *self-*

ishness—that it was selfishness alone that led the Doctor to steal the TARDIS, interfere in the affairs of others, and side mostly with pretty, friendly, grateful humans/humanoids, against ugly, unfriendly, ungrateful non-humanoids. The Doctor might then wonder whether morality and selfishness were as incompatible as Kant claims. Mightn't selfishness be the *foundation* of morality?

A Selfish Doctor?

Thomas Hobbes (1588–1679) would assure the Doctor that all of his behavior was indeed motivated solely by a concern for his own interest, but stress that this was no aberration, since it's true of *every* sentient creature. For Hobbes believed that absolutely all behavior is rooted in selfishness, so that altruism—acting for what one takes to be the benefit of others, with no concern for one's own well-being—is a psychological impossibility. This view is known as psychological egoism.

If psychological egoism is true, is there any such thing as morality? In his book *Leviathan*, Hobbes argues that life in the "state of nature"—life without laws, morality, and society, which are wholly artificial—is a perpetual "war of all against all." Every sentient creature is engaged ceaselessly in a bitter struggle to protect and maximize its own selfish interests against being raided by other sentient creatures which are attempting to protect and maximize their own selfish interests. Humans aren't excluded. Any human with food, shelter, mate, family, possessions is a natural target for many others, so any individual human life in the state of nature is likely to be "nasty, brutish, and short."

Humans differ from other Terran animals in one salient respect, however: their capacity to reason and reflect enables them to work all this out, and to work out how to improve the quality and duration of their lives. If each of us understands that it's less likely that anyone else will rob or kill him if he agrees not to rob or kill anyone else, then each of us might "sign up" to the social contract. This social contract manifests a compromise. We agree to constrain our attempts to realize our self-perceived self-interest, in recognition of the likelihood of our being much better off thereby than if no such agreement was honored. Thus our egoism is *enlightened*, not in the sense that we become at all altruistic—for that's psychologically impossible—but in the sense that reason gives us the means to transcend the state of nature and its grim inevitabilities. A truce is called in the war of all against all.

So, Hobbes would say that every action the Doctor ever performed was selfish. Ultimately, even where he helped others at great immediate cost to himself, he acted solely in order to further what he perceived, whether consciously or unconsciously, to be in his own interests. That's okay, though, because it can't be that he *ought* to have acted *un*selfishly, given that it's impossible for any sentient creature to act unselfishly. There can be no shame in not doing what one literally can't do. (As Kant puts it, "*ought* implies *can*.") This doesn't preclude the *moral rightness* of any of the Doctor's actions, though, because the social contract *is* morality.

Given psychological egoism, there's nothing else for morality *to* be. Whenever the Doctor acted in accordance with the rules set down in the social contract, he fulfilled his moral obligations to his co-signatories. But the Daleks aren't amongst these co-signatories, and neither are many of the non-humanoid races he has encountered, for their non-humanoid proclivities and powers exclude them. He has no moral obligations to beings that are too different, but he *is* morally—that is, selfishly—obliged to uphold the social contract against those who'd destroy it. This is how the Doctor's partisan behavior is to be explained and justified.

Exterminate Egoism!

How convincing is Hobbes's explanation? Certain aspects of human behavior do seem to bear it out. Moral principles are often ignored when people believe that it's in their interest to ignore them, and that they can get away with ignoring them. Few people would avoid trampling over those who were weaker and slower, if they impeded their flight from Autons' guns and Daleks' saucers. Thus, during the Dalek occupation of the Earth in the Twenty-second century, so many humans betrayed so many others—they were out to survive even at the cost of others' misery and death under their extra-terrestrial oppressors' yoke ("The Dalek Invasion on Earth," 1964, and "Day of the Daleks").

But moral principles are re-adopted hastily whenever intelligent beings become aware that their own interests are threatened without them. The Doctor himself engineered a truce between humans and Zygons on just such grounds ("The Day of the Doctor," 2013). This does seem to suggest that selfishness underlies so-called morality. And why the need for guards, police, armed forces, Judoon, Shadow Proclamation, if anything *other* than the self-interested fear of being found out and punished can be relied upon to keep people moral? Why this need, if people can be altruistic, or motivated by the thought of duty alone?

But if morality is nothing more than the social contract signed up to by members of any given society, how could anyone belonging to that society think that some of the rules set out in its social contract are morally wrong? And yet the Doctor might recall many occasions where *apparently* brave people fought *apparently* selflessly *against* the society to which they belonged, *apparently* in order to undo injustices they believed that society to enshrine, enforce, and propagate ("Invasion of the Dinosaurs," 1974 and "The Sun Makers," 1977). In our ordinary, non-Hobbesian conception, morality transcends any social contract, and undermines many of the sanctions society imposes in order to defend its injustices. Surely such appearances aren't *always* deceptive?

Is it *really* the case that no one ever acts except out of pure selfishness? The Doctor would remember how so many people, his friends amongst them, seemed to act for others' sake, with no thought for themselves—how, for example, Sarah and Harry were prepared to endure physical torture to prevent Davros from gaining information that would help the Daleks ("Genesis of the Daleks," 1975). Hobbes purports retrospectively to re-explain their actions as entirely egoistic. But what about those who made the *ultimate* sacrifice? What about Katarina ("The Daleks' Master Plan"), or Luke Rattigan ("The Sontaran Strategem," 2008)? The list is long. Hobbes says that they, too, acted selfishly, sacrificing their own lives because they couldn't tolerate the thought of going on living if they hadn't done so, or because they didn't wish to live in a world in which the people they attempted to save went unsaved.

But even if Hobbes is right about other people, surely he's wrong about *the Doctor*! Just think of all of those times when he risked everything to help others! Well, if Hobbes knew of a

Time Lord's regenerative powers, he might claim that the Doctor knew he was never *really* at risk. He acted selfishly indeed, aiming to preserve the lives and well-being of those who amused him, perhaps in order to earn their admiration, gratitude, and love for his "sacrifice." All of which made him feel good, all the while knowing that what might have *looked like* death to them was never *really* the end for him.

But there were times, surely, when the Doctor did *not* know. Saving Peri on Androzani Minor, he didn't know whether he'd regenerate ("The Caves of Androzani," 1984). And, in "The Time of the Doctor" (2013), didn't he spend hundreds of years on Trenzalore, protecting the Time Lords and preventing the Time War from breaking out again, while all the time believing that he had no more regenerations left, and would die in that place? Surely the Doctor had no overriding thought for his own interest on such occasions.

Hobbes might concede that he had no *conscious* thought, but would insist that deep down, unbeknownst to the Doctor, self-interest had to have been directing his every move. If Hobbes's diagnosis were correct, it'd imply that very often *our reasons are not our causes*—that the reasons by which we seek to explain our behavior don't in fact explain it, for we do what we do because of causes that lie beneath what we can consciously come to know about. At this, the Doctor might shudder once again, reminded of so many attempts, by those bent on oppression and domination, to reduce rational, autonomous individuals to hive-minded automata, condemned to meaninglessness by blind, impersonal impulses.

To point out the unpalatable implications of Hobbes's account isn't to give an *argument* against it, of course. In search of one such argument, and still in pursuit of a more satisfying answer to his original question, the Doctor's last trip might be to Edinburgh in the mid-eighteenth century.

A Sympathetic Doctor

David Hume (1711–1776) argues that psychological egoism is false. As we've seen, Hobbes claims that people who help others with no apparent benefit to themselves actually do so just in order to feel good about themselves, or in order not to feel bad about themselves for not helping. But, asks Hume, if your concerns for others reduce to a concern for yourself, *why* would your helping someone else make you feel better, and *why* would your failing to help someone else make you feel worse? It seems that, where my inaction causes me no material disadvantage, my failure to help another would make me feel bad only if I had a *genuine, irreducible* concern for the well-being of that person. There are times, that is, when some degree of altruism is a necessary condition of your feeling bad if you fail to help. Thus for Hobbes to say, of those occasions that you help others only to avoid feeling bad yourself, is for him to undermine his own position.

Hume would disagree with Kant's position. Pure logic alone can't motivate anyone to do anything. Exterminating those who are different can't be universalized without some sort of logical contradiction. So what? The Daleks could agree that that's the case, and yet fail to see why they ought not to exterminate those who are different. Or they could agree with Kant that they ought not to (on purely logical grounds), yet fail to be motivated to end their genocidal mission. What motivates any agent isn't pure reason, but feeling, emotion, and preference. In the Daleks' case, fear, hatred, anger, and a burning desire for dominion are overwhelmingly in command. Likewise, the Master's rational acceptance that certain people are rational agents, and even his acceptance that rationality is especially valuable, couldn't *by themselves* dispose him not to use rational agents merely as means to his wicked ends. What motivates him to exploit them is the only thing that could ever motivate him *not* to exploit them: feeling, emotion, preference, desire.

So, in attempting to disassociate moral principles from the affective aspect of every agent's nature, Kant fails to account for the "action-guiding" power that's essential to morality. Meanwhile Hobbes's impoverished conception of human nature leaves his own account looking desperate and self-refuting. The truth, Hume would say, depends upon a better conception of what human beings are basically like.

Hard-wired into normal human psychology is a faculty Hume's calls "sympathy" and we now call "empathy." It's the capacity to resonate emotionally with the feelings of others, sharing vicariously in their pleasures and pains, joys and woes. Observing someone helpless with laughter, we're compelled to laugh. We wince if we see someone violently attack another. The sight of a starving person in a far-off country can move us to tears, and we share the relief of someone just rescued from a burning building.

Sympathy is *necessary* for moral judgment, but it isn't *sufficient*. With sympathy *only*, we'd *never* non-selfishly be compelled to help others. Instead we'd seek *always* to avoid the cause of our sympathetic unease. We'd *always* turn our backs. In reality, sometimes we do *not* turn our backs. In contrast to the Doctor, this is notably untrue of the Master. Unpleasantly affected by Vivien Rook's grisly death by Toclafane, in "The Sound of Drums" (2008), his solution is to close the door! Thus the explanation of human morality also requires us to bring in human *benevolence*. Contrary to Hobbes's account, then, benevolence joins selfishness as a basic constituent of human nature. And this benevolence can lead us to do things that go against our own interests, such as donate money or give up our seat on the bus. It can motivate the Doctor to give the last of the Queen Bat's milk to his companion, knowing that this might mean his own death, or to spend centuries aging and dying on Trenzalore, attempting to keep countless billions safe.

Together, sympathy and benevolence lead us to approve or disapprove of the actions and characters of other people. We hear of a desperate colony of humanoid settlers under siege on some remote planet. The faculty of sympathy immediately makes us feel uneasy at the prospect of their suffering. Why, then, don't we simply look away, and spare ourselves? We would, if psychological egoism were true. So the fact that we sometimes *don't* look away shows the falsity of psychological egoism, and the presence of benevolence. Our natural benevolence leads us to wish that the colonists' suffering be relieved. And when reason and experience shows this suffering to be caused by greedy corporations or corrupt politicians, we might disapprove of them, want them stopped, and even try to stop them ourselves ("Colony in Space," 1971).

Here the Doctor might interrupt David Hume, to put the question that he started with: "Why do I tend to side with humans and humanoids against non-humanoids?" Hume might reply as follows. As countless examples show, we can resonate with the feelings of those who are in many ways very different from us. Thus we may discover moral rights and wrongs, virtues and vices, in situations and peoples far away in space and time. (And even—if we may speak of "discovery" here—

amongst the characters populating works of fiction!) The operation of natural sympathy is such, however, that the more remote someone is from us—spatially, temporally, culturally, emotionally, biologically—the less we tend to resonate. Now, Kant is right that moral judgments are usually thought to be universal—to apply equally to all agents—and there are ways of "correcting" for the prejudices of natural sympathy and benevolence, in order that we might come closer to this ideal. But because natural sympathy and benevolence form the foundation and essence of morality, there are bound to be limits as to how far this attempt can succeed. The "ideal" morality envisaged by Kant surrenders all motivational force, thereby ceasing to be morality at all. Morality as such must admit, therefore, of some degree of parochialism and prejudice.

At this, the Doctor might protest that, since he has traveled throughout time and space, and met beings from a million worlds, his moral outlook is unlikely to be as parochial and prejudiced as that of even the most enlightened human being. But while Hume could agree that the Doctor is the least prejudiced among us, I think he'd continue to insist that some degree of prejudice is necessary for preference, just as preference is necessary for motivation, and motivation is necessary for moral judgment and action. As comparatively enlightened as the Doctor is, he's naturally disposed to favor those whose psychology and physiology most closely resemble his own. This is why he's naturally disposed to side with human beings and other creatures relevantly like them, for it's with their feelings, interests, and concerns that his own most readily chime.

"But why should the moral psychology you describe apply to me at all?" the Doctor might ask. "I'm a two-thousand-year-old Time Lord from the planet Gallifrey, in the constellation of Kasterborous. I'm not even half-human!"

"Be that as it may, my Lord Doctor," Hume might reply, "it seems to me that my account applies to you as well. You may not be half-human, but you are at least half-*Humean*."

25
Meeting Up with Yourself

J.J. SYLVIA IV AND HEATH STEVENS

A critical point in every child's development is when they become aware that there's something or someone other than themselves.

For example, immediately after birth the baby may think of the food-giver as just an extension of its own body, an extension which engages when hunger occurs or crying ensues. But then the baby learns to understand that there is a separation between its own Self and the Other. The separation of Other from Self heralds the way for the child to develop its own individuality. However, the time-traveling antics in *Doctor Who* complicate this simple-minded view of the Self and the Other.

The Doctor, as a Time Lord, has the ability to travel backwards and forwards in time and encounter his past and future incarnations. In fact, he's done so on several occasions: "The Three Doctors" (1972), "The Five Doctors" (1983), "The Two Doctors" (1985), and "The Day of the Doctor" (2013). These crossover situations are seemingly paradoxical in that they involve the Self *as* Other. As David Kyle Johnson has explained, the Doctor is only one person, but his many regenerations are separate personalities in different bodies. So, it's like the same body reconstructed multiple times.

Thus, in *Doctor Who*, it can be difficult to distinguish between Self and Other, but there are some philosophical conceptions that can help us understand these ideas. Applied philosophers Duane Halbur and Kimberly Halbur have written that of the many different schools of thought, the humanistic one is probably the most consciousness-based, or phenomenological, in that it primarily focuses on "here-and-now" experiences.

Humanism is primarily concerned with advancing human fulfillment, and the emphasis is always on the experiences of the present. This approach is appealing in analyzing identity issues in *Doctor Who* because it allows us to bypass some philosophical paradoxes of being and existence. For example, in most of "The Day of the Doctor" we don't have to debate which version of the Doctor—War, Ten, or Eleven—is *the* Doctor or even the "current" one (that is, the primary protagonist) because they're all interacting simultaneously in the same timeline. We can simply say that in this episode there are three unique Selves with corresponding two Others, depending on perspective. From Eleven's point-of-view, Ten and War are Others, and vice versa for each.

Existentialism, a particular subfield of humanistic philosophy, further elucidates perspectives of self. As Irvin Yalom has explained, existentialism emphasizes existence and our role in self-determining our destiny through individual choices. The major themes considered by existentialists are death, freedom, isolation, and the meaning of life, and these themes are seen throughout all of *Doctor Who*'s history.

With regards to understanding Self, the theme of meaning is most easily illustrated in "The Day of the Doctor." Apparently, Time Lords are allowed to choose their names, and the Eleventh Doctor told his companion Clara that the name chosen is a promise to be kept. She inquires as to what his promise was, and the Tenth Doctor states, "Never cruel or cowardly." The War Doctor adds, "Never give up. Never give in." This promise is thus the meaning behind the Doctor's chosen name, and it directs his actions in this story and almost all of the others. Immediately before this exchange, Clara refers to War as "the warrior" and Ten as "the hero." The Eleventh Doctor asks Clara what his description is, and she implies that he's forgotten the meaning of who he is. She tells him to "be a doctor!" The Doctor's name is therefore synonymous with his *modus operandi*.

The Self and the Other also cross paths in this existential approach to the meaning behind the Doctor's name. From the moment the audience is introduced to the War Doctor at the end of "The Name of the Doctor" (2013), through the first half of "The Day of the Doctor," Ten and Eleven both regard War as more 'Other' than they regard each other. In fact, they're united in that they're contemptuous of War because he's the incarnation responsible for ending the Time War by seemingly destroying both the Daleks and Time Lords.

Eleven confronts War at the end of "The Name of the Doctor" by stating that his actions weren't done "in the name of the Doctor." War's Other-ness is even confirmed by himself in the short "The Night of the Doctor" (2013) by saying that he's the "Doctor no more." We see this play out in "The Day of the Doctor," when War warns Ten and Eleven to leave before he destroys Gallifrey, by pleading, "Go and be the Doctor that I could never be." Throughout most of "The Day of the Doctor," War even finds it hard to accept Ten and Eleven as Self: "the man who regrets...and the man who forgets," in the words of the Interface of the Moment. However, through this contact, the Selves and the Others eventually learn from one another, and the result is a more whole Doctor who no longer rejects an aspect of his Self (namely, the War Doctor) as Other.

In many ways, this episode is an example of a resolution to an identity crisis typical of adolescents, as described by Erik Erikson in the article "Eight Ages of Man." Adolescence is often described as a period of "storm and strife" because teenagers and young adults are repeatedly asking themselves, "Who am I?" while at the same time enduring a number of physical changes (like puberty) and life-condition changes (like going into high school). In addition, this episode also changes the entire mythology of the New Series and gives the Doctor the new goal of finding Gallifrey.

The therapist Abraham Maslow unknowingly sums up the Doctor's contact between Self and Other when he described existentialism as the "human predicament presented by the gap between human aspirations and human limitations (between what the human being *is*, what he would *like* to be, and what he *could* be)." Of course, the Doctor is a Time Lord and not strictly human, but Time Lords are enough like humans for Maslow's statement to apply.

A Deleuzian Shock

How might we learn from the Self as Other? We can better understand this with Gilles Delueze's conception of learning, which relies on his very different conception of the 'virtual'. Most often applied today in terms of technology, we think of "the virtual" as something inherently unreal, or at least not physical. For Deleuze, the virtual is real and it brings about the actual. Yet, as actualized individuals, we only experience a small part of the actual, and it's only through Others that we can conceptualize the world in a manageable way. Deleuze explains this in *Logic and Sense*:

> The part of the object that I do not see I posit as visible to Others, so that when I will have walked around to reach this hidden part, I will have joined the Others behind the object, and I will have totalized it in the way that I had already anticipated. As for objects behind my back, I sense them coming together and forming a world, precisely because they are visible to, and are seen by, Others. (p. 305)

Only by conceptualizing things through the perspective of Others can we truly understand them at all. Others both enable us to conceptualize the world around us and to see ourselves as separate from it.

More specifically, for Deleuze, learning happens through a surprise, or shock, which often occurs as an encounter with the Other. Justin Marquis explains this potential for a shock in our encounter with the Other:

> if we recognize that the possible world expressed by the Other we perceive is in fact an expression of the virtual, we can allow the Other to teach us by composing ourselves to the Other, the possible world the Other expresses, and the Other's way of interacting with our world.

The encounter with the Other creates an assemblage that shocks us into seeing the world in a new way. It's the interaction with Others that opens us up to new thoughts and possibilities. Let's consider a simple example to make this more concrete. The first time that we fall in love with someone, it's the shock of our experience with the Other that opens us up to a new way of understanding and experiencing the world. Without the Other, we'd never have been able to conceive of the affection—or emotions—we experience while in love.

The Girl Who Waited Learns from Amy

AMY: Why are we still here?

THE GIRL WHO WAITED: Because they leave you. Because they get in their TARDIS and they fly away.

AMY: No. Rory wouldn't. Not ever. Something must have stopped him.

THE GIRL WHO WAITED: You did. Or rather, the old version of you. The me version of you. I refused to help them. I won't let them save myself.

AMY: Why?

THE GIRL WHO WAITED: If you escape then I was never trapped here. The last thirty-six years of my life rewrites and I cease to exist. That's why old me refused to help then. That's why I'm refusing to help now. And that's why you'll refuse to help when it's your turn. And nothing you can say will change that.

Doctor Who offers us an interesting thought experiment in exploring the challenges of confronting the Other: could another version of our Self be the Other that we meet? The Girl Who Waited literally faces this conflict when she meets the younger version of herself. Of course, this is precisely the type of paradox that any companion of the Doctor risks facing. What would it mean to meet another version of yourself? Are you meeting you—or are you meeting Other?

This question seems a little more straightforward when it's the Doctor running into different incarnations of himself, because each regeneration is clearly different on many levels, ranging from his taste in clothing—bowties, scarves, celery— and food—jelly babies or fish fingers and custard—all the way to very fundamental dispositions of his personality. Yet, the question is tougher in the case of Amy and the Girl Who Waited. Though visibly older, the Girl Who Waited is, in almost every other respect, Amy.

As this story begins, Amy, Rory, and the Doctor are planning to vacation on the planet Apalapucia, but they arrive to discover the planet is under quarantine due to a deadly plague.

Amy becomes separated from the Doctor and Rory and becomes trapped in a parallel time stream that passes much faster than the original one. Normally, the Doctor would rush in to save his companion, but he can't do so in this situation because the plague is fatal to two-hearted species such as Time Lords. Therefore, the Doctor alters some technology to allow Rory to communicate with him back in the TARDIS while Rory attempts to rescue his wife. As one might expect in *Doctor Who*, things get a little timey-wimey, and the rescue doesn't go as planned. Rory is attacked by Handbots, and Amy must save him; but the Amy who saves him is much older because she's been waiting for Rory and the Doctor's rescue for thirty-six years. Amy has become the Girl Who Waited.

Needless to say, all parties are upset at this encounter for different reasons. The Doctor is burdened by locking onto the "wrong" Amy, the sight of his aging wife shakes Rory, and the Girl Who Waited is angry with the men for abandoning her. The Doctor devises a way to return and save young Amy, but he requires the help of the Girl Who Waited. However, she's unwilling to assist because she believes it will essentially mean her death, or rather, never having existed in the first place. At this impasse, the Doctor is able to engineer a way for young Amy to remotely communicate with the Girl Who Waited across the varying time streams. The stage is thus set for a Deleuzian shock moment during this contact. The Girl Who Waited suddenly remembers this conversation and young Amy's unsuccessful supplication for help.

Yet this time, young Amy is able to do the impossible and break the laws of time by convincing the Girl Who Waited to bring her back for Rory's sake. At this point, the two women begin to enter an assemblage where the Girl Who Waited is the Self and young Amy is the Other. The Self learns from the Other how important Rory actually is to her, reminding her about the love she has for him. The Girl Who Waited then tells Rory that she's going to "pull time apart for you."

Now that everyone is helping each other, the Doctor is able to instruct them how to temporarily merge the two time streams to pull young Amy into the one with everyone else. After some awkward moments now that the two Amy's are physically in contact with one another, they have to run back to the TARDIS and avoid battalions of Handbots. The Girl

Who Waited takes some initiative and stays behind a bit to give Rory and Amy a chance to make it to the TARDIS. As soon as they enter the TARDIS, the Doctor closes the door and locks the Girl Who Waited outside. The Doctor then presents a sort of Sophie's choice to Rory explaining to him that he lied and only one Amy can leave with them. Rory will have to decide which wife to take back with him. In many ways, this scene parallels the earlier episode "Amy's Choice" (2010), in which Amy had to choose which reality she wanted: one with or without Rory. She chose Rory. The Girl Who Waited pounds on the doors of the TARDIS, and Rory is about to let her inside when she begs him not to open the door if he truly loves her (the Girl Who Waited). The assemblage is complete. The Self has truly learned from the Other what's important and how to act upon that love. The TARDIS dematerializes, Amy wakes up to ask "where is [the Girl Who Waited]?", and the curtain closes with the implication that Amy has a full memory of the events, therefore illustrating the truly unifying assemblage of the Self and Other.

The Self as Other

So what gives? How can the Girl Who Waited learn from Amy? The Girl Who Waited has thirty-six years of experience that Amy doesn't. The experiences that the Girl Who Waited has accumulated in these years have changed her personality and how she understands the world. In many ways, this is our intuitive understanding of how the world works. Do you see the world now in exactly the way you saw it five years ago, or ten? The experiences we had in those years shaped and changed the way we think about the world around us, and our memories of those experiences shape who we are. John Locke explored this particular conception of identity as related to consciousness and memory in his *Essay Concerning Human Understanding*. For Locke, personal identity is derived from our psychological continuity—our ability to be conscious of and remember our past; that is what shapes us, makes us who we are.

Acknowledging the differences in memory between Amy and the Girl Who Waited can open up the door to allow us to see an older version of ourselves as Other. In *other* words, if I meet a me that has different memories and experiences than I do, at minimum, I am faced with the very real and open question of whether that person can really be understood to *be me* at all. It's precisely my memories and experiences that have helped shape me into the very person that I am.

Yet, as Other, the Girl Who Waited also challenges our traditional notions of wisdom. We often think that with age and experience we gain wisdom. Our accumulated experiences help us understand the world better and thus make better decisions. The Girl Who Waited, however, learns from her younger self, Amy. It's Amy who can most clearly recall and articulate her love for Rory. Thirty-six years of waiting caused some of those strong feelings to fade from her memories, as the Girl Who Waited explained: "The look on your face when you [Rory] carried her . . . me . . . her. When you carried her, you used to look at me like that. I'd forgotten how much you loved me. I'd forgotten how much I loved being her. Amy Pond in the TARDIS with Rory Williams."

This emphasis and priority on the more immediate experience and feelings of Amy rather than the Girl Who Waited allows us to conceptualize Amy as Other in this case, specifically because she still has vivid access to memories that the Girl Who Waited no longer does. She vividly remembers Rory in a way that isn't immediately accessible to the Girl Who Waited. Although we undoubtedly learn more things as we grow older, it's easy to *forget* that we also lose access to many of our past experiences.

Learning from Our Own Other

If we can understand our own past selves as an Other, this opens up such confrontations to more than just the realm of time travel and science fiction. There are many ways in which we have access to our past selves, perhaps more now than ever, thanks to the ubiquity of technology. For example, I (J.J.) have over fifteen years of past versions of myself that I can access on the internet, ranging from a blog that I kept daily during nearly all of my time in high school, through Facebook and Twitter updates, all the way to a YouTube video series I created in the process of becoming a father. This type of social media gives us glimpses of our former selves. When I go back and read the words of me from high school, often I not only don't remember the events being described, but am also *shocked* at the way I thought about the world in many cases!

However, learning from my own Other rather than the Other of others does meet some potential difficulties. While discussing this potential with students at the 2014 session of North Carolina Governor's School East, they posited two challenges. Does social media show our true self, and what if we think our past self is stupid?

One popular criticism of social networking sites, such as Facebook, is that their users only post the very best and most positive things about their lives, choosing to keep private the daily problems and struggles that we all encounter. Thus, Facebook leaves us with a very one-dimensional understanding of others, often believing that others don't face the same types of problems and struggles that we do. If I look back and only see the positives that I've posted, is this really me?

First, I'm not sure how well this generalizes. I know my own Facebook feed contains a true mix of experiences that contain both triumphs and tribulations. Second, and perhaps more importantly, I think that in all of our interactions with others, we attempt to put our best foot forward, in the ways many of us might do on social media. Yet, others still learn from their interactions with us—much as we might from our past selves. And perhaps the version of ourselves that we choose to share and present with others says a great deal about who we are in the first place.

Overwhelmingly, students agreed that when they went back and read things they'd written in the past, they were most often shocked at how stupid the past versions of themselves seemed. Even in this worst-case scenario, there may be something we can learn from that version of our past selves: empathy. If we can reflect on how far we've progressed, then perhaps through the shock of experiencing our past self, we can develop a stronger empathy for those who aren't as far along that progression as we are, seeing them as a work in progress rather than making a negative judgment. And that might just be a way to help develop our own ethics of caring, much like the Doctor himself. Sylvia argues the same point in "Doctor, Who Cares?", in *Doctor Who and Philosophy: Bigger on the Inside.*

As they travel through space and time, both Amy Pond and the Doctor have had the opportunity to meet other versions of themselves. Unless we're lucky enough to hear the wheezing and groaning of the TARDIS materializing in front of us one day, we most likely won't get that same chance. However, we can muster a little bit of our own timey-wimey adventure by using social media to confront our very own Other Self. It may be scary, painful, or even humiliating to take that look back; but if we've learned anything from Amy and the Doctor, taking that risk is probably worth it.

26
Time Lords Are Us

STEPHEN FELDER

> People assume that time is a strict progression of cause to effect, but actually, from a non-linear, non-subjective viewpoint, it's more like a big ball of wibbly-wobbly, timey-wimey, stuff.
>
> —TENTH DOCTOR ("Blink," 2007)

In "The Impossible Astronaut" (2011) Rory, Amy, and River witness the Doctor being killed. The Doctor killed at Lake Silencio is 1,103 years old, but later, in the same episode, when they encounter the Doctor in a diner he is 909. The 1,103-year-old Doctor in "The Impossible Astronaut" has a diary similar to River's, and they can "catch up" with each other, but the 909-year-old Doctor in the same episode barely knows, and scarcely trusts her.

After the Doctor's murder (by a younger version of River), an old man, Canton Everett Delaware III, tells them he won't be seeing them anymore, but they will be seeing him. We find out that what he meant was that they'd be encountering a younger (version of) "him" in 1969.

At Lake Silencio we experience a "present" in which almost all of the characters have different pasts and futures. No wonder the Doctor describes time as "wibbly-wobbly." But what is it? In the famous quote from "Blink" the Doctor challenges our typical assumptions about time. He challenges the common-sense notion that time is a "strict progression of cause to effect" and asks us to consider it from a "non-linear" and "non-subjective" point of view.

But what is time? Before we consider what time might be, we should first analyze both the "linear" and the "subjective" conceptions of time and consider why the Doctor might be justified in asking us to reject them.

Both views—the linear and the subjective—begin with our most basic understanding of time: it flows. Time seems to be a movement from past to future by way of the present. It always seems to be moving. It never stands still. Time isn't a series of distinct, static moments strung together like individual beads on a necklace; it's more like a river that flows by us, or like a melody that makes sense only as a whole, and not as individual notes. So it's likely not coincidental that one of *Doctor Who*'s most important characters is River Song, herself a Time Lord.

People often try to understand our experience of time by either thinking of it in metaphorical terms as a *river* (the linear view), or by analogy to our experience of a *song* (the subjective view), both of which give us the feeling of "flow" that seems so central to what time is for us.

River Song of Time

If we use the "river" analogy, time can be thought of as an objective reality—something outside of us—ever-flowing in a linear fashion. Adopting the "river" view of time we could think of the Doctor dropping himself down at various points up and down the stream, "floating" there for a while, and then jumping to another point on the stream, with time itself a continuous, objective "flow." But there are problems with this understanding of time.

First, to suggest that we "float" on the river of time would be to suggest that all events exist for us as an *eternal present*. If I'm flowing with "time," that is, if I'm "floating" on the river of time, and time is conceived as some sort of objective, "linear" something, then I never experience time in motion because I am "floating" with it.

The point is that the *experience* of time is an experience of flowing, but when I'm floating on an actual river I feel this flow relative to the fixed objects on the shoreline. In the time-as-river metaphor, there are no fixed points, no events that occur outside of time. The river of time encompasses all existence leaving us no fixed points of reference that might generate a sense of *flow*.

What gives me the experience of a river's flow is the fixed point of the shore. But the universe has no such fixed point.

Yes, there's been a sequential succession of occurrences since the Big Bang, but I'm part of the succession, without a fixed, immobile vantage point—a God's-eye perspective, so to speak—from which to view them flowing. So, time can't be like a river, flowing past, or upon which I float since that wouldn't explain the experience of flow that seems basic to what time is.

So if describing time as an objective reality "outside" of me doesn't account for that experience of "flow," maybe the sense of flow comes from something "inside" of me—something constructed by my own mental capacities. To account for this "internal" origin of time we might opt for what I'm calling the "song" strategy. In order to experience a song, as a song, I have to be able to experience it as a flow, and not as a simple succession of isolated notes. This is similar to my experience of time. I don't experience the world as a series of individual, isolated "moments" but rather as a flow in which each "moment" seamlessly flows into the next.

The "subjective" theory of time tries to account for my experience of time as flowing by claiming it's a product of my mind's work in assembling experiences retroactively into a coherent whole. In this view, we can account for our experience of both time and music as "flow" as a construction of our minds. Thus, according to the theory that our minds somehow assemble the individual notes of the song (and, by analogy, the individual moments of experience) retroactively, the flow of the melody and the flow of time would be like a puzzle that my mind assembles once it has all of the pieces. But this doesn't actually account for the sense of flow that time seems to be.

Even assuming my consciousness could correctly assemble the notes of the melody in the correct order, my consciousness would still be assembling individual notes one at a time, not the tune as a whole, and we all realize that the experience of hearing a song isn't an experience of separate, linked moments; it's an experience of *flow*. Similarly, if my consciousness is supposed to generate the experience of flow that is time by arranging moments of experience into a succession, they'd still all be isolated packets of experience, presented to my consciousness one at a time, and not the experience of flow that I experience as time. So it seems my experience of a song, like my experience of time's flowing, can't be simply the product of my mind. It can't be purely subjective.

Both of these views are also challenged by the structure of the relationship between the Doctor and River Song. The Doctor and River experience their relationship in opposing orders. River's "earlier" encounters with the Doctor are the Doctor's "later" encounters with her. Put another way, the Doctor's future is River's past, and River's future is the Doctor's past. (The relationship between the timelines of Amy, Rory, and River/Melody are even more complex!) However, in each of their encounters they experience, for a while, a flow of time that they share. When they leave each other, each goes into *a future*, a future that's unique to each of them (since their future is the other character's past) and their current, shared experience goes into a (now) shared past. But, if time is a "strict progression from cause to effect," what is it about the experiences of the Doctor and River that accounts for the Doctor's past being River's future, and vice versa?

If time is like the objective, linear river on which we float, then we might conclude one of them would be swimming upstream. But that doesn't make sense, since both of them are passing into (their own versions of) the future (not their own past!). If time's an assemblage of events in the mind—the subjective view—then why do the Doctor and River experience things "back to front?" Why not assemble the experiences—the pieces of the puzzle—in the same direction (retroactively)? In other words, the fact that the Doctor and River can't simply arrange the events in their lives so they experience them in the same order points to the fact that our experience of time can't be purely subjective, at least not in the sense that we're free to arrange our experiences into any order that suits us. There must be something reflexive about our experience of time— something not purely external and objective and not purely internal and subjective—something that takes place by way of the engagement of persons with events in the universe that occur in something like a progression from cause to effect without time itself being a "strict progression from cause to effect."

Theorization of Time

Maurice Merleau-Ponty (1908–1961) was a French philosopher whose work emphasized the nature of bodily experience as the foundation of all thought. He argued that all of our ideas about the world are interpretations that begin with our perceptions, and these perceptions are (a) pre-conceptual (occurring prior to our reflections on them) and (b) bodily, in the sense that our bodies are both suited for perceiving the world around us and are the means by which we do so. Our bodies aren't simply one more object among the various objects in the world; they're the very means by which the world is perceived and experienced.

For Merleau-Ponty, the experience of flow we associate with time is grounded in our pre-conceptual way of experiencing the world. We feel time flowing, we sense a past and a future, as a result of our normal, bodily way of experiencing objects, persons, and even ourselves. Since we feel "time" flowing, we assume there must some "thing" out there in the universe that's causing the experience. Then, in circular fashion, we call this thing "time" and then postulate it as the cause of our experience of (the flow of) time. Others, running into the problems associated with the linear/river view of time, turn to the subjective view, imagining there must be some kind of puzzle master "inside" of us who assembles the experiences into a "strict progression" thus creating the experience of flow which we consider "time." Thus, again, in circular fashion, since the flow of time is experienced, we posit a person, a subject, as the constructor of that experience.

Both views go wrong because they focus on our conceptions of our experience of time rather than on the experience itself. This is why Merleau-Ponty argues we should look prior to our conceptions of time and analyze our pre-reflective experience of flow. We can understand this pre-reflective experience of flowing if we think of Clara Oswin Oswald's first experience of the TARDIS ("The Snowmen," 2012). Like most people she's shocked upon entering the TARDIS, but, unlike most people, who note it's "bigger on the inside," she declares "it's smaller on the outside." She then goes back outside the TARDIS and walks all the way around it before re-entering. The dislocation she (and everyone else) feels upon entering the TARDIS is the disparity between the TARDIS's exterior and interior dimensions. This disparity comes from the fact that she treats the TARDIS as a single, unified object (which it is). When she walks inside the TARDIS she expects its internal dimensions to match its external dimensions. When she walks around it she doesn't think that every time she sees a new side of the TARDIS she's seeing a different object; instead, she knows she's experiencing a different side of *the same* object.

Her way of coming to terms with the dimensions of the TARDIS is typical of the way all of us come to terms with the world around us. As we circumnavigate an object we don't feel our experience of the object divided into individual moments; to do so would be to experience multiple objects rather than multiple facets of the same object. The reason Clara feels the disjuncture of the TARDIS's dimensions is because her memory of the TARDIS's exterior doesn't match her experience of its interior. To put this in *temporal* terms, standing outside the TARDIS for the first time, the interior of the TARDIS is still in her future as she anticipates what it'll be like. When she enters the TARDIS for the first time, her memory of the TARDIS's exterior dimensions is now in her past, and to make sure her initial impressions were correct, she goes back outside, walks around the TARDIS, and re-enters. This is how we, as sensing, perceiving bodies, get a "grip" on the world around us. The flow we experience is central to our ability to experience the world as it is—a set of unified, three-dimensional objects. Clara's experience of the TARDIS, which has multiple exterior sides and both an interior and exterior, is a single object with multiple facets that can only be observed one at a time by a finite Clara. Clara's finite experience of the multiple facets of the TARDIS is unified in her experience because the TARDIS is a unified, single object, and this unified flow of experience is something accomplished through Clara's engagement with the TARDIS.

The experience of flow then is the experience of finite perspective making sense of a multifaceted world. Clara doesn't *assemble* the various facets of the TARDIS into a unified whole like someone putting together a puzzle. She experiences the TARDIS as a whole. Nor is the flow she experiences caused by something outside of her in which she and the TARDIS are flowing. *The flow is her experience itself.* So this leads us to Merleau-Ponty's surprising conclusion regarding time: "Time is the subject, and the subject is time." This formulation is counter-intuitive, but it does match our experience. By making this claim Merleau-Ponty is arguing that both "time" and "the subject" (the "self/ego/I") are ways of conceptualizing a pre-conceptual experience. We experience a sense of flow in our encounters with the world that we then conceptualize as "time." Similarly, we experience a unity of our observations ("I" was outside the TARDIS, now "I" am inside) that we conceptualize as the subject. But in both cases there's a pre-conceptual, more immediate experience of the world grounded in our bodily engagement with it.

You Don't Know Me, But You Will

If we return to Lake Silencio for a moment we can work out Merleau-Ponty's ideas of time a bit further. We can take Amy's perspective as roughly corresponding to our own. When we first viewed the episode, we knew roughly what Amy knew. Only when we get to the crucial reveal toward the end of "The Wedding of River Song" (2011) do we begin to understand how all the events fit into the pasts and futures of all of the characters. We can then assemble a coherent timeline for any one of the characters, but not for all of them at once. Yes, we can trace a sequence of events from 1969 to 2011, but none of this accounts for what each character actually experiences as time (and to do so would be to think of time as a "strict progression from cause to effect"—something the Doctor suggested might be misleading).

What makes an event past is that one of the characters has already experienced it. What makes it future is that for at least one of the characters it hasn't yet been experienced. But there's no objective, total future (or past) that applies to all the characters at once. If time is the flow from past to future by way of the present what makes time, time, is this finite, reflexive experience of the world. Temporal experience is "reflexive" in the sense that it's neither a "God's-eye" view that can stand back, apart from time, and observe it flowing by, but neither is it a construction of the mind that creates a fictional flow. Time is real experience that must be lived through. At the end of "The Wedding of River Song" Amy frets that she's killed someone in cold blood. River reminds her that it was in a timeline that never existed. But this way of viewing the events—as occurring in a timeline that never existed—doesn't help, because Amy lived the experience. It's part of her past. It's part of her experience (of time). This is why it leads her to wonder what those actions say about her, about the Amy who's the subject of all of her experience.

This finite, bodily, personal perspective is what time is, according to Merleau-Ponty, so that we should "no longer say that time is a 'given of consciousness', but rather, more precisely, that consciousness unfolds or constitutes time." As Merleau-Ponty points out in *Phenomenology of Perception*, "I do not think about the passage from the present to another, I am not the spectator of this passage, I accomplish it. . . . I myself am time, a time that 'perdures' and that neither 'flows by' nor 'changes' . . . " Time "perdures" because "I" am time and time is "me."

We lose sight of this when we try to observe the "observer" who's observing our experience of time because, as Merleau-Ponty would argue, there's no observer who's observing time (that we in turn could observe observing it). Instead, observation is possible only in a temporal way. There's time because, as a bodies, we can't see everything at once, think everything at once, hear everything at once, be everywhere at once, experience everything at once. Our embodied experience is a finite one, and because it's finite there's time—there's the experience of flow. Time is something accomplished by finite, sensing bodies being in the world.

Take Me Back to the River Song

None of this explains how, or even whether, physics might allow for someone to travel back to 1969 from 2011. Merleau-Ponty's isn't an account of time travel; it's an account of time itself. It doesn't explain how the TARDIS can transport people to and from various points in time-space, but it does account for how the Doctor, his various companions, and we, the viewers, are able to experience time regardless of where the TARDIS might take us.

In giving this account, Merleau-Ponty suggested that time and the "self" are inextricably linked. To be a self is to be temporal, and temporality—the flow of past to future by way of the present—is a quality of our bodily existence. By showing that the subject/self is time, Merleau-Ponty has also explained how experience can be shared. Some have wondered if such sharing, such having experience in common, is even possible. Since our consciousness is private, how can we know what others are really feeling, thinking, or perceiving and how can we relate to others without knowing what's really going on "inside" of them (or that there is anything "inside" them at all)?

Merleau-Ponty suggests that "unlike two consciousnesses, two temporalities aren't mutually incompatible, because each one only knows itself by projecting itself in the present, and because they can intertwine there." According to Merleau-Ponty, time is what makes it possible for us to be in relationship with others. I connect with others both within finite experiences of seeing, hearing, and feeling the same things in similar ways (think of how everyone experiences the same "it's bigger on the inside" feeling upon entering the TARDIS), and by sharing pasts and futures that can be present for us in either memory or anticipation (think again of the Doctor, Amy, Rory, and River at Lake Silencio). A childhood friend and I can reminisce about a high school baseball game that occurred decades ago. My college literature professor continues to affect me as his questions, ideas, and general approach to life modify my own. My girlfriend and I are joined in anticipation of the Red Sox baseball game we'll attend together in a couple of weeks. My friend and I sit in the coffee shop and discuss *Doctor Who* for hours in a shared present that's continuously creating a shared past. Amy can fret about the Doctor's murder (which is in her past) while the Doctor is standing right in front of her.

This experience of time is at the core of the relationship between the Doctor and River Song. River poignantly illustrates this point when she tells Amy that she doesn't fear her own death, or the Doctor's, because she knows there's something worse waiting for her. Later, we find out that what she meant was the moment when the Doctor would no longer know her. "The trouble is it's all back to front," she explains in "The Impossible Astronaut." "I know him more, he knows me less . . . The day's coming when he won't have the faintest idea who I am . . . and I think it's going to kill me." In the next episode, "Day of the Moon" (2011), when she kisses the Doctor, the first time for him, she realizes it's the last time for her.

But the fact that they're experiencing each other "back to front" doesn't prevent their developing a deeply personal relationship. This is because time, rather than being an objective linear flow, or a subjective psychological construct, is experience itself. For Merleau-Ponty, because we're temporal, because "time" is the very nature of our experience as "subjects," the Doctor and River can "intertwine." With each encounter the bank of shared "pasts" increases and forms the basis of their relationship, with both the Doctor and River's presents always being the site where their shared past is realized and (re-)experienced in constructing a (shared) present. This occurs even though everything is "back to front" (and even though they each have a privileged access to the other's future). In "Flesh and Stone" (2010), when speaking of the opening of the Pandorica, the Doctor says "I look forward to it," and River says, "I remember it well." At that point, the opening of the Pandorica, which is in the past for River but in the future for the Doctor, "intertwines" in the present for both—and the present is where they, and we, always live. What makes their relationship a relationship is a sharing of experience, and what they show us is that experience is always temporal, which is precisely why it can be shared.

However, if, as some people imagine, there is a "self," a subject, hidden "inside" our body—something like the Teselecta ("Let's Kill Hitler," 2011, and "The Wedding of River Song")—then we're all alone. Others would present themselves to us as either objects of our perception or unverifiable constructs of our consciousness with no independent existence. In this case, all our experiences would ultimately be private. But if subjectivity is temporality, we can intertwine in the present with other temporalities that know themselves by projecting themselves into the same present. Merleau-Ponty described this relationship to the present as "projecting" because time isn't individual moments, but the constant flow of past into future. The present is the realization of our situation between past and future. (A moment, unlike a musical note, has no specific duration.)

I use Merleau-Ponty's term "temporalities" to describe the relationship between River and the Doctor, not because they're Time Lords, which they are, but because they, like us, are what time is. If time, at least as we know and experience it, is the past "flowing" through the present into the future, we're this flow. It's we, with our own "presents" that provide the means by which something can be either past or future. Isn't that exactly what the Doctor and River do? Isn't this how they manage, on each encounter, to catch up with each other—by projecting themselves into a present they share, even (especially) when they project themselves into the present by way of memory and anticipation? This is because, as Merleau-Ponty put it: "Time must be understood as the subject, and the subject must be understood as time."

Shortly before his death, in some working notes for what would've been his next book, *The Visible and the Invisible*, he asserted that "time must be understood as a system that embraces everything—Although it is graspable only for him who *is there*, is at a present." Without us as the one who is "there," who is "at a present," the "big ball of wibbly-wobbly, timey-wimey stuff" can't be grasped. But this isn't because we constitute the past and the future through an act of our "minds." I don't think up the past or the future even when I daydream about a future that doesn't happen or incorrectly remember a past event. Still, Merleau-Ponty argues there is "time" because there is "consciousness," and there is "consciousness" because there is "time." It's time that allows for perspective and perspective that allows for time. It's time that allows for shared perspectives and shared perspectives that allow for relationships.

I've been arguing, following Merleau-Ponty, that time is subjectivity. "Time" describes what's involved in being a body with a finite perspective. This finite perspective, open as it is to the world (like Clara getting a grip on the TARDIS), is what gives us the experience of flow, and thus, a sense of the past and the future. This sense of flow—of there being a past and future—allows us to think of ourselves in the present, and this ability to be present is what makes relationships possible at all.

Time is what allows the Doctor and River to have a relationship, and despite the many apparent paradoxes that relationship entails, it makes sense to us because we, like them, are time, and time is us. We, as viewers of *Doctor Who,* experience their relationship in time, which is to say, we experience it as unfolding before our finite perspective, but a finite perspective that experiences the Doctor(s) as a single, but multifaceted person, just as River does. So in this regard, the Doctor and River are like the rest of us. As they each move towards their own unique futures, they increase the pasts that can modify, and be part of, a (shared) present. Isn't this our situation, too? We can't know our futures (spoilers!), but what builds our relationships is our shared pasts formed in experiences of presence that allow us to experience others as somehow *with us*.

Tragedies can be especially illustrative of this—September 11, 2001, the *Challenger* disaster, the assassination of JFK, ("remember where you were when . . . ?")—but tragedies aren't the only such experiences. Because we are time and time is us, we engage the world in meaningful ways, connecting our present experiences to our memories of the past and our plans for the future. This connecting of past and future in our experience of the present is what creates our sense of self. It's in this way that we find connection with others who share those memories and hopes and in them come to know us as unified, enduring persons.

Each "present" is a future that goes into the past by passing through our experience of it. There isn't a succession of presents, but a perduring, living present, and this present is, in some sense, what each of us like to call "me." These me's, are what some scholars call, "the subject," and they intertwine in this perduring because "time is the subject, and the subject is time."

Time is us, and we are time. In this sense, we're all Time Lords.[1]

---

[1] Thanks to Maren Felder and Annalise Felder for introducing me to *Doctor Who* and spending countless hours watching and discussing it with me. Special thanks to Maren Felder for compiling a database of episodes and scenes relevant to this topic.

More Matrix of Time-Lord Bibliographic Sources

Abraham, Lyndy. 2001. *A Dictionary of Alchemical Imagery*. Cambridge: Cambridge University Press.

Akers, Laura Geuy. 2010. Empathy, Ethics, and Wonder. In *Doctor Who and Philosophy: Bigger on the Inside*, edited by Courtland Lewis and Paula Smithka. Chicago: Open Court.

Alcubierre, M. 1994. The Warp Drive: Hyper-fast Travel within General Relativity. *Class Lectures on Quantum Gravity*.

Aristotle. 1975. *Categories and De Interpretatione*. New York: Oxford University Press.

———. 1999. *Nicomachean Ethics*. Indianapolis: Hackett.

———. 2012. *Magna Moralia*. Miami: Hardpress.

Arlo-Costa, H. 2007. The Logic of Conditionals. In *Stanford Encyclopedia of Philosophy*. <http://plato.stanford.edu/entries/logic-conditionals>.

Augustine. 1990. *Retractationes*. In *The Works of Saint Augustine: A Translation for the 21st Century*, Volume I.2. Hyde Park: New City Press.

Baggott, Jim. Accessed 2014. The Evidence Crisis. *Scientia Salon*. <http://wp.me/p4rWb7-5N>.

Bailey, Eaton Edward and Francis Trevelyan Miller. 1910. *Portrait Life of Lincoln: Life of Abraham Lincoln, the Greatest American*. Charleston: Nabu.

Bentham, Jeremy. 2007 [1789]. *An Introduction to the Principles of Morals and Legislation*. Mineola: Dover

Bignell, Jonathan. 2005. Space for 'Quality': Negotiating with the Daleks. In *Popular Television Drama*, edited by Jonathan Bignell and Stephen Lacey. Manchester: Manchester University Press.

Bloom, Harold. 2007. *The Best Poems of the English Language: Chaucer through Frost*. New York: Harper Perennial.

Blustein, Jeffrey. 2007. Doctoring and Self-Forgiveness. In *Working Virtue: Virtue Ethics and Contemporary Moral Problems*, edited by Rebecca L. Walker and Philip J. Ivanhoe. Oxford: Oxford University Press.

Burckhardt, Titus. 1971. *Alchemy: Science of the Cosmos, Science of the Soul*. Baltimore: Penguin.

Butler, Judith. 2006 [1990]. *Gender Trouble: Feminism and the Subversion of Identity*. New York: Routledge.

Carman, Taylor and Mark B. N. Hansen. 2004. *The Cambridge Companion to Merleau-Ponty*. Cambridge: Cambridge University Press.

Carroll, Sean. Accessed 2011. Are Many Worlds and the Multiverse the Same Idea? <www.preposterousuniverse.com/blog/2011/05/26/are-many-worlds-and-the-multiverse-the-same-idea>.

———. 2013. The Most Embarrassing Graph in Modern Physics. <http://goo.gl/Zx0tvi>.

———. Accessed 2014. Why the Many-Worlds Formulation of Quantum Mechanics Is Probably Correct. <www.preposterousuniverse.com/blog/2014/06/30/why-the-many-worlds-formulation-of-quantum-mechanics-is-probably-correct>.

Chown, Marcus. Accessed 2001. Taming the Multiverse. *The New Scientist*. <http://goo.gl/byWhfU>.

Corvino, John. 1999. *Same Sex: Debating the Ethics, Science, and Culture of Homosexuality*. Lanham: Rowman and Littlefield.

Crumley, Jack S., III. 2009. *An Introduction to Epistemology*. Peterborough, Ontario: Broadview.

Dalberg-Acton, John. 1907. Letter to Bishop Mandell Creighton. In *Historical Essays and Studies*, edited by J.N. Figgis and R.V. Laurence. London: Macmillan.

Damasio, Antonio. 1994. *Descartes' Error: Emotion, Reason, and the Human Brain*. New York: Penguin.

Davidson, Donald. 1973–1974. On the Very Idea of a Conceptual Scheme. *Proceedings and Addresses of the American Philosophical Association* 47.

Davies, Russell T. 2009. Interview with Alan Sepinwall of *The Star-Ledger*. *The Star-Ledger* (June 26th).

———. Accessed 2014. "Midnight" Shooting Script. <www.TheWritersTale.com>.

Davies, Russell T, and Benjamin Cook. 2010. *The Writer's Tale: The Final Chapter*. Chatham: BBC Books.

DeCelles, K.A., D.S DeRue, J. Margolis, and T.L. Ceranic. 2012. "Does Power Corrupt or Enable: Moral Identity, Power and Self-Serving Behavior." *Journal of Applied Psychology* 97:3.

Decker, Kevin S. 2010. The Ethics of the Last of the Time Lords. In *Doctor Who and Philosophy: Bigger on the Inside*, edited by Courtland Lewis and Paula Smithka. Chicago: Open Court.

Deleuze, Gilles. 2001 [1968]. *Difference and Repetition*. London: Continuum.

Descartes, René. 1993 [1641]. *Meditations on First Philosophy*. Indianapolis: Hackett.

———. 1994 [1637]. *Discourse on the Method of Conducting One's Reason Well and of Seeking the Truth in the Sciences*. In *A Bilingual Edition and an Interpretation of René Descartes's Philosophy of Method*, edited and translated by George Heffernan. Notre Dame: University of Notre Dame Press.

Dictionary of Spiritual Terms. Accessed 2014. <www.dictionaryofspiritualterms.com/public/home.aspx>.

Dillon, Robin S. 2001. Self-Forgiveness and Self-Respect. *Ethics* 112:1.

Eaton, William. 2010. The Doctor on Reversed Causation and Closed Causal Chains. In *Doctor Who and Philosophy: Bigger on the Inside*, edited by Courtland Lewis and Paula Smithka. Chicago: Open Court.

Echeverria, F., G. Klinkhammer, and K. S. Thorne. 1991. Billiard Balls in Wormhole Spacetimes with Closed Timelike Curves: Classical Theory. *Physical Review* 4.

Erikson, E. H. 1966. Eight Ages of Man. *International Journal of Psychiatry* 2.

Erion, Gerald J., and Barry Smith. 2002. Skepticism, Morality, and *The Matrix*. In *The Matrix and Philosophy: Welcome to the Desert of the Real*, edited by William Irwin.

Everett, A. E. 1996. Warp Drive and Causality. *Physical Review* 53:12.

Everett, C.W.F., et al. 2011. Gravity Probe B: Final Results of a Space Experiment to Test General Relativity. *Physical Review* 106.

Faye, Jan. Accessed 2008. Copenhagen Interpretation of Quantum Mechanics. In *Stanford Encyclopedia of Philosophy*. <http://plato.stanford.edu/entries/qm-copenhagen>.

Freud, Sigmund. 1950. *The Interpretation of Dreams*. New York: Modern Library.

Freud, Sigmund, and Josef Breuer. 2000. *Studies on Hysteria (1893–1895): The Definitive Edition*. New York: Basic Books.

Friedman, J., K. Schleich, and D. Witt. 1995. Topological Censorship. *Physical Review* 75.

Friedman, J., M.S. Morris, I.D. Novikov, F. Echeverria, G. Klinkhammer, K. S. Thorne, and U. Yurtsever. 1990. Cauchy Problem in Spacetimes with Closed Timelike Curves. *Physical Review* 42:6.

Goldman, Alvin. 1988. Discrimination and Perceptual Knowledge. In *Perceptual Knowledge*, edited by Jonathan Dancy. Oxford: Oxford University Press.

Granger, John. 2008. *How Harry Cast His Spell: The Meaning Behind the Mania for J.K. Rowling's Bestselling Books*. Carol Stream: Tyndale House.

Green, Melody. 2010. *Doctor Who* and the Idea of Sacrificial Death. In *The Mythological Dimensions of Doctor Who*, edited by Anthony Burdge, Jessica Burke, and Kristine Larsen. Crawfordville: Kitsune.

Griswold, Charles L. 2007. *Forgiveness: A Philosophical Exploration*. Cambridge University Press.

Halbur, D.A., and K.V. Halbur. 2011. *Developing Your Theoretical Orientation in Counseling and Psychotherapy*. Second edition. Upper Saddle River: Pearson.

Hamilton, Paul. 2003. *Metaromanticism: Aesthetics, Literature, Theory*. Chicago: University of Chicago Press.

Hobbes, Thomas. 1994 [1668]. *Leviathan*. Indianapolis: Hackett.

Hume, David. 1983 [1751]. *An Enquiry Concerning the Principles of Morals*. Indianapolis: Hackett.

Irwin, William, ed. 2002. *The Matrix and Philosophy: Welcome to the Desert of the Real*. Chicago: Open Court.

Israel, Jonathan. 2002. *Radical Enlightenment*. New York: Oxford University Press.

Johnson, David Kyle. 2010. Is the Doctor Still the Doctor—Am I Still Me? In *Doctor Who and Philosophy: Bigger on the Inside*, edited by Courtland Lewis and Paula Smithka. Chicago: Open Court.

Jung, Carl G.. 1968. *Man and His Symbols*. New York: Dell.

Kant, Immanuel. 2005 [1790]. *Critique of Judgement*. Translated by J.H. Bernard. New York: Macmillan.

———. 1981 [1785]. *Grounding of the Metaphysics of Morals*. Indianapolis: Hackett.

Kelly, Michael R. Accessed 2014. Phenomenology and Time Consciousness. *The Internet Encyclopedia of Philosophy*. <www.iep.utm.edu>.

Kenny, Anthony. 2007. *Philosophy in the Modern World*. Oxford: Clarendon.

Kihlstrom, John F., Jennifer S. Beer, and Stanley B. Klein. 2002. Self and Identity as Memory. In *Handbook of Self and Identity*, edited by Mark R. Leary and June Price Tangney, New York: Guilford.

Langer, Monika M. 1989. *Merleau-Ponty's Phenomenology of Perception: A Guide and Commentary*. Tallahassee: Florida State University Press.

Lewis, C.S. 1952. *Mere Christianity*. New York: HarperCollins.

———. 1964. *The Discarded Image: An Introduction to Medieval and Renaissance Literature*. Cambridge: Cambridge University Press.

Lewis, Courtland, and Paula Smithka, eds. 2010. *Doctor Who and Philosophy: Bigger on the Inside*. Chicago: Open Court.

Linden, Stanton J. 1996. *Darke Hierogliphicks: Alchemy in English Literature from Chaucer to the Restoration*. Lexington: The University Press of Kentucky.

Littmann, Greg. 2010. Who Is the Doctor? For That Matter, Who Are You? In *Doctor Who and Philosophy: Bigger on the Inside*, edited by Courtland Lewis and Paula Smithka. Chicago: Open Court.

Livy. 2015. *The History of Rome*. Chios Classics.

Locke, John. 1979 [1689]. *An Essay Concerning Human Understanding*. Oxford: Oxford University Press.

Marquis, Justin. Accessed 2014. Deleuze and the Encounter with the Other. <www.academia.edu/2203174/Deleuze_and_the_Encounter_with_the_Other>.

Martin, Raymond, and John Barressi. 2006. *The Rise and Fall of Soul and Self: An Intellectual History of Personal Identity*. New York: Columbia University Press.

Maslow, Abraham H. 1969. Existential Psychology—What's in It for Us? In *Existential Psychology*, edited by Rollo May. New York: Random House.

Merleau-Ponty, Maurice. 1968 [1964]. *The Visible and the Invisible: Followed by Working Notes*. Evanston: Northwestern University Press.

———. 2012 [1945]. *Phenomenology of Perception*. Abingdon: Routledge.

Mettrie, J.O. de la. Accessed 2012. *Man a Machine*. <http://cscs.umich.edu/~crshalizi/LaMettrie/Machine>.

Mill, John Stuart. 2002 [1861]. *Utilitarianism*. Indianapolis: Hackett.

Miller, Arthur. 1982 [1953]. *The Crucible*. New York: Dramatists Play Service.

Minow, Newton N. 1961. Television and the Public Interest. *Address to the National Association of Broadcasters*.

Moffat, Steven. 2013. 'The Day of the Doctor' Preview. *Doctor Who Magazine* 467.

Morris, M.S., K.S. Thorne, and U. Yurtsever. 1988. Wormholes, Time Machines, and the Weak Energy Condition. *Physical Review* 61:13.

Murphy, Jeffrie G. 1998. Jean Hampton on Immorality, Self-Hatred, and Self-Forgiveness. *Philosophical Studies* 89:2–3.

———. 2009. The Case of Dostoevsky's General: Some Ruminations on Forgiving the Unforgivable. *The Monist* 92:4.

Nietzsche, Friedrich. 1966 [1883]. *Thus Spoke Zarathustra*. Translated by Walter Kaufmann. New York: Vintage.

———. *Human, All Too Human: A Book for Free Spirits*. Cambridge: Cambridge University Press.

————. 2000. *Basic Writings of Nietzsche*. Translated by Walter Kaufmann. New York: Modern Library.

Novalis. 1997. General Draft. In *Novalis: Philosophical Writings*, Translated by Margaret Mahony Stoljar. Albany: State University of New York Press.

————. 2003. Miscellaneous Remarks. In *Classical and Romantic German Aesthetics*, edited by J.M. Bernstein. New York: Cambridge University Press.

Plato. 1961 [360 B.C.E.]. *Republic*. In *The Collected Dialogues of Plato*, edited by Edith Hamilton and Huntington Cairns. Princeton: Princeton University Press.

Plato. 1961 [360 B.C.E.]. *Theaetetus*. In *The Collected Dialogues of Plato*.

Pollock, John. 1986. Brain in a Vat. In *Contemporary Theories of Knowledge*. Lanham: Rowman and Littlefield.

Putnam, Hilary. 1982. *Reason, Truth, and History*. Cambridge: Cambridge University Press.

Ryle, Gilbert. 2009. *The Concept of Mind*. London: Routledge.

Sallis, John. 1971. Time, Subjectivity, and the Phenomenology of Perception. *The Modern Schoolman* 48.

Sandifer, Phillip. 2013. *TARDIS Eruditorum: An Unofficial Critical History of* Doctor Who, *Volume 1*. Eruditorum Press.

Schiller, Friedrich. 2009. Letter of an Aesthetic Education of Man. In *Aesthetics: A Comprehensive Anthology*, edited by Steve Cahn and Aaron Meskin. Malden: Blackwell.

Sidgwick, Henry. 1907. *The Methods of Ethics*. London: Macmillan.

Siegfried, Tom. Accessed 2014. Tom's Top 10 Interpretations of Quantum Mechanics. *Science News*. <http://goo.gl/TbThDB>.

Simpson, Jacqueline, and Steve Roud. 2000. *The Dictionary of English Folklore*. Oxford: Oxford University Press.

Solomon, Robert C. 2009. Self, Deception, and Self-Deception in Philosophy. In *The Philosophy of Deception*, edited by Clancy Martin. New York: Oxford University Press.

Sternberg, Eliezer J. 2007. *Are You a Machine? The Brain, the Mind, and What It Means to Be Human*. Amherst: Humanity Books.

Stokes, Patrick. 2010. Just as I Was Getting to Know Me. In *Doctor Who and Philosophy: Bigger on the Inside*, edited by Courtland Lewis and Paula Smithka. Chicago: Open Court.

Stone, Curtis. 2013. *The Science Delusion*. Brooklyn: Melville House.

Streetmentioner, Daniel. 1979. *Time Traveler's Handbook of 1001 Tense Formations V1 and V2*. San Francisco: Megadodo.

Sylvia, J.J. 2010. Doctor, Who Cares? In *Doctor Who and Philosophy: Bigger on the Inside*, edited by Courtland Lewis and Paula Smithka. Chicago: Open Court.

Tipler, F.J. 1974. Rotating Cylinders and the Possibility of Global Causality Violation. *Physical Review* 9:8.

Tippett, B. K. 2011. Gravitational Lensing as a Mechanism for Effective Cloaking. *Physical Review* 84.

Tolkien, J.R.R. 2001. *Tree and Leaf: Including the Poem Mythopoeia; The Homecoming of Beorhtnoth*. London: HarperCollins.

Turing, Alan M. 1950. Computing Machinery and Intelligence. *Mind: A Quarterly Review of Psychology and Philosophy* 59:236.

Vaidman, Lev. 2014. Many Worlds Interpretation of Quantum Mechanics. *Stanford Encyclopedia of Philosophy*. <http://plato.stanford.edu/entries/qm-manyworlds>.

Watson, Gary 2003. *Free Will: Oxford Readings in Philosophy*. Second edition. Oxford: Oxford University Press.

Waugh, Kirsty. 2009. *Mixing Memory and Desire: Recollecting the Self in Harry Potter and His Dark Materials*. MA thesis. Massey University.

Wenzel, Michael, Lydia Woodyatt, and Kyli Hedrick. 2012. No Genuine Self-forgiveness Without Accepting Responsibility: Value Reaffirmation as a Key to Maintaining Positive Self-Regard. *European Journal of Social Psychology* 42.

Westlund, Andrea C. 2009. Anger, Faith, and Forgiveness. *The Monist* 92.4.

Wilkinson, Philip. 2008. *Signs and Symbols: An Illustrated Guide to Their Origins and Meanings*. New York: Metro.

Williams, Bernard. 2002. *Truth and Truthfulness*. Princeton: Princeton University Press.

Wordsworth, William. 2012 [1798]. *The Tables Turned*. Amazon Digital Services.

Worley, Peter. 2010. Timey-Wimey Stuff. In *Doctor Who and Philosophy: Bigger on the Inside*, edited by Courtland Lewis and Paula Smithka. Chicago: Open Court.

Yalom, Irvin D. 1980. *Existential Psychotherapy*. New York: Basic Books.

The Second Great
Gallifreyan High Council

While writing her PhD thesis on Søren Kierkegaard's repetition of philosophy, HJÖRDIS BECKER-LINDENTHAL ran away with the Eleventh Doctor, who not only changed her perception of time and space, but also her shoe style. When she isn't traveling in the TARDIS, Hjördis mostly finds herself in Cambridge, England, where she enjoys discussing the cosmological argument with students at the Faculty of Divinity, excavating the traces of medieval thinkers in the works of nineteenth-century philosophers, and advocating the benefits of winter swimming.

COLE BOWMAN is a writer and independent scholar living in Portland, Oregon. She's contributed to other volumes in the Popular Culture and Philosophy series, including *Dracula and Philosophy: Dying to Know* (2015), and the forthcoming titles *Divergent and Philosophy,* and *The Ultimate Walking Dead and Philosophy.* When not doing philosophy, Cole occupies her time by opening old fob watches in the hopes of freeing Time Lords that might be hiding from the forces of evil.

ANGEL M. COOPER is an Adjunct Professor at Bridgewater State University. Her research interests include existentialism, Friedrich Nietzsche, ethics, and philosophy of popular culture. She contributed to *The Ultimate Walking Dead and Philosophy*, and is developing a paper on video games and virtue ethics. She teaches a seminar on *Doctor Who* and philosophy, where she tries to impart the important rules of the universe to her students, such as: "Crossing into established events is strictly forbidden. Except for cheap tricks," "Never interfere in the affairs of other peoples or planets unless there's children crying," and "Always take a banana to a party."

Though **PAUL DAWSON** was born between "The Edge of Destruction" and "The Roof of the World" (which might help explain his mood swings), his love of *Doctor Who* was innate. Consciously recollecting this innate passion during Patrick Troughton's tenure, full-blown fandom gripped him like a benign tentacle in the early 1970s, when he almost convinced himself that he too had been exiled to Earth, and would one day rediscover the secret of the TARDIS (or disguised wardrobe), and escape the tedium and terror of his schooldays. While this never quite happened, in later years he acquired a PhD in Philosophy, which meant that people could call him "Doctor," and he could feel happy and somewhat vindicated if they did. Paul now teaches Philosophy at University College School and King Alfred's School, both in London.

AUDREY DELAMONT is an envatted brain who works primarily in epistemology (skepticism) and action (or at least she thinks she does). Audrey's brain was awarded a BA and an MA in philosophy from the University of Calgary, where she lives with her husband and horde of dogs. She's an expert procrastinator and connoisseur of the awesome, so when she discovered *Doctor Who* she devoured all of the seasons immediately, much to the dismay of her own companion who continually wanted to know if she had done the dishes or merely watched "that weird British show all day." When Audrey's envatted brain isn't watching *Doctor Who* it's pretending to make art and play instruments, babble about philosophy, and avoid angel statues. She might make a good companion for the Doctor as long as she wasn't given anything of great importance to hold onto (she has a disposition to lose absolutely everything, and there are far too many places inside of the Tardis to look).

MICHAEL DODGE is Research Counsel and Instructor at the University of Mississippi, School of Law. A long-time science fiction fan, he's written on ancient skepticism, the nature of time, the history of biology, the concept of sovereignty, and how science and law influence one another. He contributed to *Mr. Monk and Philosophy: The Curious Case of the Defective Detective*, as well as *SpongeBob SquarePants and Philosophy: Soaking Up Secrets Under the Sea!* He's fond of Matt Smith as the Eleventh Doctor, and shares the Doctor's penchant for "cool" headwear. He hopes, in time, to find the perfect fez to compliment his teaching methodology.

COLIN DRAY is a lecturer in literature at Campion College of the Liberal Arts, Australia, and has previously taught at the University of Wollongong. His work has appeared in *Australian Literary Studies*,

Meanjin, Antipodes, and *Joss Whedon: The Complete Companion*. He's a contributor to *PopMatters*, and to his own blog *Themenastics*. His favorite Doctor is Matt Smith (although he considered his hand gestures a little understated), and he once, derisively, described Colin Baker's costume as "Something hosed out of a unicorn enclosure," before twiddling the tassels on his floor length scarf, dusting off his question mark sweater vest, taking a bite from the celery stalk on his lapel, and driving off in a canary yellow roadster.

CHARLENE ELSBY, PhD, is an Assistant Professor at Indiana University-Purdue University, Fort Wayne. She maintains that "The Doctor told us so," is a completely acceptable appeal to authority.

STEPHEN FELDER is an intellectual and cultural historian who frequently uses psychic paper to pass himself off as a philosopher. He holds a PhD in history from the University of California, Irvine. He's a Professor of Humanities at Irvine Valley College in Irvine, California.

CHRISTOPHER GADSDEN is a third-generation Whovian raising his four children in the same noble tradition. He resides with his wife Kristin (also a fan) in Columbia, Missouri, where he teaches philosophy at the University of Missouri and Heritage Academy of Columbia, and serves with a campus ministry (Cru). Unlike Chris's other heroes (Jesus and Socrates) the Doctor provides far more interesting costume possibilities, Chris's proudest accomplishment to date is being told that, with properly coiffed hair, a brown pin-stripe suit, and a bit of imagination, he doesn't look entirely unlike the Tenth Doctor.

MARTIN STONE HENNESSEE is a graphic designer and opera chorister who co-chairs the *Doctor Who* programming at Atlanta's TimeGate convention. He'd really like to know more about the unseen adventure wherein Gilbert and Sullivan gave the First Doctor a too-large Ulster coat. Perhaps he filled in for Richard Temple in *Ruddigore*? Or maybe he used it to smuggle Susan out of the chorus of sisters and cousins and aunts? Either way it was doubtless a Cotton-esque romp ending in some sort of bloodbath, with Hartnell tittering merrily, if inappropriately, while fleeing the scene.

MATTHEW A. HOFFMAN is a PhD student at Florida State University. Formerly interested in ancient and political philosophy, he regenerated a few years back into an ethicist of the Wittgensteinian variety. Growing up during the wilderness years, he was deprived of *Doctor Who* until its revival in 2005. Instead, his time was consumed by comics, *Star Trek*, and *Harry Potter*. Since there's no point being grown-up if you can't be childish sometimes, they remain a major part of his life. He has difficulty deciding whether Tom Baker or Matt Smith is his favorite Doctor. He agrees with the Eleventh Doctor that bow ties are cool, but that might be because they're the only neckwear he can tie properly.

A.G. HOLDIER is an ethics instructor for Colorado Technical University (in between TARDIS trips and teaching high school theology classes in his own personal Pandorica—Southern Idaho). Having first met David Tennant's Doctor during his graduate studies in philosophy at Denver Seminary, he's wondered how much of his life dances from one fixed point in time to another. Since his future incarnations have not yet returned to rescue him from his present fate, he's content for now to continue his research in aesthetics, environmental ethics, the ontology of fiction, and contributing to several previous volumes of the Popular Culture and Philosophy series. Lately, though, he's been feeling this strange ice-cream pain on the side of his head, but it's probably not a big deal.

NATHAN KELLEN is a PhD candidate at the University of Connecticut. His dissertation is on the nature of truth and logic, and he soon hopes to regenerate into a professor. Nathan has a fondness for the Scottish Doctors, and hopes the next is both a Scot and a ginger. If the next Doctor were to appear at his doorstep, he'd ask her to arrange a picnic and tea with Plato, Immanuel Kant, Ludwig Wittgenstein, and River Song on Asgard.

Doctor **COURTLAND LEWIS** became a companion of both the Fourth and Fifth Doctors in September 1983, but the BBC decided not to transmit his adventures. Though he spends most of his time with the Doctor, he also teaches at Owensboro Community and Technical College, writes and edits books, sits on his porch, and attends sci-fi conventions. Courtland edited both *Futurama and Philosophy* and *Divergent and Philosophy*, is completing work on *The Way of the Doctor*, and contributed to *Time and Relative Dimensions in Faith* and *Behind the Sofa* (a collection to aid Alzheimer's research).

You're dreaming now. **GREG LITTMANN** is a green, six-legged Dream Crab that dropped onto your face (*splat!*) and is keeping you asleep. The frustrated little crab is forcing you to live in its fantasy world, one where it's associate professor of philosophy at SIUE, publishing in the philosophy of logic, epistemology, and the philosophy of professional philosophy. Though it can't even hold a pen, it's making you dream that it's published numerous chapters for books that relate philosophy to popular culture, including volumes on *Planet of the Apes*, *Star Trek*, *Star Wars* and *The Walking Dead*. Then, when it has broken down your brain to liquid protein, you will die.

ROB LUZECKY is a Lecturer at Indiana University-Purdue University, Fort Wayne. After criss-crossing a few countries and continents, this reformed Time Lord spends his days trying to fix his TARDIS and teaching students about ethics, aesthetics, and ontology.

KEVIN MCCAIN is Assistant Professor of Philosophy at the University of Alabama at Birmingham. Rumors of his travels through time and space abound. The latest have it that he occasionally engages the Master in battles of wit, and that the pocket universe in which the Time Lords are trapped is contained in the space between two particular books on his office bookshelf. Currently, he refuses to confirm or deny either rumor. However, McCain has said that as soon as the Doctor pays him the money owed from a bet they made concerning certain events on Trenzalore, he'll happily reveal the truth of such matters.

MASSIMO PIGLIUCCI travels through time and space as the K.D. Irani Professor of Philosophy at the City College of New York, author of almost 150 technical papers, and author or editor of ten books, including *Answers for Aristotle: How Science and Philosophy Can Lead Us to A More Meaningful Life*. He also edits the web magazine Scientia Salon (scientiasalon.org). More importantly, though, after taking BBC America's official test (www.bbcamerica.com/anglophenia/2013/11/personality-quiz-doctor/) he has found out for sure what he always suspected: in another time line he would've been the Ninth Doctor.

DEBORAH PLESS got her BA in philosophy from Hamilton College, her MA in screenwriting from New York Film Academy, and her PhD in life from life itself. When not dashing off through time and space with the Ninth Doctor and Donna Noble, she contents herself to run *Kiss My Wonder Woman*, a pop culture analysis blog. Her work has also appeared in *Doctor Who and Philosophy*, *Futurama and Philosophy*, *Divergent and Philosophy*, and of course several other works that won't be published for another thousand years or so because, you know, time travel.

KATHERINE SAS received her BA in English from Messiah College, works as an academic coordinator at the University of Pennsylvania, and is pursuing an MA in English with the Mythgard Institute at Signum University. Her interests include the Inklings, *Doctor Who*, and the imaginative tradition in literature, television, and film. She has a blog called Raving Sanity and co-hosts Kat and Curt's TV Review, a weekly podcast on *Doctor Who* and *Buffy the Vampire Slayer*. After years of hesitating at the sheer bulk of *Doctor Who*, the Narnia pastiche of "The Doctor, the Widow and the Wardrobe" convinced her to take the plunge. She's a devoted Adherent of the Repeated Meme and loves round things.

JESSICA SEYMOUR recently completed her PhD with Southern Cross University in Australia, where she researched how power and agency are portrayed in Young Adult (YA) speculative fiction. She's a recipient of the Australian Postgraduate Award, and her research interests include children's and YA literature, popular culture, and fan studies. She'd trade her TARDIS tea cup for the Twelfth Doctor's attack eyebrows, but sadly has to make do with Rory Williams's nose.

R. ALAN SILER has been a Whovian since November 23rd, 1983—the Twentieth Anniversary of the show. Since then, he's founded a *Doctor Who* fan club (the Atlanta Gallifreyans), was a contributing editor on a *Doctor Who* web service, started and runs a *Doctor Who* convention (www.timegatecon.org) now in its tenth year, and is currently writing a book about *Doctor Who* with two additional ones planned. He's a little bit obsessed. His favorite Doctor is the Sixth. His least favorite is . . . well, he doesn't really have a least favorite Doctor.

DONNA MARIE SMITH is the Assistant Manager of the Acreage Library, a branch of the Palm Beach County Library System in Florida that is next to a small forest of trees. She hasn't spotted any Vashta Nerada lurking in the shadows, but she occasionally sees a horse from eighteenth-century France wandering through the parking lot. Like the Doctor, Donna is fascinated with the wonders of the universe, and her love of knowledge led her to earn degrees in Library Science, Journalism, and English. She's contributed to *Doctor Who and Philosophy: Bigger on the Inside*, *The Catcher in the Rye and Philosophy: A Book for Bastards, Morons, and Madmen*, and the forthcoming *Downton Abbey and Philosophy*. She reviews books on media studies for *Library Journal* and likes to travel to new places within our space-time continuum.

PAULA SMITHKA is an associate professor of philosophy at the University of Southern Mississippi when she's not on board the

TARDIS. She is forever grateful to Court and the Doctor for her abduction. Her interests are in philosophy of science, particularly philosophy of biology. She also teaches a Philosophy through Science Fiction course where more companions for the Doctor are frequently created. Naturally, one of the texts for the course is a brilliant book called *Doctor Who and Philosophy: Bigger on the Inside*. The course is Paula's attempt to help students avoid being fluorescent pudding brains. She also cautions them to "Count the shadows" and "Don't blink."

KEN SPIVEY is a songwriter, *Doctor Who* and *Harry Potter* expert, award-winning convention runner, and band leader of the MTV.com-and-*Creative Loafing*-praised-Steam-Punk-Time-Lord-and-Wizard-Rock-Band, "The Ken Spivey Band."

HEATH STEVENS is a professional school counselor and instructor in psychology at the Mississippi School for Mathematics and Science, and earned his BA and MA from the University of Mississippi. He's usually quite vague about what he's a doctor of, but he sometimes tells inquirers that his doctorate in educational psychology comes from Southern Illinois University Carbondale. Heath survived his dissertation by taking breaks to watch every single episode (or reconstruction) of the Classic Series, NewWho, *Torchwood*, *The Sarah Jane Adventures*, and *K-9 and Company*. The best advice he gives his students comes from the Fourth Doctor: "There's no point being grown-up if you can't be childish sometimes." Out of respect for the Doctor, Heath doesn't insist on being called by that prefix. However, he does appreciate being referred to as The Legend.

PETER SUTTON is an associate professor of philosophy at Virginia Union University in Richmond, Virginia. His favorite companion is Martha. Except really it's Amy. Actually it's Rory, but only because of when Rory says, "Would you like me to repeat the question?"

J.J. SYLVIA IV spends most of his days watching his one-year-old running around the house adeptly wielding her very own sonic screwdriver as she squeals in delight. When he's not at home, he's busy being a PhD student in the Communication, Rhetoric, and Digital Media Program at North Carolina State University, where his research interests include the philosophy of communication, big data, affirmative critical theory, and digital pedagogy. His current projects involve incorporating Google Glasses into his public speaking classes, gamifying higher education, and attempting to grow his very own attack eyebrows.

DOCTOR BEN TIPPETT is an expert in Einstein's theory of general relativity, and he studies black holes. He's written several papers on fiction science, including his *Unified Theory of Superman's Powers*, and a paper describing the gravitational warping of spacetime generated by Cthulhu's tomb city of R'lyeh. He's currently a sessional lecturer at the University of British Columbia Okanagan, where he teaches mathematics. You can follow him on twitter at @bnprime. Ben and Dave Tsang collaborate on *The Titanium Physicists Podcast* (titaniumphysics.com). If you'd like to learn more about quantum mechanics, spacetime curvature, and black holes, why not listen while you drive to work? It's available on Stitcher, iTunes, the Apple Podcast App, and other places podcasts are found.

DOCTOR DAVE TSANG is an astrophysicist who studies planets, black holes and neutron stars. He loves *Doctor Who*, drawing silly pictures and thinking about physics. He's currently a postdoctoral researcher in Physics at McGill University. You can follow him on twitter at @DrDa5id. Dave and Ben Tippett collaborate on *The Titanium Physicists Podcast* (titaniumphysics.com).

DR. SCOTT VIGUIÉ holds two doctoral degrees and is an archaeologist and an attorney who's done extensive research on myths and their impact on modern archaeology and storytelling. He's the creator of *Dr. Geek's Laboratory of Applied Geekdom* and *The Science from Fiction* audio show, where audiences are brought closer to those who are attempting to bring about the world of tomorrow. A lifelong Whovian, Dr. Viguié routinely appears at such conventions as Gallifrey One, where he speaks on such topics as the science of *Doctor Who*. His love of all things *Who* can also be heard on the podcast *Articles of the Shadow Proclamation*.

Higher–Order Logical Index for the Cyberman and Dalek in All of Us